The
Liberation of
Christmas

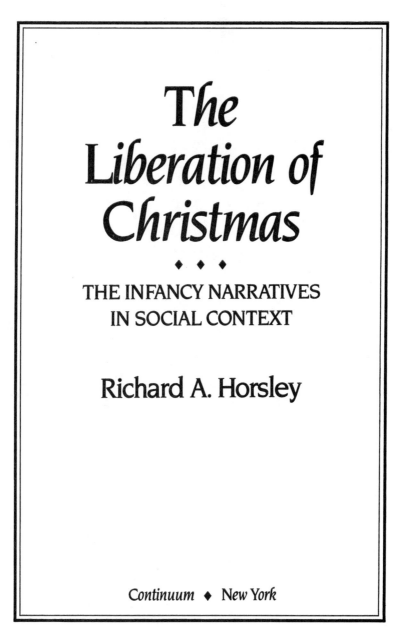

The
Liberation of
Christmas

◆ ◆ ◆

THE INFANCY NARRATIVES
IN SOCIAL CONTEXT

Richard A. Horsley

Continuum ◆ New York

Dedicated to the Memory of
Elaine Baskerville Horsley

1993

The Continuum Publishing Company
370 Lexington Avenue, New York, N.Y. 10017

Printed in the United States of America

Library of Congress Cataloging-in-Publication Data

Horsley, Richard A.
  The liberation of Christmas / Richard A. Horsley.
    p. cm.
  Bibliography: p.
  Includes index.
  ISBN 0-8264-0592-4 (pbk.)
  1. Bible. N.T. Matthew I, 18-II, 23—Criticism, interpretation,
etc. 2. Bible. N.T. Luke I, 5-II, 23—Criticism, interpretation,
etc. 3. Jesus Christ—Nativity. 4. Christmas. 5. United States—
—Social conditions—1980— 6. Central America—Social
conditions—1979— 7. Christianity and politics. I. Title.
BS2575.2.H65   1989
232.9'2—dc19   88-25114
                                                                CIP

Contents

Acknowledgments

A number of colleagues and friends have provided stimulation and insights into various aspects of the infancy narratives and the difficulties of interpretation. Special appreciation in this regard is due to Tim Buckley, Mike LaFargue, Mary Malone, Chris Motta, Max Myers, Teri Ortiz, Andy Overman, Jim Pasto, Jack Spence, Clark Taylor, Pat Turner, and Tim Wise. Special thanks also to Kate DeRubeis, Erin O'Brien, and Deborah Rich for valuable research assistance. Randy Huntsberry, Mike LaFargue, Max Myers, Andy Overman, Kathy Sands, and R. J. Schork read parts or all of an earlier draft and provided incisive criticism and valuable suggestions.

The book is dedicated to the memory of Elaine Baskerville Horsley, my mother. Besides being an energetic and gifted teacher who inspired young people to sing joyfully, she worked tirelessly for justice and peace, in her own home community, in her country, and among the peoples of the world. She took special delight in children and was uncommonly effective with young people; in addition to her own children and grandchildren, she nurtured more than twenty foster children and young people over several decades. She understood and lived the Christmas story. When she died her family and friends sang for her the choruses of Handel's *Messiah,* from "Comfort Ye, My People" and "The Glory of the Lord Shall Be Revealed" to "Unto Us a Child Is Born" and "Hallelujah!"

Introduction

Christmas is supposedly a religious celebration. But Christmastime is also an all-important festival of consumption, at least in North America. In the United States, which consumes 70 percent of the world's resources, 40 percent of all goods retailed annually are sold during the four weeks between Thanksgiving Day and December 25. Thus Christmas is a crucial force driving the economy. Santa Claus has clearly become the principal symbol that inspires all this consumption. But underlying Santa's prominence in recent decades is the original Christmas story, which is deeply rooted in Western culture through years of reading, hearing, and reenactment. Indirectly at least, the giving, hence the buying, of gifts is rooted in the paradigms of God's gift of the Christ-child and the costly gifts of the Magi. The Christmas story has clearly come to have a material significance: it helps to legitimate the festival of retailing and consumption of goods. The Christmas story has thus also become subservient to contemporary economic ends as well as subjected to modern cultural presuppositions.

Traditionally Christmas was the celebration of the birth of Christ, and the birth narratives in the Gospels of Matthew and Luke constituted the Christmas story. The sensitive or critical reader of the birth narratives in the Gospels may thus wonder what the original Christmas story could possibly have to do with the contemporary celebration of Christmas in the United States. Yet, Christmastime remains the principal, perhaps the only, context in which "the Christmas story" is read and considered. And the American Christmas festival is a dominating cultural context indeed, given the conjunction of aggressive advertising in the media, shopping for gift exchange, school vacations, holiday performances, gatherings of friends and family, and even church services. Particularly important has been the incorporation of features of what was once the story of Christ's historical birth into a wonderland of fantasy scenes in store windows, such as Santa with his elves and reindeer. Most effective of all, probably, has been the transformation of the Christmas story into one among several "fairy tales' in the plethora of "Christmas specials" on television, such as "Rudolph the Red-nosed Reindeer," "Frosty the Snowman," or "The Grinch Who Stole Christmas." Whether downtown or in one's living room, Christmas is now a fantasy that has considerable commercial but little historical significance. It would be difficult indeed for the Christmas story to be heard in such an overwhelming cultural context.

A principal reason why we have been slow to discern that aspects of the Christmas story actually function to legitimate this annual festival of consumption is that we have learned to assume that "religion" is somehow separate from "politics" and "economics." Indeed, in many modern societies religion is legally separated as well as structurally differentiated from polictical and economic institutions. We are beginning to realize, however, that no matter how institutionally differentiated our society may be, religion and politics and economics cannot in fact be separated in the actual functioning of people and institutions. For more than two decades now we have been aware that a "civil religion" is alive and well in the United States, serving to unify the country in celebrations such as the Fourth of July and the inaguration of presidents and to integrate individual families with the nation as a whole in the celebration of Thanksgiving. Often the inseparability is hidden and indirect. The more spirituality and morality become privatized, for example, the more the ends or values that individuals serve are determined by the large economic institutions for which they work. Thus also, in indirect as well as direct ways, aspects of the Christmas story have become integral to the Christmas festival, which is as important economically as it is religiously in the United States.

The conflict that the sensitive reader may feel between the infancy narratives of Jesus and the current celebration of Christmas, therefore, cannot be understood in terms of a conflict between religion and economics or "materialism." We think of the Bible and biblical narratives as religious, perhaps largely because of the aforementioned structural differentiation undergone by modern societies. It may thus be necessary to remind ourselves that, however religious it has become, the Bible is about the whole of life, political and economic as well as religious, material as well as spiritual. In the ancient Israelite-Jewish and Christian communities that produced biblical literature, life was not separated into different dimensions. Indeed, the presupposition in biblical literature appears to be that life cannot be so divided. There are no words or concepts in biblical literature that correspond to the modern "religion." When we interpret the Bible as something primarily or only religious, therefore, we are distorting it, reducing it to something less than literature concerned with the whole of life. The conflict that we sense between the infancy narratives and the contemporary celebration of Christmas may be one between one whole way of life and another, that is, not between religion and materialism, but between religion *and* politics on the one hand and religion *and* politics on the other.

Biblical studies is a product of the modern world. Christian biblical study particularly has been, to a considerable degree, determined by the institutional differentiation of modern society and presuppositions of modern life. The role and responsibility of biblical scholars has thus been to interpret biblical literature for faithful Christians. That role and responsibility, that literature, and the Christian faith are understood as religious. Because the Bible also deals with political and economic matters and much of biblical narrative is about historical events in a broader than religious sense, biblical scholars do take note of basic historical, including political, data pertinent to biblical materials. But such data usually are not allowed to influence the basically religious or theological interpretations that biblical studies produce.

If we want to appreciate biblical literature on its own terms, particularly if we allow the Bible to address us on its own terms, we must adjust our mode of appropriation, especially the scope with which we allow the Bible to stand over against us. This means not simply taking political and economic matters as well as religious affairs more adequately into account. It means attempting to understand that politicoeconomic affairs are inseparable from religious matters in most biblical material, and, correspondingly, that the import of the biblical material is thus also broader than simply religious. Our perspective and our reading will likely be seriously altered.

Biblical studies has also been the product largely of the established churches, theological schools, and universities of North Atlantic societies—that is, of white males who have a position of power and privilege in the world (regardless of how they perceive their own social status). The voices of women, blacks, and third-world interpreters, however, are making themselves heard. Because of their affinities and affiliations, these new voices are to a degree articulating the concerns of poor and powerless peoples more generally. Perspective and reading must change. One important change emerging already is the increasing awareness that biblical literature, while certainly compiled and written into the form in which we have it by a literate elite, includes much material from popular traditions, narratives, prophecies, songs, and so forth, which originated from and express the concerns of poor and powerless people.

From these and other realizations we are beginning to discover more generally how our reading and interpretation of the Bible have been determined by modern cultural and social history. With regard to the infancy narratives some focused discussion must be devoted to certain aspects of this influence, such as how the rationalist critique of these narratives as "myth" and not "history" led to their relative neglect by mainline biblical studies (chap. 1) or how, after our pretensions to objective investigation, we must now acknowledge that no neutral stance is possible (chap. 8). In particular, it is important to attempt to compensate for the location of established biblical studies in the relatively affluent universities and theological schools of the North Atlantic and its embodiment largely in white male intellectuals (esp. chaps 5, 7–8). Throughout the book, of course, we will be attempting to compensate for our modern presuppositions about religion as a separable dimension as we deal with narratives concerned with and addressed to the whole of life. Similarly, but to a lesser degree, we will be attempting to recognize our modern individualistic bias, while focusing on stories concerned with "all the people."

Treatment of the infancy narratives in the following chapters will be primarily historical, in the broadest sense. The focus and emphasis will be on the social relationships reflected in the narratives. Certain traditional theological issues will simply be left unaddressed. For example, although the infancy narratives provide the principal textual basis for the doctrine of "virginal conception," it is possible to treat the social role of Mary in the deliverance of the people without opening up this controversial issue. It has already been dealt with critically and sensitively by Raymond Brown and others.[1] While the doctrine of the incarnation will not be dealt with explicitly at any point, the chapters below will, in effect, be exploring its implication extensively, as the salvation embodied in Jesus is examined in its historical context of concrete political, economic, religious relationships.

Another issue that will not be treated is the relation of the infancy narratives to the rest of the New Testament. There appears to be no more direct relation between Paul and the infancy stories than there was between Paul and other materials in the Gospels. However remarkable it may seem to us, Paul apparently knew next to nothing of Jesus' sayings. Similarly, beyond the formulaic statement at the beginning of Romans that Jesus was "descended from David according to the flesh," Paul displays no knowledge of or interest in Jesus' birth. The Gospel of John provides a highly distinctive account of the "incarnation" of the Word, but nothing similar to the infancy narratives. Even within the Gospels of Matthew and Luke there is very little direct interrelationship between the infancy narratives and the rest of the Gospel material, and the way in which Mary is referred to later is quite different in tone.

The infancy narratives, however, are integral and instrumental parts of both Matthew and Luke. In these two Gospels the birth stories and the crucifixion-resurrection stories form both the framing for the ministry of Jesus, and the links of Jesus' life and significance with the broader historical context. The teaching and healing ministry are directed to "the lost sheep of the house of Israel," mostly in Galilee. The birth narratives and the crucifixion-resurrection narratives link Jesus explicitly with the history of Israel or even humankind, and more directly and immediately with the imperial Roman rulers and the Jewish rulers. Moreover, the latter are not simply the background or setting for the teachings and healings but are essential forces and actors in the overall history and historical significance of Jesus. Thus is should also be clear as well that the Gospels do not simply take the political situation into account; rather, it is an integral part, the framing of the story as a whole.

With regard to the infancy narratives and the rest of the New Testament, it is most important procedurally that we not conform the former to any other viewpoint represented in biblical literature. Our concern ought to be rather to discern the distinctive features and message of the infancy narratives, however much they may turn out to stand in tension, for example, with Pauline theology.

I should indicate briefly that I am attempting to avoid some concepts that have been central to previous interpretation of Jesus and the Gospels. One concept that may be obscuring more than enhancing understanding of biblical history and literature is *eschatology*. The term ostensibly refers to understanding of "last things." But however rich the overall gospel tradition may be in apocalyptic lore and language, there is almost nothing in the Gospels that could be called eschatological in the sense of "final" or "endtime." Many biblical scholars of earlier generations took apocalyptic language far too literally and misunderstood imagery of fulfillment (of historical hopes or promises) and vindication (of the suffering faithful) in terms of "the end of history," "the end of the world," or even "cosmic catastrophe." Of course the reading of apocalyptic imagery as eschatological is useful for those who want to avoid the historical references and particularly the political implications of certain gospel traditions. If the references are to the endtime and not to a historical situation or possibility, then the sayings or prophecies can more easily be avoided as irrelevant or, at most, function simply as sanctions.

Of special pertinence to the infancy narratives is the concept of the messiah and messianic expectations. Close analysis of the relevant texts in recent decades has indicated that there is little evidence from the time of Jesus for any messianic expectations, certainly not for any standard Jewish expectation of "the Messiah." Previous discussions of how Jesus differed from supposedly typical Jewish expectations of a political or military messiah (being instead some sort of religious or spiritual messiah) were therefore pursuing a false issue. The fact that there is so little evidence of expectations of a messiah from educated groups that produced literary remains makes all the more striking and important the evidence of concrete movements led by popularly acclaimed kings as comparative material for evaluating the stories about Jesus as the newborn messiah and "king of the Jews."

After the extensive, detailed, and comprehensive examination of the infancy narratives in Matthew and Luke by Raymond E. Brown, it might seem inappropriate as well as impossible, only a decade later, to say anything more, let alone new, on the subject. As will be evident from the scores of references to *The Birth of the Messiah,* the discussions below are heavily indebted to Brown's magisterial work. Shifts in our interests and perspectives, however, require that we reexamine materials and issues that only recently appeared to have been dealt with definitively. The chapters below have a particular focus, of course, and do not pretend to provide the kind of comprehensive coverage of the infancy narratives offered by Brown.

The attempt in Chapter 7 below to draw a broad analogy between ancient and modern history may seem problematic to some. It is a self-critical and historical-critical pursuit of what has been called a "dynamic analogy" in hermeneutical discussions and has nothing to do with the overly specific and inappropriate applications of biblical prophecies to contemporary nations, persons, and events by certain fundamentalist or sectarian groups. Procedurally, in order to avoid the analogy's influencing my presentation of ancient historical relations, I did not research and reflect on the modern case until after chapters 2 through 6 were written. Morever, the differences as well as the similarities are presented, particularly in the politicoeconomic systems involved. Some may feel that the presentation of the modern analogy of Central America under the *pax Americana* includes more detail than necessary. At least some exposition is needed, however, in order to appreciate the network of politicoeconomic relations that has emerged and the differences with the ancient world as well as the validity of the broad analogy being drawn.

What follows in the chapters below is not close, word-by-word exegesis of biblical texts. There is a good deal of such close analysis behind many of the socioeconomic expositions. But I am attempting to back away from, and to sacrifice, a close textual engagement here in the hope of gaining a broader perspective on social relationships portrayed or reflected in the text and of seeing those relationships in broad but concrete historical context.

·1·

The Christmas Story

HISTORY OR MYTH?

A wide gulf often exists between popular understanding of the Bible and the sophisticated exegesis of professional biblical scholarship. Nowhere is this gap more pronounced than with regard to the stories of Jesus' birth and those of his resurrection. The very stories that provide the basis for the two fundamental Christian festivals of Christmas and Easter are viewed by professional scriptural scholars as historically the least trustworthy.

It was not always so. The Renaissance and Reformation brought a victory of sorts for the literal or historical meaning, as opposed to the allegorical or other understandings of the Bible. Most readers in early modern Europe, like Paul and Augustine before them, understood biblical narratives to refer for the most part to real events that formed part of a broader world history running from the creation to the last judgment and new creation. The Renaissance and Reformation, however, also saw the revival of rationalism and a more critical historical awareness. Conflict was virtually inevitable, particularly in Protestant circles proclaiming *sola scriptura,* where the Bible was made to carry much of the authority lost by the institutional church. Biblical narratives were attacked as incredible and unrealiable by deists and rationalists from without, and domesticated by intellectual leaders from within the churches. Particularly objectionable or indefensible were reports about the origins of the world or of Christ that no one could have witnessed, portrayals of actions and personal appearances by God or heavenly beings, bodily or empirical representation of what seemed rather to be imaginary, and the portrayal of happenings that contradict the ordinary patterns of nature. Most such reports and portrayals came to be understood as myths, as opposed to reliable historical reports.

Not surprisingly, the stories of the annunciation, virgin birth, and other

1

incidents surrounding the birth of Christ, along with the stories of the resurrection or the transfiguration of Jesus, were among the first to be relinquished. By the end of the eighteenth century, the more rational, critical
theologians, particularly in German Protestant circles, no longer claimed any
historical veracity for the narratives of incarnation or resurrection. David
Friedrich Strauss cannot be blamed for undermining the Christmas story. He
simply had the audacity in 1835 to view much of the rest of the gospel tradition in the same way that naturalists and rationalists had long understood
the infancy narratives—that is, as myths.

Rationalism and a more critical awareness of history were driving a wedge
between what was depicted in biblical narratives and the "real" world of conceivable events. No longer able to defend or believe in the literal meaning
of obviously mythical biblical stories, theologians and churchmen sought security in inward or abstract spiritual forms. Since narratives such as the creation
or infancy stories were mythical or miraculous, the scholars detached the
meaning of Scripture from the narratives themselves and located it in theological ideas, religious truths, or moral values. With regard to the story of
Satan's temptation of Jesus, "the dominant idea of the time that evil comes
from the devil lent the vision the more definite form. As soon as the pure
soul of Jesus revolted against the ideas that were introduced by sensuousness,
then the fantasy submerged the image of the devil, in whose mouth it placed
these sensual promptings characteristic of him; but it was reason that
triumphed."[1] Strauss claimed that his "mythical interpretation, by renouncing
the historical body of such narratives, rescues and preserves the idea which
resides in them, and which alone constitutes their vitality and spirit." He
apparently believed that what he had just annihilated with his historical criticism of mythical contents of the Gospels was all the more secure as religious
doctrine: "All that the Scriptures declare and the church believes of Christ
will still subsist as eternal truth."[2] Particularly in the German university circles
from which biblical scholarship developed, the intellectual freedom to explore
the Scripture critically was combined with a strong individualistic pietism.
Historical skepticism regarding what might be known about Jesus through
the mythical materials in the Gospels was linked with—indeed made possible
by—devout personal faith in Christ.

The location of the meaning of Scripture in theological ideas or religious
truth, besides being a defensive search for security in a private, spiritual refuge,
was thus also a withdrawal from historical, political, and economic life into
a purely religious realm. It may have been motivated by the modern Christians'
own cultural circumstances, but it was grounded in their reading of Scripture.
The great German New Testament scholar Ferdinand Christian Baur was
clear that Jesus wished to be messiah only in a spirtual sense. And at the
climax of "liberal theology," Harnack asserted that Jesus' message of the king-

dom of God, which was "purely religious," could be summarized in the idea of "God the Father and the infinite value of the human soul."[3] In their defensive reaction against the attacks from without and within by naturalism and rationalism, theologians and biblical scholars relinquished narratives such as those of Jesus' birth as belonging to myth as opposed to history and abandoned any political or other real-worldly dimensions of biblical narratives. Insofar as the meaning of Scripture was found not in the narratives themselves but in some religious truth or theological doctrine or moral value—as discerned by modern interpreters—the infancy narratives were now subjected to modern culture. The Christmas story no longer had any reliable historical standing over against the readers or hearers but was dependent on them for an infusion of private spiritual or doctrinal meaning.

Scholarly Skepticism and Spiritualization of the Infancy Narratives

In their quest for historical knowledge about Jesus, critical scholars understandably avoided the "mythical" infancy narratives and the "miraculous" healing stories as the least reliable of the generally suspect narrative material and concentrated on the more reliable traditions of Jesus' teachings. That concentration, of course, also suited theological and other scholarly interest in doctrine and ideas, and it meant relatively less tension with the modern scientific cultural ethos. Although the healings and other miracle stories were virtually ignored for decades earlier in this century, the infancy narratives have been perhaps the material in the synoptic Gospels most neglected by established biblical scholarship. Certain passages from Matthew's and Luke's infancy stories, of course, have been examined frequently in connection with issues such as the virgin birth. But the energies of critical scholarship on the synoptic Gospel materials were concentrated on Jesus' teachings. For example, the most influential books on Jesus in the twentieth century, such as those by Bultmann and Bornkamm, ignore the birth narratives.[4] Even interpretations of broader scope, such as the most respected of so-called New Testament Theologies, neglect the infancy stories.

Some minimal attention was required, of course, in the writing of commentaries on Matthew and Luke. In that connection, however, there has been remarkably little change in the discussion of relevant historical and comparative cultural information for a century.[5] More important, the basic interpretative options have remained virtually the same since the end of the eighteenth century. The supernaturalist position takes the text literally, the subject matter being the spatiotemporal occurrences described in the narrative, and affirms the historical factuality of the miraculous elements, ironically on the same literalistic presuppositions as its original rationalist (now "scientistic") opponents. The naturalist view still looks for the subject matter of the narratives in real historical events but critically cuts through the miraculous or mythical depiction to some sort of nonmiraculous, natural occurrence. The rationalist position locates the subject matter not in what is narrated itself but in theological ideas of religious truths stated by the Bible in narrative form. Thus the meaning could be quite independent of the author's intention for the narrative. The mythicist approach locates the meaning of such miraculous narratives as the infancy stories in the frame of mind or consciousness that permeated bygone ages and claims to possess the scholarly tools or analytical keys that can provide access to the enduring meaning (thus returning virtually to the rationalist position for the ultimate meaning). As noted above, once the crucial step in the rationalist position is taken, locating the meaning in something other than what is referred to in the narrative itself, then the subject matter and meaning can be virtually anything: a system of ideas, particular Christian doctrines, inward moral or religious experience, a particular mentality (e.g., mythical), or the structure of human existence generally.

For the last century, commentaries on the Gospels of Matthew and Luke have followed these principal options, often mixing or juxtaposing two or three of them in interpreting the same item in the narrative. A somewhat cursory survey of several commentaries from the turn of the century, some from around 1930, and several from recent decades is perhaps sufficient to indicate both the continuation of these basic interpretative options and the typical Christian theological ideas or concerns presented as the meaning of items in the narratives. Overshadowing all is the continuing apologetic struggle with the marvelous elements in the narratives such as angelic appearances and prophetic predictions. Although they are "difficult to reconcile with the known facts of history," the narratives nevertheless "abound in historical features and are eminently true to life"; we even hear that "the dignity, beauty, and spirituality of these narratives is strong evidence of their authenticity."[6] Commentators frequently resort to naturalistic explanations, such as a shock to the nervous system through some abnormal strain to explain Zechariah's dumbness in Luke 1.[7] More common in dealing with the marvelous features in the narratives is a combination of the mythicist and rationalist positions. It has to be acknowledged that the infancy narratives are "not free of the instinct of religious minds to clothe in poetic form the truths in which they believe. . . . But from the imaginative symbolism of the narrative we will necessarily distinguish the fundamental religious realities from which the representation proceeds,"[8] The stories may speak of physical miracles and of contemporaneous history in stories that belong "to the poetry of worship," but they present "theological truth" and theological answers to the meaning of that history.[9]

Most commentators do discern the political implications and conflicts in the narratives. It is recognized by some that the newborn "king of the Jews" poses a threat to Herod's rule; that enemies, most likely the Romans and the Jewish high priests, are proclaimed as overcome; and that there is a "political note" in the deliverance of Israel from its enemies.[10] But twentieth-century commentators, like their predecessors, are concerned to explain away any political implications in the narratives. Granted, "Israel has lain crushed under the foreign despotism of Rome"; and yes, "redemption is envisaged as a drastic revolution by which the mighty are dethroned, the rich dispossessed and the proud humiliated" in the Magnificat of Luke 2: "This language," however, "is not to be taken literally but in a spiritual sense."[11] The Benedictus may portray God's plan in political terms, but at least the song closes "on a more definitely religious note."[12] The apparent direct political confrontation portrayed in the infancy narratives can be placed instead into a Christian theological scheme, "the inevitable conflict between the earthly and the heavenly kingdom, the world and the Church."[13] Once the meaning is located in such doctrines and not in the narrative itself, of course, the savior announced in Luke 2:11 is naturally read as referring to the "deity" of Jesus, and the peace announced in verse 14 is read as the atonement between "sinful men and a holy God."[14]

Commentaries thus interpret the meaning of the ordinary nonmarvelous or nonmiraculous items in the narrative as lying elsewhere, usually in Christian theological ideas. A few examples of interpretations that recur in several commentaries over the generations can also illustrate how such interpretations serve to spiritualize and depoliticize the infancy stories even further. Thus, with certain variations, the Magi are read as representatives of the Gentiles who came to accept Christ, while the Jews, supposedly here symbolized by Herod and the high priests, rejected and persecuted him.[15] The Magnificat, however powerful the imagery, is really a song of "mystical devotion."[16] Simeon, Anna, Zechariah, and Elizabeth are lauded as representatives of the finest Old Testament or Israelite holiness or piety that, against the supposedly dominant deadness or externalities of Judaism of the time, had somehow managed to survive.[17] The "messianic hope" in the Magnificat and Benedictus is admittedly expressed "in terms of a national deliverance from human oppressors," but this hope is explained as *eschatologically* redefined and transferred to the *parousia* or as "rid of its limitations of nationalism and self-righteousness."[18] The hope expressed in these songs still "involves a confusion of Israel's political destiny with her religious vocation, and national self-concern from which Jesus had to dissociate himself before he could accept the role of Messiah."[19]

Twentieth-century commentaries on Matthew and Luke thus repeat the standard interpretative options and standard Christian theological concerns that derive from earlier generations when they treat the infancy narratives. The rationalist location of the meaning elsewhere than in the narrative may originally have been motivated by a defensive reaction to the more fantastic elements in the stories of Jesus' birth. This reaction swept the ordinary, non-miraculous sociopolitical items into its defensive spiritualizing and depoliticizing reduction of the narrative elements to theological doctrines. The infancy narratives were effectively subjected to modern theology and, insofar as the latter was shaped apologetically, were considered under the impact of modern rationalism and according to the canons of modern cultural generally.

The Infancy Narratives and the Theology of Matthew and Luke

In the second half of the twentieth century, biblical scholars discovered Matthew and Luke as theologians and authors in their own right, not simply as stages in the development of gospel traditions. "Redaction criticism" is both an outgrowth of and a comfortable solution to the problem posed by "myths" in the Gospel narratives. Skeptical that synoptic narratives and other materials provided adequate historical evidence for dealing with Jesus, scholars shifted attention to how the Gospel writers used gospel traditions in their respective interpretations of Jesus. The problem of mythical narratives was thus avoided by focusing on how Matthew or Luke utilized the various traditions and motifs available to them. Like previous studies of synoptic Gospel materials that assumed the rationalist or mythologist positions, redaction criticism locates the meaning or the subject matter of its texts not in the narratives or sayings themselves. Redaction critics now look for meaning in the intention or interpretation of the writer, that is, in the "theology" (or "christology" or "soteriology," etc.) of Matthew or Luke or the communities from and for whom they wrote). Thus the theology or the purpose that scholars discover in Matthew and Luke may reflect modern apologetic and other theological concerns more than the designs of the evangelists themselves.

Since there is virtually no overlapping between the stories in Matthew and those in Luke, their respective infancy narratives would appear to be prime material in which to find their creative work as authors and theologians. On the other hand, because redaction criticism works by comparisons between traditions and their treatment by Matthew and Luke, and because the infancy narratives had been relatively neglected by synoptic Gospel studies, it may not be surprising that perhaps the most influential early redaction study virtually ignored the infancy stories.[20] That fact simply points to the difficulty that scholarly studies have experienced in determining the "theology" delineated in Matthew 1–2 of Luke 1–2 and particularly in understanding how their respective infancy narratives also are used to express the overall theology of each Gospel. This problem can be seen in a few representative treatments of each.

Recognition of Matthew's distinctive use of "formula quotations" ("this was to fulfill what was spoken by the prophet . . . ") led to the claim that

Matthew 2 (which contains several such quotations) "is dominated by geographical names," which are "what is really important to him."[21] The purpose of Matthew in Chapter 2 was apologetic: how did Jesus the messiah come from Nazareth in Galilee and not from Bethlehem, the village of David, as it said in Scripture, according to the questioning in John 7:41–42.[22]

However, the claim that the geographical names, even as emphasized by the formula quotations, dominate Matthew 2 seems highly questionable. What dominates the narrative is clearly the conflict between the newborn king of the Jews and the reigning king, Herod. The threatened Herod figures directly or indirectly at every point in the narrative except the actual visit of the Magi in verses 9–11 and the naming in verse 23.[23] Moreover, the notion that Matthew is pursuing an apologetic purpose is derived not from Matthew but only from the dispute in John 7. From the lack of textual evidence, we are increasingly aware that at the time of Jesus there were almost certainly no standard or widely acknowledged "Jewish expectations about the Messiah" such as birth in Bethlehem, about which Matthew or other followers of Jesus of Nazareth would supposedly have been embarrassed.[24] Just because the followers of Jesus early on applied to their "messiah" phrases from psalms that stemmed originally from the established Davidic royal theology (esp. Pss. 2 and 110) does not mean that they were defensively oriented toward some hypothetical established view of the proper pedigree of the messiah. Indeed, the royal Herodian and aristocratic priestly families that dominated Jewish Palestinian society would hardly have been entertaining messianic expectations, which could only have been threatening to their own position. Precisely that is the principal point of Matthew 2! The popularly acclaimed "kings" among the Jewish people who were active around the time of Jesus' birth surely did not have Davidic pedigrees.[25] There is little in the Gospel of Matthew itself or in the Palestinian Jewish milieu out of which the traditions he used emerged to suggest an apologetic motive. The typical early Christian concern to interpret Jesus according to fulfillment of biblical promise and prophecy (and prototype) would appear to be the operative motive in Matthew's use of the formula quotations to embellish the significance of the events narrated in chapter 2.

While affirming Matthew's apologetic concern, Brown concludes that it is secondary to the broader Matthean scheme of revelation followed by a twofold reaction of acceptance by the Gentiles and rejection by the Jews. He thus escalates what was a Christian exegetical observation in earlier interpretations to a schema that dominates Matthew 2: "The wise men of the Gentiles accept and pay homage; but the ruler of Jerusalem and all the chief priests and scribes of the people do not believe."[26] But such a reading grossly simplifies and homogenizes a more complex writing. Herod is Herod, and the Magi are the Magi in Matthew 2. The absurdity of taking them as representatives of something else can be illustrated by trying to pursue such a reading consistently throughout the Gospel. Brown suggests that in chapter 2 Matthew is thinking of the parallel scene of the passion in chapter 27.[27] Thus, if Herod is a representative of the Jews generally in chapter 2, then Pilate should be a representative of the Gentiles generally in chapter 27. A consistent reading along these lines suggests that both Gentiles and Jews have thus rejected Jesus. In the Gospel of Matthew, however, Herod and Pilate are not representative figures but particular rulers, both of whom recognize the challenge posed by Jesus "the king of the Jews."

It is understandable that theologically oriented New Testament scholars would conclude that christology is the principal concern of a writer presenting the "good news" of Jesus Christ. More precisely, it has been claimed that the title "son of God" provides the key to Matthew's christology, which is in turn the key to understanding Matthew. But the argument for this position from the text of Matthew 2 is surely unconvincing. "The newborn child of Mary . . . is indeed the King of the Jews. As such, he is Israel's royal Messiah. Still, he is most assuredly not a political figure, as Herod mistakenly assumes. Instead, he is, as God says through the prophet, the eschatological Shepherd . . . (who) is more than simply the scion of David. He is, as God again says through the prophet, 'my Son.' "[28]

The events in Matthew 2, however, are surely not simply pegs on which to hang a chain of titles that increase in significance until they reach "my son." The latter, moreover, in the statement "out of Egypt I called my son" (Hos. 11:1) makes a pointed comparison of Jesus with Israel, whose origins he is recapitulating, and is not an (escalated) equivalent to king, messiah, shepherd, son of David, or other such title. And "child" in Matthew 2:11, 13 can hardly be twisted to mean "son of God." There is simply no indication—let alone the title "son of God" itself (cf., rather, 4:3, 6)—in chapter 2 that might indicate that Matthew is articulating a "son of God" christology. In fact, nothing in Matthew 2 suggests that in chapters 1–4 Matthew might be concerned principally with "the person" of Jesus.[29] It should also be noted, against the persistence of the anxious attempt to deny or avoid any political dimensions of the narratives, that Herod is no more mistaken than Pilate: the newborn, like the crucified "king of the Jews," most assuredly *is* a political figure and most assuredly is not an eschatological one, at least not in Matthew, where he clearly stands in conflict with the established authorities, both in his ministry and in his resurrection-exaltation (28:20).

Luke 1–2 have come to be understood as fitting Luke's broader theological interpretation of history. But despite an initial sense that this meant "world history,"[30] subsequent discussions have focused largely on the narrower (and less vulnerable) "salvation history." Thus, whereas the author "Luke" himself places his history in the broad context of the Roman *oikoumenē* and world history since the creation, recent discussions of Luke reduce his concern to whether one religion (Christianity) is the legitimate successor to another (Judaism) and reduce his characters in the infancy narratives to representatives of the *piety* of Israel.[31] The way is thus opened for a return of something similar to the Lutheran pietism behind the earlier scholarly retreat into a depoliticizing spiritualization of infancy materials such as the Magnificat and its singer. "Mary is the model disciple." She is the "ideal believer" who totally abandons herself to God's will in "an absolute self-surrender."[32] In addition to belittling Mary, such a view also misses (1) the world-historical significance of the events of deliverance in which Mary and the other actors/speakers in Luke's stories are principal participants as well as (2) their excitement over the deliverance.

These representative treatments of the infancy narratives as integral parts of the theologies or purposes of Matthew and Luke indicate how sophisticated those evangelists were in the manipulation of their materials. Such studies also demonstrate how certain items in the infancy stories may fit into particular christological or soteriological interpretations; but the latter often appear to be more a reflection of modern religious concerns than of the Gospel writers' designs. The principal problem with many redactional studies is that they tend to draw attention away from, or even to obscure, the actual narratives and the characters, social relations, or hymnic statements in them. Such studies make us more alert and sensitive as religious readers but do not appear fully open to the broader challenges that the infancy narratives may pose.

It would thus appear that, as a result initially of Western cultural developments and then of its own development as an academic enterprise, biblical scholarship has offered little beyond spiritual edification by way of elucidation of the very stories that form the basis of the celebration of Christmas. Having acknowledged that the extraordinary narratives of Christ's birth were quite unreliable and incredible as accounts of actual events, biblical scholars sought some minimal security in an inward spiritual or higher theological meaning. They effectively abandoned any attempt to maintain or to recover any implications the Christmas stories might have for the "real" world of politicoeconomic or general historical life. Meanwhile, the celebration of Christmas, along with the Christmas stories themselves, has moved increasingly into a world of fantasy in a cultural milieu that no longer has a sense of historical events that are being celebrated (or reenacted). Christ may now be born in our hearts, but little attention is given to the implications of Jesus' having been born historically.

HERO-LEGENDS OR NARRATIVES OF LIBERATION?

Legends of the Birth of the Hero: Definition and Motifs

While biblical scholars tended to ignore the infancy narratives of Jesus because of their indefensible mythical character and because of the retreat customarily made into inward spiritual interpretations, psychologists, myth-ophiles, and folklorists were finding them highly attractive. The basic Christmas story was now no longer so untouchable as Holy Writ, as *sui generis,* direct divine revelation, but with its marvelous mythical features it still held a certain mystique for those exploring the inner life. While scholars of the so-called history of religions school were attempting to explain certain "folk-loric motifs" and particularly the virgin birth from various Hellenistic religious sources,[33] the Freudian Otto Rank utilized the story of Jesus' birth and those of fourteen other heroes such as Oedipus, Romulus, and Lohengrin to construct a standard myth of the birth of the hero.[34] This myth, alongside other materials such as dreams, infantile imaginings, and neurotic fantasies, was then useful for Rank and others exploring individual psychological development, particularly the dynamics between the child and its parents. Even more significant for subsequent consumption in North America, C. G. Jung and his disciples used the story of Jesus' birth along with wide-ranging mythical materials to explore "the mythological stages in the evolution of consciousness" for the light it shed upon the development of personality.[35] Joseph Campbell then furnished a popularized, if vague and diffuse, discussion of what he called "the Monomyth," in *The Hero with a Thousand Faces.*[36]

During the early 1970s, as attention in academic circles returned from concern with sociopolitical issues to quest for personal meaning, certain motifs from the infancy stories of Jesus played a role in the largely Jungian quest for a significant sense of the self.[37] Even in New Testament courses, "the myth of the birth of the hero" rivaled redaction criticism as an approach to the infancy narratives. This was surely at least partly because the former approach provided a way to appreciate the stories as a whole with intriguing cross-cultural parallels, while redactional analysis tended toward a more abstract appreciation of the "theology" of Matthew or Luke, however sophisticated it may have been.

It may well be an indication of the significance that biblical scholars suspected lay in the broader comparative mythological and psychological analysis of the Jesus story that, at two major conferences in 1977, distinguished folklorists were invited to address groups consisting primarily of New Testament scholars. Their presentations were entitled "The Hero Pattern and the Life of Jesus" and "The Gospels as Oral Traditional Literature."[38] Discussions between biblical scholars and those in other disciplines such as folklore and literary analysis offer much promise of further understanding of materials of mutual interest. From these two recent interpretations of the Jesus story in the context of hero patterns, however, it is evident that many scholars are not yet familiar with the presuppositions, or adept in the sophisticated analytical techniques, of each others' fields.

The diverse, inconsistent, and imprecise use of fundamental interpretive categories presents a major obstacle to interdisciplinary study. During the last decade or two there has been at least some minimal convergence between some folklorists, anthropologists, and classicists in the way they define the concepts of myth, legend, and folktale as three different forms of "prose narrative." One highly important feature of these converging interdisciplinary distinctions and definitions is the attention to sociohistorical context. It may prove useful in biblical studies to utilize these cross-culturally derived and applicable distinctions and definitions—and thus simply to sidestep the heavily charged discussions within biblical studies both of Strauss's "mythological" interpretation of Jesus traditions and more recently of Bultmann's "demythologizing."

According to these converging definitions *myths* are accounts dealing with origins, whose main characters are not usually human beings but gods or spirits, and which are considered truthful in the society in which they are told.[39] *Legends,* like myths, are regarded as true by their tellers and audience; unlike myths, however, they are about humans, are set in a period less remote, and are not necessarily viewed as sacred. *Folktales* (including but not confined to what has been called "fairy tales"), unlike either myths or legends, are regarded as fiction, are not taken seriously, and are virtually timeless and placeless.[40]

It has been suggested recently that most of the narratives in the Hebrew Bible and the Gospels are myths, according to the definition just given.[41] Of course, New Testament materials have been viewed as mythical by their theological interpreters from the eighteenth century through Bultmann, in contrast to Old Testament narratives, whose scholarly defenders distinguished them particularly from ancient Near Eastern myths. According to the recently converging definitions of folklorists, classicists, and anthropologists, however, very few biblical narratives would qualify as myths. Nearly all biblical narratives are about people in ordinary, often conflictual sociohistorical interaction. With notable exceptions such as the molding of Adam out of the ground, the one transcendent "god" influences the action through certain forms of communication. God is occasionally praised in hymns as doing battle, but the enemies are not gods but human forces such as Pharaoh's armies. The Gospel infancy stories in particular are primarily about interaction between people, with divine guidance through angelic appearances as God's purpose or plan is accomplished through the actions of people. By contrast with the myths of other societies, the narratives in the Hebrew bible and the Christian Gospels cannot be categorized as sacred narratives about gods, spirits, or other superhuman beings. But neither are many of these narratives reliable accounts of events that actually happened—hence their rejection, long since, as history. It should be clear that the recently converging interdisciplinary definition of myth, like the old conceptual alternatives of "myth" versus "history," is unable to deal adequately with biblical narratives, a subject to which we must return later in the chapter.[42]

If we focus on the infancy narrative of Jesus and the other "myths of the birth of the hero" discussed by Rank and other mythophiles, it is clear that very little of this material fits the recently converging definition of myth. Such hero stories are rather examples of what folklorists are calling *legends*. The stories of Romulus, of Oedipus king of Thebes, and of Moses were all taken seriously and took place in particular times and places, unlike folktales, but they took place in the "remembered," and not completely remote, past and were not about gods but about people, unlike myths. The use of the term *legend* for the infancy narratives and pertinent comparative materials is attractive also because it enables us to refer to certain marvelous or fantastic features such as angelic appearances, divine parentage, floating in a basket, or nursing by a she-wolf as "legendary" without getting bogged down in the morass of previous debates regarding the meaning of myth.

Further procedural flexibility is necessary, however, in order to avoid winding up in a museum-like taxonomy of definitions by narrative type. In addition to the sensitivity to context already evident in the definitions above, it is important to maintain a sensitivity to the particular use or function of a given narrative or of a given motif and to changes in cultural or social presuppositions and contexts. For example, if a story usually told of a hero is applied to a figure traditionally understood as a god in Greek culture, is the narrative then a myth or a legend? If stories originally about a human hero are transformed into sacred narratives about the same figure now understood as a god, are they myths in the new sociocultural context? Or if the traditional cultural presuppositions shift dramatically in modern society, are stories that traditionally functioned as myths or legends still to be so classified?

The need for flexibility is vividly illustrated precisely by the changes in function of the infancy stories about Jesus in connection with the changes in cultural context. When, in the context of highly ritualized and established ecclesial Christianity, the abbreviated Christmas story of the divine Christ's incarnation formed part of an annual cycle of highly sacralized stories grounding the sequence of sacred festivals (such as Christmas itself, Holy Week, and Easter), in which the principal actors were divine (God, Jesus, the Holy Spirit) or superhuman (the blessed virgin, angels), then it came close to being a myth, functionally speaking. When the infancy stories are presented in the contemporary Christmas fantasy of manger scenes alongside scenes of Santa's elves and reindeer or in cartooned television specials in the same vein as "The Grinch Who Stole Christmas" or "Rudolf the Red-nosed Reindeer," then they would appear to be more like folktales, that is, virtually timeless and placeless (although seasonal), not to be taken too seriously, and even, in some cases, taken as the adventures of animal characters. As the stories stand in the Gospels, or were traditionally read or enacted in churches or homes, they appear to be legends.

For exploration of the infancy narratives in comparison with stories of heroes, of course, the appropriate concept clearly is legends, and the latter category should be substituted for "myth" in further discussion of Rank's and others' heroes. Rank suggested that "a standard saga" of the hero's birth could be reconstructed from "a series of uniformly common features" found in stories about such figures as Cyrus, Oedipus, Perseus, Romulus, Hercules, Moses, and Jesus:[43] the hero is the child of distinguished parents; his origin is preceded by difficulties; an oracle cautions against his birth, threatening danger to his "father"; he is exposed in a box on the water but then saved by animals or lowly people; after growing up, he takes revenge on his father and achieves honors. Enough of the particulars mentioned about Jesus in Matthew 1–2 and Luke 1–2, on the other hand, appear sufficiently similar to the principal motifs in the pattern we adapted from Rank that the legendary pattern of "the birth of the hero" seems applicable.

More Complex Patterns: Stories of Liberation

One has the uneasy feeling, however, that the legends of the birth of the hero do not comprise the whole story in the case of the birth narratives about Jesus. Interpretation of the latter in terms of the hero legends rests on the important assumption that the pattern of motifs implicit in a particular set of legends is the bearer of meaning. Hence, interpretation concentrates on the motifs that persist through legends about many heroes across several cultures and through several centuries. It is obvious, however, that such an assumption and procedure are biased in favor of the recurrent pattern, to the neglect (if not exclusion) of the particular details that give a given set of legends concrete references and implications.

Indeed, when we examine the details in the Jesus stories more carefully, a number of differences begin to appear with many of the typical motifs in the hero legends. While Jesus' mother, Mary, is a virgin, she is apparently an ordinary peasant girl, and not of royal or distinguished ancestry. The father, Joseph, while he stands in the Davidic line according to both Matthew's and Luke's genealogies, is also not distinguished and certainly not a king, in contrast with the grandfathers, fathers, or uncles in the typical hero legends. Correspondingly, the ruler, Herod (and Augustus Caesar) is totally unrelated to Jesus. In the Gospel stories, furthermore, Jesus is not exposed by the father-ruler on a mountain or in a field, much less in a box on the water. Jesus is indeed rescued and raised by lowly people, but they are his parents, not foster parents.

In many of these differences from the typical hero legends, the stories of infancy narratives of Jesus are similar to the story of Moses in Exodus 1–2, which, significantly, has been thought to have influenced the Jesus stories. The exposure of Moses in a basket in the Nile, of course, has one dramatic parallel to the stories of Sargon and Romulus. But the details of Moses' birth and infancy make Exodus 1–2 as dissimilar to the typical hero legends as they are similar to the stories about Jesus. For example, his parents are not distinguished but common, and the ruler, Pharaoh, is unrelated.[44]

More decisive than their differences in detail from the other hero legends, however, is the different pattern of relationships that the biblical narratives of Jesus and of Moses display. The pattern in the biblical stories is more complex, and it involves a differently defined fundamental conflict. In the typical hero legends the current ruler, who is also (grand)father of the hero, is threatened by the birth of the hero and seeks to eliminate him by exposure, but the hero is rescued and raised by (usually) lowly foster parents and eventually takes the place of (grand)father as ruler, establishing a new regime. In the Gospel narratives, the current ruler—a tyrant who is totally unrelated to Jesus—is threatened by the birth of the king-to-be and seeks to kill him by action that involves more general political repression, while Jesus' parents, in rescuing him, become refugees from the political repression that continues under the ruler's son and successor.

The fundamental relationship and basic conflict is not the simple one between current "father" (= current ruler) and child-hero (= future ruler) but a far more political conflict between current ruler, who takes repressive measures to counter the challenge posed by the child, on the one hand, and the child-liberator along with the parents and other lowly people, on the other. If we include the canticles from Luke 1–2, the conflict is articulated explicitly as one between the lowly (whom God is delivering) and the ruling potentates (whose reign God is terminating). The Magi, moreover, if we take them seriously as royal-priestly advisers from the Eastern empire (see chap. 2), add yet a further political complication. In Exodus 1–2, similarly, the conflict is not simply one between (foster) father-ruler and (adopted) son as a potential successor but one between Pharaoh's highly repressive rule and the future liberator (who, ironically, escapes from the Pharaoh's repressive measures directly into the royal court) and his own people, the Hebrews. In both the stories about Jesus and those about Moses, the purpose is liberation of the oppressed, and the tone or emphasis in the narratives is concern for them over against their tyrannical rulers. More precisely, not only in Exodus 1–2 but in in the infancy narratives of Jesus as well, the lowly people who are to be saved from their rulers are the Israelites.

A consideration of the language and cultural traditions in Matthew 1–2 and Luke 1–2 indicates that the stories of Jesus' birth reflect and almost certainly emerged from a Palestinian Jewish milieu and thus reinforce the explicit indications that the stories focus on the redemption of Israel from its rulers. Back at the turn of the century, with interest focused on the virgin birth, scholars were fascinated with possible parallels from Hellenistic religion. In recent decades scholarly attention has more carefully explored the infancy narratives' roots in and parallels with Palestinian Jewish literature. It is now often observed that the language, characters, and ideas both in Luke 1–2 and in Matthew 1–2 are so traditionally Jewish that there is little in them that is distinctively Christian.

There is wide recognition now that Luke 1–2 reflect a Palestinian Jewish milieu. Not only are there far more "Semiticisms" in these narratives than in the rest of Luke (with the canticles often being labeled as Jewish psalms, perhaps originally in Hebrew or Aramaic), but the characters in Luke 1 are representatives of typical Israelite or "Old Testament piety," according to long-standing consensus. "Luke" is thought to have composed much of the narrative in chapters 1–2, but in doing so he drew not only on traditional biblical terms and phrases but on particular biblical forms and figures as well.[45] Most determinative of the overall organization of his materials, perhaps, he utilized the biblical form of the annunciation of the birth of a significant leader or liberator, such as those of Ishmael and Isaac (Gen. 16:7–13; 17:1–3, 15–21; 18:1–2, 10–15) and Samson (Judg. 13).[46] Most influential of all on the portrayal of the annunciation and birth of both John the Baptist and Jesus is the story of the annunication and birth of Samuel to Hannah and Elkanah (1 Sam. 1). Luke's close adherence to the traditional form, in five major steps, with several subsidiary steps within the divine message, means that the narrative in Luke 1 resonates with important Jewish biblical figures and events. And those figures and events are highly significant, including the issue of the fulfillment of the promises to Abraham, one of the great "liberators" of Israel, as well as Samuel, the last great charismatic liberator who also was the prototypical prophet in the anointing of the first two kings. It is worth noting as well that similar steps occur in the divine commissioning of other great leaders of the people's liberation, such as Moses and Gideon (Exod. 3:2–12; Judg. 6:12–22).

Some would go as far as to claim that the genre as well as the style of Matthew's narratives are those of Jewish midrash.[47] Although that claim has not found general acceptance, Matthew like Luke is clearly following traditional biblical literary forms, such as the annunciation of a great leader's birth.[48] As noted above, a highly distinctive feature of Matthew 1–2 is the prominence of "formula quotations" of biblical prophecies at crucial points in the story. The importance of these quotations in the present context is that they illustrate explicitly and vividly that in certain crucial ways the birth of Jesus was a fulfillment of Israel's biblical prophecies.

Moreover, Matthew more clearly than Luke is using already formed narratives. Analysts do not agree about the precise scope, shape, and form of such pre-Matthean material. The "main pre-Matthean narrative" may well have been structured along the lines of a series of three angelic dream appearances (basically Matt. 1:20–21, 24–25; 2:13–15a; and 2:19–21).[49] There was also likely a pre-Matthean story about the visit of the Magi.[50] The importance of recognizing such pre-Matthean traditions in the present connection is that we thus have evidence of narratives, however "legendary," about the birth of Jesus that originated apparently from a Palestinian Jewish milieu probably during the first generation after Jesus' ministry. Such narratives, moreover, included portrayal of the central conflict with Herod and a portrayal of the child Jesus as repeating the formative history of Israel (going down into Egypt in time of distress and then returning to its own homeland) and the experiences of Moses (including the hostility of Herod and Pharaoh, the kings' repressive measures, and the return home).[51] In any case, the pre-Matthean as well as the Matthean narratives are both deeply rooted in, and make clear reference to, the tradition of God's liberation of Israel from its enemies. This has always been recognized as a vivid feature of the canticles in Luke 1. But it is no less prominent, if in less explicit hymnic terminology, in Matthew as well.

Josephus's retelling of stories of Moses in Exodus 1–2 provides a striking illustration of how resilient the dominant biblical concern with the people's liberation could be, precisely when those stories were being further conformed to the birth-of-the-hero pattern. The passage in Josephus is doubly interesting in this connection because it has some other, more particular parallels with Matthew 1–2.[52] The story in Exodus 1 starts with Pharaoh's attempt to kill the males born to the Hebrews, one of whom happened to be the infant Moses. Josephus, in an apparent attempt to conform the story to the standard Greco-Roman hero motifs, has a sacred scribe prophecy to the king that an Israelite would be born who would end the sovereignty of the Egyptians and exalt the Israelites, in response to which the king ordered the newborn Israelite males cast into the river (*Ant.* 2.205–6). But not simply the king is threatened, as in the hero legends, but the Egyptians generally were filled with dread, like "Herod and all Jerusalem" in Matthew 2. Moreover, Moses' father, Amram (whose wife was already pregnant), was told by God in a dream that the soon-to-be-born Moses would deliver his people from bondage (*Ant.* 2.212, 215–16; cf. Matt. 2:1–3; 1:18–21). The prophecy to the old king is inserted into the story, but the overall point of the story is made even more explicit earlier than in the biblical source: the deliverance of the people from bondage.

The stories of Jesus' infancy may well be interpretable according to the fundamental pattern of the legends of the birth of the hero. Indeed, it appears that this may well have been the way the traditional Christmas story was understood in many contexts since Christianity became established in the Hellenistic-Roman world. Moreover, such a meaning or understanding of the basic story must be seen to have a clear political dimension interrelated with the psychospiritual significance so attractive to recent mythographers and psychologists. Without the concrete particulars of the story, however, there are fewer "controls" on the way the narrative functions or is understood in a given cultural situation. There is thus serious reason to attend to those concrete particulars in the infancy narratives of Jesus as potential controls on our proclivities to adapt the recurrent pattern (with "universal" pretentions) to certain questionable Christian theological viewpoints.[53]

REALISTIC NARRATIVE AND HISTORICAL CONTEXT

Another reason why the infancy narratives of Jesus cannot simply be classified with legends of the birth of the hero—or neglected as mere unhistorical myths or treated simply as illustrations of Matthean or Lucan theology—is that they refer to historical figures. Greco-Roman legends and mythography fixed supposed burial places for some of the heroes cited by Rank, but the likes of Perseus, Theseus, and Romulus were fictional figures. Jesus, like Cyrus and perhaps Moses and Zoroaster, however, was a historical figure. However legendary he appears in Herodotus and other literature, Cyrus was the historical founder of the Persian empire.[54] And while we cannot move directly or even indirectly from the exodus narratives to actual events in Egypt or on Mount Sinai, there may well have been one or more leaders of proto-Israelites in those generations and locations in which earliest "Israel" had its origins. The infancy stories about Jesus tell of a figure of very recent memory, one now generally accepted as historical, despite the lack of extra-Christian documentary evidence. Moreover, the infancy narratives of Jesus, like those of Cyrus, also mention other historical figures.[55] The integral roles played by Herod the Great and Augustus Caesar in particular ground the infancy stories of Jesus firmly in world history. These narratives also refer to particular concrete historical circumstances such as the subjection of the people of Israel to Roman tribute and repressive measures taken by a threatened King Herod. Under the impact of modern rationalism early historical criticism rightly discerned that these narratives did not refer to actual historical events. But it will hardly help to continue to treat as myths these narratives that, besides displaying a cast of characters and a pattern of interaction far more complex than those in the typical hero legends, refer to historical figures and concrete historical circumstances and relationships.

One suspects that the earlier modern understanding of myth and of the contrast "myth *versus* history" involves a serious confusion between two different issues: types of narrative, on the one hand, and the ways in which they were "true" or reliable as information or representation, on the other. With regard to the latter issue, we have long since recognized that both myths and legends, particularly as defined more carefully above, are useful as sources of historical or ethnographic information for the societies that produced them. For example, *Enuma Elish,* a Babylonian myth of origins, can be seen to reflect certain features of imperial Babylonian civilization and the historical transition to that stage. Legends such as those in Herodotus's accounts of the birth of Cyrus not only reflect but represent, in whatever heroic form, certain historical features of the historical transition from the Median to the Persian empire that he founded. The legends of Jesus' birth provide even more complex and detailed references to historical circumstances and portrayal of historical social relations. Thus myth, legend, and history, as categories of narratives, all provide, in varying degrees and manners, references to historical events and relationships. As long as biblical studies had given up the idea that such material as the infancy narratives refers in some way to real (historical) events, then there was understandably no reason to explore the historical conditions of those (non)events. But once we begin to see more clearly that such narratives do, in however legendary a way, refer to historical figures and circumstances, then exploration of the historical conditions is essential.

The earlier understanding of "myth versus history" also left us confused about narrative forms and their subject matter or meaning. If a narrative appeared to be a myth, then the subject matter or meaning had to be located somewhere else than in the narrative—for example, in the "folk" mentality that produced the myth, or in some higher theological or inner spiritual truth. With respect to particular narratives, the interpretation in terms of "mythical pattern" of heroes' birth legends is of a similar character. The meaning is located not in the narrative itself but in some transcultural pattern that is only incidentally concretized by particular narratives. Closer examination of the infancy narratives of Jesus (and Moses), however, suggested that the concretizing details in these narratives make their meaning more complex and more political than the hypothetical "mythical pattern" might allow. It would appear to be important to take seriously the concrete, ostensibly historical details, perhaps including the angelic appearances, which allude to other concrete figures or events in biblical memory or tradition, in order to comprehend or at least be open to the meaning of these narratives.

In order to understand such stories adequately, we apparently need a concept of realistic or history-like narrative for which one does not seek the subject matter or meaning outside the narrative itself. In such narrative, as in historical narrative itself, not only do characters and circumstances belong together, but the subject matter or meaning is located in the narrated relations and interaction of those characters and circumstances. That a historical novel is fiction does not mean that it should not be read as realistic narrative. Similarly, that the infancy stories of Jesus are legendary, with some of the incidents being fictional or fantastic, does not mean that we should reduce the narratives to christological truth or a mythical pattern. Partly as a result of its defensive reaction to the challenge of considering biblical stories as myth and not history, biblical studies lost a sense of narrative. Biblical interpreters are now regaining an appreciation for narrative form, but this is often without any relation to concrete circumstances and social relations, and sometimes consciously unrelated to historical or even cultural context.[56] If we are dealing with realistic or history-like narrative, whatever its factual or fictional character, and particularly if it ostensibly refers to certain historical circumstances, then simply in order to take the narrative itself seriously, we must seek to understand it against the historical background of its origin and reference.

If we no longer feel compelled defensively and categorically to dismiss the stories of Jesus' birth, or the narrative details in them, as "myth"—or to insist that they are after all historical "truth"—then perhaps we could read the stories as history-like narratives (or "historical legends" or "ledendary history") that provide a meaningful presentation or representation of certain historical circumstances and relationships. To do so, however, we need to have a more adequate acquaintance with the particular historical circumstances and social relations that provide the background from which the narratives emerged and to which they refer. Then we can better evaluate and appreciate the ways in which the infancy narratives of Jesus portray those circumstances and relationships.

PART ONE

◆

The Infancy Narratives in Historical Context: The Rulers

·2·

Caesar and Census

As we stand before the idyllic Christmas scenes of the Christ-child in the manger, adored by Mary and surrounded by happy shepherds and the gentle ox and ass, political conflict may be the furthest thing from our minds. We are vaguely aware that Mary, Joseph, and the shepherds are humble folk, and probably poor as well, and that the "three kings" who bring such valuable gifts are wealthy. Our usual hearing of the Christmas story, however, misses or perhaps avoids the politicoeconomic as well as the religiocultural conflict that is implicit throughout the stories and that at points even comes explicitly to expression. It may be useful, therefore, stepping outside of both the established holiday context and traditional christological frame of reference, to make a brief overview of the fundamental conflict articulated in the infancy narratives before exploring the principal figures, institutions, and social relationships involved in greater detail. (At this point we will leave aside the Lucan "canticles" both because of their more traditional religious or even devotional use and because they are semiseparable from the stories in which they are now embedded.)

The most obvious conflict, and the most explicit violence, appears in Matthew's depiction of Herod's "massacre of the innocents" (2:16). But that horrendous slaughter of babies is rooted in the primary conflict portrayed in Matthew's narrative, namely, that the child has been born "king of the Jews" precisely in order to deliver the people from the rule of the established king, Herod. The very structure of the story is the mutual threat that the child and Herod pose to each other. Along the way of his itinerary, moreover, Jesus repeats the formative history of his people, its original story of liberation from bondage and a hostile king.

As in Matthew, the point of Luke's narrative, which recurs in several of the component stories or songs, is the birth of a king. Luke's narrative, however, is less explicit and graphic about how the birth of Jesus as the new king of Israel stands in direct opposition to the established rule of Herod and Caesar, so we must attend to the principal indicators in the component stories. First of all, Jesus is announced by the angel to Mary in Luke 1:32–33 as the one who would restore the Davidic kingship in Israel (i.e., in Palestinian Jewish society). The words of the divine messenger are a direct allusion to the original founding oracle of the Davidic dynasty, 2 Samuel 7. But Herod was still king over Jewish society, and any ancient hearer or reader would have taken the Roman imperial context for granted. As was the case with earlier empires, so too the Romans placed their own clients in power as local dynasts. Thus in causing Jesus to be proclaimed and born as the new king who would reinstitute the glorious Davidic kingship in Israel, God was directly opposing the Roman empire as well as its client-king Herod.

Of course, such opposition was nothing new in the sacred biblical traditions of the Jewish people. Saul and then David himself had been "anointed" (i.e., *messiah*) by God as well as by the people themselves to oppose the Philistines, who were threatening to subject the people of Israel. And Elijah was commissioned by God on Mount Horeb (= Sinai) to anoint Jehu as king in order to lead a revolution against the oppressive regime of Ahab. Elijah, of course, was well remembered as one "who brought kings down to destruction, . . . who anointed kings to inflict retribution, . . . (and) who was ready to restore the tribes of Jacob" (Sirach 48:6, 8, 10). That is the background and connotation when the divine messenger Gabriel (= God is my warrior) announces to Zechariah that his son, John, will go before the Lord "in the spirit and power of Elijah, . . . to make ready for the Lord a people prepared" (Luke 1:17).

There is a similar background and connotation to the way in which the Spirit-filled Elizabeth greets the pregnant Mary: "Blessed are you among women!" (Luke 1:42). Anyone familiar with the sacred traditions of the people would immediately be led to think of Mary as another Jael or Judith. They were *the* two women to be greeted in this way, because of their heroic action directly against enemy rulers in the liberation of their people. In giving birth to the new Davidic king, Mary also is acting in opposition to the established ruler(s).

The scope of the conflict is dramatically broadened and its intensity escalated with the beginning of the story in Luke 2:1–20. The opposition could not be clearer for those with eyes to see. Caesar's decree that the whole world must be assessed for taxation is the occasion for the actual birth of the new Dividic king of Israel. The latter, moreover, is announced as "savior," as well as messiah, and the heavenly army proclaims "peace" on the earth. But (as we shall see further below) Caesar was already being given divine honors around the empire as the savior who had brought peace. Finally, in what is really the terminal, prophetic story in Luke's infancy narrative, the Spirit-filled Simeon and the prophetess Anna and her listeners receive the child with joy because they have been longing for the liberation of their people (2:25, 38).

The principal thrust of the infancy narratives would appear to be that God, through the birth of Jesus as the anointed Davidic king, is effecting the deliverance of Israel from its Herodian and Roman rulers. Since the basic conflict appears to be between the rulers and ruled, the exploration of the fundamental social relationships reflected in the infancy narratives that follows will be organized according to that division, with chapters 2 and 3 focused on the Roman and the Jewish rulers, respectively. Chapters 4, 5, and 6, are then devoted to the Palestinian Jewish people, starting with the peasantry in general, then exploring the situations of women, priests, and shepherds in particular, and concluding with the people's songs of liberation.

CAESAR THE SAVIOR

Highly regarded biblical scholars interpret the appearance of Caesar Augustus in Luke 2:1–20 as merely a setting for the birth of Jesus. The emperor's decree of a census is correspondingly viewed as a literary device. Neither Caesar Augustus nor the census are important in themselves. At most, the most powerful figure in the world serves as a facilitating "agent of God, who by his edict of registration brings it about that Jesus is born in the town of David."[1] Besides providing a "chronological framework," the Roman emperor Augustus is "ironically . . . serving God's plan" in his decree.[2] Luke thus associates the birth of the messiah with "a famous Roman emperor" whose lengthy reign was "widely regarded as the era of peace."[3] Augustus had "pacified the world" and then been widely celebrated as "savior of the whole world." Luke, of course, was not "denying the imperial ideals" but merely presenting "an implicit challenge to the imperial propaganda."[4]

One must wonder, however, whether Luke is all that timid and apologetic, and whether the appearance of Caesar Augustus and his decree are all that innocuous in this story. The contents of the angel's message to the shepherds and of the heavenly hosts' chorus later in the story fly directly in the face of those "imperial ideals." Jesus is announced not just as "the messiah, the lord," but as "savior" as well. Now "messiah" and "lord" may very well be interpreted as "kerygmatic titles, stemming from the Jewish Christian community of Palestine." However, "savior" (*sōtēr*) is not a major title for Jesus in the New Testament; this is the only application of the term to Jesus in the synoptic Gospels. And in narrative context it is juxtaposed with Augustus Caesar, who was known far and wide as the "savior" of the world. Moreover, the only time Paul uses the term is in a revealed "word of the Lord" in which the return of Christ to earth is portrayed in terms of the triumphal *parousia* of the Roman emperor (the "savior") to a city that joyously celebrates his coming.[5]

The story in Luke 2:1–20 clearly announces the birth of a savior. But in the context of the Roman empire, and especially after the reign of Augustus, there would have been no doubt whatever about who the savior was. What, moreover, would be the point in the story of the heavenly host's singing of peace? Augustus had already brought peace, which is why he was honored as savior.

The Savior Who Brings Peace

For two or three generations prior to the victory of Augustus at the battle of Actium, the cities and peoples of the eastern Mediterranean had experienced virtually continuous political conflict and chaos. If anything, it intensified after Rome determined to impose order, for Pompey's conquests were followed by the wars against the rising Parthian empire to the east, and then by the empirewide and decade-long Roman civil war. The Roman republic was tearing itself apart, and the rest of the world with it. With his victory at Actium, Augustus was able to bring peace and order into the world for the first time in anyone's memory. The empire he established was *salvation,* and he himself was the *savior.*

Starting almost immediately, and continuing into subsequent generations, there was an outpouring of gratitude and good will toward Augustus himself as well as Rome for bringing the peace for which people had yearned so long. From all corners of the empire came paeans of praise for the ruler who had brought peace, order, harmony, and prosperity. It appears in every genre of literature, such as poetry, history, and philosophy, as well as in inscriptions, temples, and official communications. And there is a genuinely religious feeling coming to expression in the explicitly religious language and concepts, some of which are highly familiar from the New Testament and subsequent Christian usage. Dominant is the praise of the all-powerful, wise, and virtuous ruler Augustus (or his successor) who has brought peace and prosperity to the world in fulfillment of the hopes of humankind. Therefore, particularly in the cities of the eastern Mediterranean, the imperial savior is honored, indeed worshiped, as divine.

Panegyrics from Roman poets seem extravagant by modern standards:

> Thine age, O Caesar, has brought back fertile crops to the fields, ... has wiped away our sins and revived the ancient virtues, ... and the fame and majesty of our empire were spread from the sun's bed in the west to the east. As long as Caesar is the guardian of the state, neither civil dissension nor violence shall banish peace. (Horace, *Odes* 4.15)

> Lo! under his auspices, my son, that glorious Rome shall bound

her empire by earth, (and) her pride by heaven. . . . This, this is he whom thou so oft hearest promised to thee, Augustus Caesar, son of a god, who shall again set up the Golden Age. (Virgil, *Aeneid* 6.780–93)

By comparison with these, however, the divine honors Augustus received in the East are more deeply religious, even cosmic and ontological in their conception. In Halicarnassus, for example, sometime after 2 B.C.E., when Augustus received the title "Father of the Fatherland" in Rome, "Caesar Augustus, . . . Zeus Paternal, and Savior of the whole human race, in whom Providence has not only fulfilled but even surpassed the prayers of all men . . . [is to be honored as god] with public games and with statues, with sacrifices and with hymns."[6] Perhaps the most comprehensive illustration of the worship of the emperor as the savior and bringer of peace and fulfillment is the inscription of the decree of the Provincial Assembly of Asia, dated 9 B.C.E.:

The most divine Caesar . . . we should consider equal to the Beginning [*archē*] of all things . . .; for when everything was falling [into disorder] and tending toward dissolution, he restored it once more and gave to the whole world a new aspect; Caesar . . . the common good Fortune of all. . . . The Beginning of life and vitality. . . . all the cities unanimously adopt the birthday of divine Caesar as the new beginning of the year. . . . Whereas the Providence which has regulated our whole existence . . . has brought our life to the climax of perfection in giving to us [the emperor] Augustus, whom it [Providence] filled with virtue for the welfare of men, and who, being sent to us and our descendants as a Savior, has put an end to war and has set all things in order; and [whereas,] having become manifest [*phaneis*], Caesar has fulfilled all the hopes of earlier times . . . in surpassing all the benefactors [*euergetai*] who preceded him . . . , and whereas, finally, the birthday of the god [Augustus] has been for the whole world the beginning of good news [*euaggelion*] concerning him [therefore let a new era begin from his birth] (*OGIS* 2, no. 458)

Far from being a new or isolated phenomenon, moreover, this worship of the emperor as savior who instituted peace was both rooted in a long-standing Hellenistic tradition of honoring the emperor as "savior, benefactor, and (god)" manifest and supported by a broader *theology* of empire as well. Particularly in the East the veneration of the goddess Roma had become institutionalized during the late republican period; in numerous places sacrifices were apparently offered to Rome and the Roman people in the local Romaion (temple to Roma). It was clear generally to the cities of the East that God or the gods were with Rome. Even the Jewish Pharisee and historian Josephus appeals to his rebellious fellow Jews from the theological view that "God who went the round of the nations, bringing to each in turn the rod of empire, now rested over Italy" (*War* 5.367). Needless to say, the Romans themselves were convinced that the gods had richly blessed their undertakings. One is almost tempted to see a prefiguration of later (Christian) trinitarian doctrine in the formulation of the oath of allegiance (to Gaius, 37 C.E.) sworn by both citizen-bodies in eastern cities and Roman "businessmen" there: "We swear by Zeus the Savior and the God Caesar Augustus [Octavian] and the holy Virgin of our city [Athena Polias] that we are loyally disposed to Gaius Caesar Augustus."[7] How political theology was integrated into natural theology can be illustrated from the Pythagorean Diotogenes: "It is right for a king to act as does God in his reign and command over the universe. . . . And king bears the same relation to state as God to universe; and state is to universe as king is to God."[8]

As Ernst Barker pointed out some time ago, the Roman empire was a religious as well as a political reality. Just as a city-state entailed a civic religion, "an Empire-State entailed an empire-worship; and an empire-worship in turn . . . entailed the worship of an emperor."[9] And, in connection with the nativity narrative in Luke 2, the important point is to realize that the key symbols of the sacral imperial politics were that Caesar (Augustus and his successors) was the divine savior who had brought peace to the world.

The *pax Romana*, of course, was a peace imposed by military might. "You O Roman, remember to rule the nations with might. This will be your genius—to impose the way of peace, to spare the conquered and crush the proud" (Virgil, *Aeneid* 6.850–53). Peace and military victory were literally two sides of the same coin, as is illustrated many times over in numismatic finds from the early empire. Typically on one side appears the head of the goddess Pax, with Augustus on the other side in military garb with a spear in hand.[10]

The imposition of the *pax Romana*, of course, meant subjection. As Tacitus has a Roman governor say to a leader of the Germans: "All men have to bow to their betters; it had been decreed by those gods . . . that with the Roman people should rest the decision what to give and what to take away" (*Annals* 13.56.1). And subjection by military conquest, a principal point of which was to terrorize the subjected people, could get brutal and bloody. On Germanicus's operations in Germany in 14 C.E., Tacitus reports that "for fifty miles around he wasted the country with sword and flame. Neither age nor sex inspired pity. Places sacred and profane were razed indifferently to the ground" (*Annals* 1.51.1). The main thing, however, was to terrorize and subject, not utterly to destroy, other cities and peoples. As Augustus himself says in his *res gestae:* "Foreign peoples who could safely be pardoned I preferred to spare rather than to extirpate." Toward the end of the republic, as Rome expanded its empire dramatically, its conquest combined mass slaughter with mass enslavement. Economic motives were clearly operative here. The Roman patricians had steadily been taking over the land from the plebians, who had to serve in the legions, and required large gangs of slaves to operate their large agrarian estates, or latifundia. In their spectacular series of conquests around the Mediterranean basin, they brought hundreds of thousands of slaves to Italy. Of course in many cases, particularly in the East, it was more beneficial economically simply to lay the people under tribute.

Once conquered, the subjected peoples were henceforth controlled by their "savior." As Seneca suggests to the young Nero in a soliloquy, the emperor had "been chosen to serve on earth as vicar of the gods" and was "the arbiter of life and death for the nations" (*Chem.* 1.1, 2). It behooved the subject peoples to "preserve mutual goodwill with peace and concord and friendship," which meant basically recognition of Roman rule and obedience to it. As Plutarch declared, the peoples of the empire had no need of political activity, since, with the Roman peace, all war had ceased. And "of liberty the people enjoy as much as our rulers allot them, and perhaps more would not be better" (Plutarch, *Precepts of Statecraft,* 32). In controlling and exploiting the subject peoples, the Romans collaborated with the native rulers or upper class. Not surprisingly, it was the urban aristocracies in the East who engaged so eagerly in the worship of the emperor. Tacitus mentions that it was an "old and long-standing principle of Roman policy [to] employ kings among the instruments of servitude" (*Agricola* 14.1).

For subject peoples, the *pax Romana* thus meant subordination as a system, and the system as subordination. "Like one continuous country and one people, all the world quietly obeys. Everything is carried out by command or nod. . . . The constitution is a universal democracy under the one man that can rule and govern best."[11] If on occasion there was some unrest, a cohort of the emperor's soldiery could be sent in, "the terrors of which, along with a few executions, restored things to concord" (Tacitus, *Annals* 13.48, slightly paraphrased). How the subject peoples likely felt about the Roman peace is suggested in a famous passage where Tacitus has the Caledonian chieftain say to his fellow Britons: "You have sought in vain to escape [the Romans'] oppression by obedience and submissiveness. [They are] the plunderers of the world. . . . If the enemy is rich, they are rapacious, if poor, they lust for dominion. Not East, not West has sated them. . . . They rob, butcher, plunder,

and call it 'empire'; and where they make a desolation, they call it 'peace' "
(*Agricola* 30).

The Roman Peace versus the Palestinian Jewish People

How this peace bore on the Palestinian Jews of Jesus' time is portrayed
vividly in an abundant literature, from cryptic allusions in some of the Dead
Sea Scrolls, to lurid visions in apocalyptic literature, to caustic comments in
rabbinic debates. The most direct and descriptive statements perhaps come
from the historian Flavius Josephus, who participated in the great Jewish
War of 66–70, first as a Jewish general, and then as an adviser to the Roman
troops. Although he writes history basically from the Roman point of view,
he is also sensitive to what happened to his people, even if from his own
aristocratic standpoint. Thus by focusing on his reports, we can gain a sense
not only of the Roman viewpoint but of both the Jewish resistance generally
and a significant form of leadership in that resistance as well.

The stubborn Palestinian Jews were conquered four times in the course of
two centuries before they acquiesced in the *pax Romana*—twice by around
the time Jesus was born, once more before Matthew and Luke were written,
and once again before those Gospels were very widely read. The initial phase
of conquest lasted for a generation, from Pompey's initial subjection of the
country in 63 B.C.E. until the Romans' client-king Herod had finally conquered
the people with the help of Roman troops in 37 B.C.E. The slaughter and
enslavement were not extreme in the initial conquest by Pompey—a mere
twelve thousand in the capture of Jerusalem, including many priests and others
engaged in sacrifices at the altar on the sabbath (*War* 1.148–51; *Ant.* 14.64–
71). But thereafter the Palestinian Jews suffered repeated brutality, partly as
the result of Roman attempts to suppress continuing resistance led by rival
Hasmonean figures, and partly because of the struggle among powerful Roman leaders for control of the empire. Crassus heavily plundered the Temple
(two thousand talents had been left untouched by Pompey) to fund his expedition against the Parthian empire to the east (54–53 B.C.E.). A few years
later Cassius, in connection with further attempts to check the Parthians,
captured the Galilean town of Tarichea, "where he reduced thirty thousand
Jews to slavery" (*War* 1.179–80; *Ant.* 14.105, 120). Jewish resistance and
Roman military operations continued periodically until Herod finally beat
the Jews into submission.

The second Roman conquest, in response to massive popular Jewish rebellions in every major Jewish district of Palestine, occurred right around the
time Jesus was supposedly born, that is, at the death of Herod, in 4 B.C.E.
Roughly contemporaneous with the birth of Jesus, the messianic king of the
Jews and savior in the Lucan story, there were three major "messianic move-

ments" led by popularly acclaimed "kings" of masses of Jewish peasants, and the Romans had to reconquer the country with sizable contingents of troops. The slaughter and enslavement that ensued is noteworthy because it occurred in places in which Jesus and his followers lived or were active, according to gospel traditions. The Roman troops "captured and burned the city of Sepphoris [a few miles from Nazareth] and reduced its inhabitants to slavery." In northwestern Judea (apparently), says Josephus, "the whole district became a scene of fire and blood. . . . Emmaus [cf. Luke 24], the inhabitants of which had fled, was burned to the ground." The Romans then scoured the countryside for rebels, imprisoned many, and crucified about two thousand (*War* 2.68, 70–71, 75; *Ant.* 17.289, 290–91, 295).

The most fully documented Roman conquest of the Jews—and Jewish rebellion—was the great Jewish War of 66–70, in which Josephus was a principal actor, often an eyewitness. The Romans, having been completely driven out of Palestine by a massive popular revolt, had to make a major military mobilization to retake the country and were merciless in reconquest. A few brief illustrations from Josephus tell the story of slaughter and devastation. At the town of Japhia, a few miles southwest of Nazareth, after six hours of fighting, "the more efficient combatants were at length exterminated, and the rest of the population was then massacred in the open or in their houses, young and old alike. For no males were spared except infants; these along with the women the Romans sold as slaves. The slain . . . amounted to fifteen thousand; the captives numbered 2,130" (*War* 3.304–5). In many other districts, the Roman army systematically implemented what was apparently a "scorched-earth policy," then set out on what has in recent times been called "search and destroy." Those who did not flee the Roman advance were either slaughtered or enslaved. Those who fled were hunted down by the cavalry. In Perea, for example, "the whole countryside through which their flight had lain was one scene of carnage, and the Jordan choked with dead." Judea and Idumea were similarly devastated, with fire, slaughter, and enslavement (see *War* 4.419–48; esp. secs. 437, 443–48). After a prolonged siege, Jerusalem was taken, the defenders killed or enslaved, and the Temple and city destroyed.

The Arch of Titus stands in the Roman forum to this day as a vivid reminder of the great victory of the Romans over the intransigent Jewish people. Even more revealing of the devastation and brutality on which the Roman "peace" was founded, and of its bearing on the Jewish society in which the infancy narratives were taking shape, was the great triumph celebrated in Rome by the victorious generals, the emperor Vespasian and his son Titus. To focus on only two aspects from the detailed description by Josephus of this grand display of the majesty of the Roman empire:

The war was shown in numerous representations, in separate sections, affording a very vivid picture of its episodes. Here was to be seen a prosperous country being devastated, there whole battalions of the enemy slaughtered; here a party in flight, there others being led into captivity; . . . an area all deluged with blood, . . . houses pulled down over their owners' heads; and, after general desolation and woe, . . . a country still on every side in flames. . . . The triumphal procession ended at the temple of Jupiter Capitolinus, . . . for it was a time-honored custom to wait there until the execution of the enemy's general was announced. This was Simon bar Giora . . . with a noose around him and scourged meanwhile by his escorts . . . dragged to a spot abutting on the Forum. . . . After the announcement that Simon was no more and the shouts of universal applause which greeted it, the princes began the sacrifices and, having duly offered these with the customary prayers, withdrew to the palace. (*War* 7.122–56)

It is significant again to note that the "enemy general" here ceremonially executed by the Romans as they triumphally reestablished their "peace," was yet another "king of the Jews," having come into leadership of the revolt as a popularly acclaimed king.

The final Roman conquest of Jews in Palestine, from 132 to 135 C.E., was yet another long war of attrition that devastated the land and people. Again the revolt was led by a popularly recognized king, Bar Kochba, whom even Rabbi Akiba proclaimed as the messiah, the "son of the star."

Implications for Luke 2:1–20

It is often suggested that the story in Luke 2:1–20 is contrasting the (true) spiritual or religious ruler/savior with the (false) secular or political ruler/savior. But nothing in the story itself indicates such a contrast. And not only were "politics" and "religion" inseparable in both Jewish and Hellenistic-Roman culture, but the connotations of Caesar Augustus as savior are explicitly religious as well. Nor is there any indication in the story that the child Jesus is somehow to be a nonviolent messiah or savior, in contrast with some hypothetical standard Jewish messianic expectation of a military leader. We have no evidence of any standard Jewish expectation of a military messiah. And the "great heavenly army" of verse 13 suggests rather that the story has roots in the biblical tradition of God's battling on behalf of a beleaguered people. The circumstances of the birth of the infant savior are humble, to be sure, in contrast with the supreme station of the emperor, but the story is about a far more serious and substantial contrast.

Regardless of what Luke or a conceivable pre-Lucan story had in mind, any reader or hearer of this story in the Hellenistic-Roman world, particularly in Palestine, would have understood here a direct opposition between Caesar, the savior who had supposedly brought peace, and the child proclaimed as the savior, whose birth means peace. Luke clearly understands Jesus to be in direct confrontation with the emperor, for here finally is the birth of the messiah in the city of David that the stories and particularly the songs in Luke 1 are proclaiming and eagerly anticipating.

In a Jewish milieu in particular, the period from well before the birth of Jesus through the time of his birth and well beyond the point at which Luke was written was dominated by continuous tension and periodic outbreak of overt conflict between Roman imperial rule and the people in Palestine. More particularly yet, about the time Jesus was born and again just before Luke would have been written, movements led by popularly acclaimed "kings" attempted to assert their independence and came into direct confrontation with the imperial "peace." Although these other popular "kings of the Jews" are not mentioned in the New Testament, they were clearly remembered, as were the Roman responses, such as the slaughter and enslavement in Sepphoris near Nazareth in 4 B.C.E. or in the hill country of Judea in 4 B.C.E. and 69 C.E. Whereas the emperor cult celebrated the birthday of the god Augustus as "good news for the whole world" (i.e., the gospel of *world order* maintained by Roman military might), in Luke's story God's messenger announces the birth of Jesus as "good news for the whole people" (i.e., the gospel of *liberation* for a people subjected to that world order).

CAESAR'S CENSUS

The general tension between Roman imperial rule and the Palestinian Jewish people was focused on the tribute that Rome demanded. This is precisely the framing, the heading of the story of Jesus' actual birth in Luke 2:1–20. Yet, studies of this story, even more than those of other parts of the nativity narrative, become bogged down in intricate debates regarding precise details of character and chronology.

Because Luke presents the census under Quirinius, which apparently took place in 6 C.E., as the occasion for Jesus' birth, his story appears to stand in contradiction with the ostensible date of Jesus' birth in Matthew 2 as under King Herod, who died in 4 B.C.E. Luke himself implies the same earlier date for Jesus' birth in placing John the Baptist's birth under Herod and then portraying Jesus' birth as simply a few months after John's. Scholarly study has become obsessed with resolving the difficulties that the stories of Jesus' birth present for the dating of his birth. Lengthy notes and appendices are written, for example, to establish precisely when Quirinius was legate in Syria or whether there was an empirewide census in or around 4 B.C.E. or 6 C.E.[12]

The obsession with pursuing and resolving the chronological discrepancies between the various stories is understandable, given the importance of fixing the date of Jesus' birth for Christian faith as well as the study of the Gospels. But overshadowed in the process is what Roman taxation meant for people such as Mary and Joseph, the shepherds, or the readers of this story—along with what the birth of a "savior" may have meant in relation to that taxation.

Scholarly interpreters have been led to the disconcerting conclusion that Luke simply failed to understand the date of the census of Quirinius, despite his presentations of a two-volume history of Christian origins ostensibly correlated with key events and figures of universal history (e.g., Luke 1:5 and 2:1). The scholarly discomfort, however, may stem at least partly from the failure to discern that neither Luke nor the story he presents in 2:1–20 may be primarily interested in historical accuracy. Whether or not this story was composed entirely by Luke himself, it is legendary in character. This narrative and surely Luke himself as well are interested in the significance of the census itself, not its chronological accuracy. Perhaps the clearest indication of this interest is the awkwardness of verses 1–2: The decree of Caesar Augustus is that " the whole world" should be enrolled, to which is then added parenthetically the highly problematic particulars that this was "the first census" under Quirinius as "governor of Syria." Indeed, Luke's confused memory and dubious "historical" information should be taken as clues leading us to a more appropriate approach to the census as the ostensible occasion for Jesus' birth.

Similarly, on the level of literary analysis, the observation that it is "paradoxical" that the description of the census (the "elaborate setting" in 2:1–5) is longer than the description of the birth itself (vv. 6–7)[13] suggests that the census itself was of some significance. Both the Lucan and the Matthean birth stories had to deal with the discrepancy between the historical tradition that Jesus was from Nazareth and the prophetically rooted expectation that the (Davidic) messiah would come from Bethlehem (cf. John 7:41–42). Thus once we recognize Luke's chronological confusion, it is tempting to view the census as "a purely literary device" to bring Mary and Joseph who were residents of Nazareth to Bethlehem, the city of David, so that Jesus could be born according to messianic expectation.[14] But Luke could have found "a less complicated way" of getting Mary and Joseph into the appropriate location for the birth of the messiah. Far from being "a purely literary device," the census is itself an important component in the overall story. Such stories are complex as well as compact. The census as the occasion for Joseph and Mary to journey to Bethlehem may well be the device that resolves a christological problem, but it is more than that.

That the census or tribute to Rome is in itself important for this story is confirmed by the importance of the tribute issue toward the end of Luke's

Gospel. In a uniquely Lucan passage Jesus is accused of "forbidding us to give tribute to Caesar" as well as claiming to be "Christ a king" and of "perverting our nation" or "stirring up the people" (Luke 23:2, 5). Scholarly treatments often claim that these accusations are false. But in Luke's presentations of Jesus' preaching and actions, the latter two of these accusations are clearly true.[15] Whether the charge of forbidding the people to pay tribute to Caesar is true depends on how 20:19–26 is understood, particularly the phrases "the things that are Caesar's" and "the things that are God's." The interpretation that Jesus instructs payment to Caesar depends heavily upon the modern assumption of separate realms of "politics" and "religion." But if politics and religion are inseparable, as they were in the ancient world, then the issue is one of direct confrontation and mutual contradiction (the presupposition in the question of entrapment put to Jesus in the first place!). Jesus may not have said anything culpable in so many words, but his hearers would have assumed that all things "belong to God."[16] It would therefore appear that, both in the beginning and at the end of his Gospel, Luke understood Jesus to oppose the Roman tribute.

Tribute to Rome

In the ancient world, the rulers of imperial societies lived by conquest, and none more aggressively than the dominant Roman aristocracy. Following the initial conquest, in which they plundered temples and palaces for booty and towns and villages for slaves, they then exacted tribute from the conquered peoples. The tribute was intended as a means of demeaning the subject people as well as a source of support for the imperial apparatus. By contrast with what Tacitus says about the Batavians, we can appreciate the situation everwhere else: "They are not insulted, that is, with the exaction of tribute, and there is no tax-farmer to oppress them; they are immune from burdens and contributions" (*Germania* 29.1). The tribute provided the means of financing the imperial domination and, to a degree, the income of the dominant society or ruling circles. Says a Roman general to the Gauls after suppressing their revolt in 70 C.E., "We, though so often provoked, have used the right of conquest to burden you only with the cost of maintaining peace. For the tranquility of peoples cannot be had without armies, nor armies without pay, nor pay without tribute" (Tacitus. *Hist.* 4.74). Directly or indirectly through the taking of tribute, however, not only was the army supported, but tax farmers, governors, and many other Romans acquired great wealth. The Roman imperial regime also utilized tribute to pacify the Roman mob with "bread and circus," much of the former made from the taxes extracted from Egypt.

The ancient Palestinian Jewish peasants may not have been used for the direct subsidy of the Roman "bread and circus," but their produce paid as

tribute was used, for example, to help feed Sidon, which had a limited ex-
ploitable agricultural base itself but was important to the Romans for commercial and strategic reasons. In any case, from the time of Julius Caesar, the
Palestinian Jewish peasants rendered to Caesar roughly 12.5 percent of their
crops annually except in sabbatical years. Julius Caesar had ordained "that all
the country of the Jews, excepting Joppa, pay a tribute yearly for the city of
Jerusalem, excepting on the seventh (which they call the sabbatical year),
because therein they neither receive the fruits of the trees nor do they sow
their land; and that they pay as their tribute in Sidon on the second year the
fourth part of what was sown; and besides this, they are to pay the same
tithes to Hyrcanus [high priest] and his sons which they paid to their forefathers" (*Ant.* 14.200–201). Rendering tribute to Caesar of course did not
involve any mitigation of the traditional economic burden of rendering tithes
to the high-priestly government of the Jerusalem Temple-state, which was
also ostensibly a duty owed to God. That the high priests, who were the
principal beneficiaries of the traditional Jewish tithes and offerings owed to
the Temple and priests, were also those responsible for collecting the tribute
under the Roman governors in the first century C.E. is a telling illustration
of the politicoeconomic chain of domination under the *pax Romana.*

Payment of the tribute demanded by Rome was a serious matter indeed
for the subject people. Because the tribute was a symbol of domination and
subjection as well as the economic means by which the Romans supported
their empire, Rome regarded nonpayment as tantamount to rebellion. Imperial
officials were ready to mount punitive military expeditions to enforce their
demands. Palestinian Jews had experienced the Roman wrath even for a delay
in the rendering of tribute. When the great Roman civil war broke out, Cassius
laid Syria and Palestine under excessively heavy tribute. When certain Jewish
areas were slow to respond, he ordered the men of the four principal district
towns of Gophna, Emmaus, Lydda, and Thamna sold as slaves (*Ant.* 14.271–
76; *War* 1.220–22). Thus Caesar's decree of the census provides far more
than an occasion for the christologically necessary shift of scene from Nazareth
to "the city of David." The decree that all must go to their ancestral house
or town of origin to be enrolled for taxation in this story reveals the whole
system of domination and exploitation.

Popular Jewish Resistance to the Tribute

The tribute as a symbolic as well as substantive subjection gains additional
significance when we recognize that, according to Jewish biblical traditions,
at least as popularly understood, tribute to Caesar stood diametrically opposed
to loyalty to God. According to the first commandment and related biblical
traditions, the Jews owed exclusive loyalty to God, who was understood not
simply as the ideal or spiritual leader but as the actual king and ruler of the

society. Because the tribute/census was symbolic of submission to the alien rule of Caesar, to acquiesce in payment was virtually tantamount to disloyalty to God for a faithful Palestinian Jew. Not surprisingly, the tribute became a focus of Jewish resistance to Roman rule during the first century. This fact is dramatically illustrated by two events, the first mentioned in Luke 2 around the time of Jesus' birth, and the second a generation after Jesus' ministry and crucifixion as a leader of popular resistance (i.e., just prior to the time Luke-Acts was written). Besides illustrating the popular attitude toward the tribute, both events also indicate the class conflict between the Jewish priestly aristocracy, who collected the tribute for the Romans, and the people, who resented and resisted its payment on religious as well as economic grounds.

The imposition of tribute as well as direct Roman rule in Judea in 6 C.E. evoked a serious resistance movement. This group, which Josephus labeled "the fourth philosophy," has been misunderstood as the "Zealots," supposedly a widespread organization advocating armed rebellion against the Romans in defense of Torah and Temple. But there is no historical evidence for such a movement. The so-called fourth philosophy was specifically focused on resistance to the tribute. Apparently the presence of a Herodian king who was at least half-Jewish at the head of Jewish society provided a buffer that mediated Roman rule and tribute. Once Herod's incompetent son, Archelaus, was deposed and direct Roman rule imposed in 6 C.E., however, the contradiction between Caesar's rule and God's rule was more obvious and unavoidable. The scholar-teacher Judas of Galilee and the Pharisee Saddok admonished the people "not to consent to the tribute to the Romans and not to tolerate mortal masters, since they had God as their lord" (*War* 2.118; cf. 2.433). In his parallel account of the fourth philosophy, Josephus describes their resistance to the tribute as based in the conviction "that God alone is their leader and master" and that they should submit to torture and death rather than be subjected to any man as master (*despotēs; Ant.* 18.23).

The high priest Joazar, in opposition to the popular resistance led by Judas and Saddok, energetically advocated submission to the assessment. Josephus's passing comment that Joazar was later "overpowered by the multitude" (*Ant.* 18.26) suggests that there was serious conflict between the high-priestly collaborators in Roman rule and at least some of the resistant Jewish populace over the Roman census in 6 C.E.

Another major protest against the tribute emerged in the summer of 66 C.E. After steadily deteriorating economic and political conditions in the 50s and 60s, the Judean people were seriously in arrears in their payment of tribute. Knowing that the Romans regarded nonpayment as tantamount to rebellion, the priestly aristocracy brought the Herodian king Agrippa II up to Jerusalem, where he admonished the people to pay the tribute without delay, urging that "there is nothing to check blows like submission" (*War*

2.345–404). The priestly rulers then set out to collect the tribute in the towns and villages. The people, however, at least the Jerusalemites, exasperated at numerous insulting provocations and abuses by the Roman governor Florus and at Agrippa himself, "heaped abuse on the king and formally proclaimed his banishment from the city; some of the insurgents even ventured to throw stones at him" (*War* 2.406).

It is significant to note in this connection that the only place other than Luke's birth narrative where Caesar is mentioned in the synoptic Gospel is in connection with the tribute as the focus of conflict between the Jewish people and their ruling aristocracy, who were collaborating in the Roman imperial system. The high-priestly rulers, desperate to lay hands on Jesus, who had been "teaching and healing" in the Temple courtyard, "sent to him some of the Pharisees and some of the Herodians, to entrap him in his talk." The issue on which they thought to trap Jesus into a declaration that would justify his arrest: "Is it lawful to give tribute to Caesar, or not?" (Mark 12:13–14). If Jesus answered yes, he would forfeit the support of the people, but if he answered no, they could arrest him as an advocate of rebellion against the *pax Romana*. The whole story is premised on the expectation that he would declare that "rendering to Caesar" was not lawful according to the "way of God" which Jesus was "truly teaching" (note the questioners' deliberate and pointed flattery in v. 14). Jesus of course wriggled out of the trap by teaching, "Render to Caesar the things that are Caesar's, and to God the things that are God's." But it is quite clear from this story that the ruling groups—and the Gospel writers—knew which side of the issue Jesus and his followers stood on. There was no question in the minds of the Jewish people that all things properly belonged to God, their exclusive lord and master.

The census decreed by Caesar would have been recognized as against the will of God as revealed in the Torah. Indeed, when King David had conducted a census, even the prototype of the messianic king, and his society along with him, had been severely punished by God (2 Sam. 24). To have a decree of an alien imperial census juxtaposed with the birth of the messiah is the height of political-economic-religious conflict: the messiah now being born would lead the people's successful resistance against that false and intolerable lordship and subjection.

·3·

Herod, Jerusalem,
and the Magi

HEROD AND THE MASSACRE OF THE INNOCENTS

It has been determined that Matthew 2 is a brilliantly edited apology explaining that, even though Jesus came from Nazareth, he really does meet "the strictest Jewish expectations about the Messiah," having been born in Bethlehem as a son of David. But one wonders if perhaps all the recent scholarly emphasis on the sophisticated apologetic editing of Matthew is not really also an apologetic effort by modern interpreters to avoid the otherwise unsettling sociopolitical implications of this narrative.

Without doubt, Matthew has shown great sophistication in articulating at least two highly important christological points by working his "formula quotations" into the story. The newborn "king of the Jews" explicitly recapitulates the key sequence of events in the origins of Israel itself, starting in the promised land, sojourning in Egypt, and then being called out of Egypt as God's chosen child. And of course the "itinerary" also serves the purpose of explaining how the messiah was indeed born in Bethlehem as expected, even though he was known as coming from Nazareth.[1]

As with all great literature, there are also other levels of significance in this part of the Gospel in addition to Matthew's own sophisticated theological emphases. It has been suggested that one of the principal goals in Matthew 2 was to move the christological moment of revelation to the conception of Jesus and portray the twofold response to that revelation as recognition by the Gentiles (the Magi) but rejection by the Jews.[2] It is hardly the case that Matthew here portrays the Jews generally as rejecting the revelation in Christ, for neither in Matthew nor in any other Gospel does Herod or all Jerusalem represent the Jews generally. If anything, they stand over against the people generally.

The suggestion, however, that Matthew is here portraying the Jews as rejecting the messiah illustrates the general lack of attention to the sociopolitical dimension of the nativity narratives. (As if it were not clear, even on a superficial reading of the story, that Herod is portrayed here as a cruel tyrant— or to a reader more aquainted with formative biblical history, that Jesus here recapitulates the people's formative sojourn in and calling out of Egypt!) Perhaps a cursory review of the text will refresh our sense of what is happening in this narrative.

The most fundamental theme of the story in Matthew 2, the irreducible basis of the story, has to be the opposition of the threatened king Herod to the child Jesus. The birth of a new "king of the Jews" would obviously pose a threat to the reigning monarch, for his purpose or role would be to overthrow or at least replace the established ruler. And here are the Magi from the East, inquiring where the new king is so that they can pay homage— homage that Herod himself might reasonably expect to receive as the reigning king. Not surprisingly Herod (and all Jerusalem with him) was "startled" or "perturbed."[3] The fact that Herod has to inquire of the chief priests and scribes where "the anointed one" was to be born indicates that he himself was definitely not the divinely anointed king of the Jews, shepherd of God's people Israel. His own illegitimacy as king is thus set in sharp relief. The threat that the newborn baby poses to his rule is unmistakable. Hence even the first-time reader or hearer of the story would recognize that Herod's own stated intention to pay homage to the newborn is utter pretense, a ruse to discover the whereabouts of the threatening child. This understanding is confirmed by the warning to the Magi. Then comes the messenger's warning to Joseph that Herod seeks to destroy the child, then the flight to Egypt, and finally the massacre itself. But even the death of Herod does not remove the threat to the child, for the new king, Archelaus, is hostile as well. This is a story of sharp, violent political conflict. A new king has been born and constitutes an obvious threat to the established king. The latter takes the most gruesome measures to eliminate the threat before it can really get started.

The debate over whether this story reproduces an actual historical event has diverted our attention from the central theme of the story and its connotations and implications. Quite apart from any particular incident that may underlie it, the story portrays a network of historical relationships that prevailed in the general circumstances of the birth of the messiah. It is important, therefore, to recover a sense of who Herod was, what he represented, and what relations he had with his subjects.

Client-King of the Romans

Herod was king by the grace of Rome, and he conquered the Jews with the help of Roman legions. By skillful and consistently pro-Roman maneuvering, his father, Antipater, had become, for all practical purposes, the ruler of Jewish Palestine under the nominal authority of the last Hasmonean high priest, Hyrcanus, after the Roman conquest under Pompey in 63 B.C.E. Herod thus got his start as a sort of governor or sheriff of Galilee under his father's authority. He immediately came into sharp conflict with the people there and even with many of the leading figures on the Sanhedrin (governing council) in Jerusalem itself when he aggressively pursued and murdered the popular brigand-chief Hezekiah. When summoned before the high court in Jerusalem, he arrogantly appeared in the royal purple with an armed body-guard instead of as a humble supplicant (*War* 1.204–12; *Ant.* 14.158–84). When in connection with the Roman civil war following the assassination of Julius Caesar, Cassius imposed an excessively heavy levy of extraordinary tribute from Palestine (in 44 B.C.E.), Herod very expeditiously brought in his quota of one hundred talents from Galilee (*War* 1.218–21; *Ant.* 14.271–74). Herod and his brother Phasael skillfully switched their allegiance to and heavily bribed each successive Roman leader who became dominant in the East. Despite the general hatred of the Jews and the appeals of large high-level delegations against them, Mark Antony appointed the brothers tetrarchs and imprisoned or killed many of the Jewish envoys (*War* 1.242–45; *Ant.* 14.301–3, 324–29).

Just at this time, the Romans were struggling to maintain their imperial control in the eastern Mediterranean against the powerful Parthian empire to the East. Indeed, Antigonus, one of the last remaining Hasmonean princes, cast his lot with the Parthians in order to obtain their help in taking control of Jewish Palestine. When Antigonus and Parthian troops moved in, Herod fled to Rome.[4] There, with an anxious eye on the Parthian threat in the East, the Roman Senate made Herod king of the Jews, with the appropriate cer-emonial celebration: "The meeting was dissolved and Antony and Caesar (Augustus) left the senate-house with Herod between them, preceded by the consuls and the other officials, as they went to offer sacrifice and to lay up the decree in the Capitol. On this, the first day of his reign, Herod was given a banquet by Antony" (*War* 1.285). "Thus did Herod take over royal power" (*Ant.* 14.381–89)—as a client-king of Rome.

Taking possession of his kingdom, however, was quite another matter. Antigonus and the Parthians still controlled the country, and substantial numbers of Jews in the ruling city of Jersualem and apparently in the coun-tryside as well preferred them to the hated Roman puppet Herod. Thus it took Herod three years to conquer his kingdom with the help of Roman troops. Resistance was strong everywhere, but particularly intense and resilient in Galilee. We must weave our way between seemingly contradictory reports by Josephus. He says, on the one hand, that the peasantry in Herod's native Idumea rallied to him, whereas some months later it was apparently necessary for him to station two thousand infantry and four hundred cavalry there to prevent insurrection (*War* 1.293, 303). He says initially that "all Galilee" came over to Herod but then relates repeated, stubborn resistance in Galilee that Herod had difficulty suppressing (*War* 1.291, 303–7, 309–13, 315–16, 326; *Ant.* 14.395, 413–17, 420–30, 432–33, 450). In order to feed and support his own and the Roman troops, Herod raided the countryside for provisions (*War* 1.299; *Ant.* 14.408). The slaughter of the people in villages and towns was extensive at points (including towns known in Gospel stories, such as Emmaus; *War* 1.319, 334; *Ant.* 14.435–36, 457–61). After spending three years in conquering the rest of the country, Herod was finally able to besiege Jerusalem in 37 B.C.E. with a huge army of eleven battalions of infantry and six thousand cavalry (*War* 1.342–46). "When the troops poured in, a scene of wholesale massacre ensued; for the Romans were infuriated by the length of the siege, and the Jews of Herod's army were determined to leave none of their opponents alive. Masses were butchered in the alleys, crowded together in the houses, and flying into the sanctuary" (*War* 1.351).

Once he had conquered the country, and especially after his kingship was confirmed by Augustus after the battle of Actium, Herod set up a model client-kingdom in grand Hellenistic style, "one of the most impressive demonstration of the new order Augustus had introduced into the Roman empire."[5] Militarily strong kingdoms such as Herod's continued to be important to Roman imperial rule to ensure the security of the empire over against the Parthian empire to the east. As an official "friend and ally of the Roman people," Herod's job was to maintain law and order in his own realm and to implement Roman policy or defend Roman interests in the eastern Mediterranean and on the frontier with the Parthian empire. Various inscriptions indicate that Herod adopted the titles "Admirer of the Romans" and "Admirer of Caesar."[6]

Because the whole eastern Mediterranean was now pacified in subjection to imperial rule, much of Herod's energy as ruler went into what we would now call cultural activities, although the economic, political, and religious implications should be immediately obvious. Herod engaged in extensive building projects, filled the country with temples and other monuments dedicated to Caesar, and in virtually unprecedented munificence lavished gifts and endowments upon the emperor and other imperial figures, on numerous Hellenistic cities, and on the Olympic games.

For the pleasure and security of his extensive family and elaborate court, Herod built magnificent palaces in Jerusalem and in other cities and fortresses around the country, the most famous of which are Herodium and Masada (*War* 1.419–21; 7.285–91; *Ant.* 16.142–45; etc.). He also built several new cities around his realm, some named after his relatives. Herod's most famous project of all was the rebuilding of the Temple in Jerusalem.

> In the fifteenth year of his reign, he restored the Temple and, by erecting new foundation-walls, enlarged he surrounding area to

double its former extent. The expenditure devoted to this work was incalculable, its magnificence never surpassed. . . . The fortress which dominated it on the north . . . he restored at a lavish cost in a style no way inferior to that of a palace, and called it Antonia in honor of Antony. (*War* 1.401)

Much of Herod's building programs, in fact, were in homage to Caesar. The two most famous new cities were named after the emperor—Sebaste (= Augustus), in Samaria, and Caesarea, which later became the governor's seat in the Roman province of Judea. The latter city, involving the creation of a seaport "larger than Piraeus" (near Rome), "materials brought from outside at great expense," and twelve years for its construction, was entirely rebuilt with white stone and adorned with magnificent palaces, amphitheater, theater, public places, and quinquennial games. "On an eminence facing the harbor stood Caesar's temple . . ., it contained a colossal statue of the emperor, not inferior to the Olympian Zeus, which served for its model, and another of Rome, rivalling that of Hera at Argos" (*War* 1.413–15; *Ant.* 15.331–41). Later, Herod had a temple dedicated to Caesar built of white marble on a mountain near the sources of the Jordan (*War* 1.404). Among numerous other dedications to Caesar were the honorary inscriptions that he placed in the theater he built in Jerusalem (*Ant.* 14.272). "In short," says Josephus, "one can mention no suitable spot within his realm which he left destitute of some mark of his homage to Caesar" (*War* 1.407).

Herod's munificence and benefactions were astounding even to the ancients, accustomed to such conspicuous display. "In all things he undertook he was ambitious to surpass what had been done before. . . . They say that Caesar himself and Agrippa often remarked that the extent of Herod's realm was not equal to his magnanimity" (*Ant.* 16.141). Throughout his life, from the liberal bribes he provided to Antony, Augustus, and others and through the large sums and endowments he left to emperor and empress, he lavished gifts on imperial figures. He gave special attention to courting Agrippa's friendship (e.g., *Ant.* 16.12–116). "But it would be difficult to mention all his other benefactions, such as those that he conferred on the cities in Syria and throughout Greece and on whatever places he may have happened to visit" (*Ant.* 16.146; cf. sec. 24). Thus "he provided gymnasia for Tripolis, Damascus, and Ptolemais; a wall for Byblus; halls, porticoes, temples, and marketplaces for Berytus and Tyre; theaters for Sidon and Damascus; an aqueduct for Laodicea on sea; baths, sumptuous fountains, and colonnades for Ascalon" (*War* 1.422). And he financed the rebuilding of the portico for the city of Chios, endowed the office of gymnasiarch for Cos, and lightened the burden of taxes and debts for Phaselis, Balanea, and other towns in Cilicia in addition to gifts to Athens and numerous other Greek cities. His most celebrated benefactions were the erection of the Pythian temple in Rhodes, the financing of paving and colonnade for the twenty-furlong main street in Syrian Antioch, and the endowment of the Olympic Games (*Ant.* 16.18, 23–24, 142–49; *War* 1.422–28).

Exploitation and Tyranny

The economic implications of the foregoing are perhaps as obvious as they are ominous. Herod's extraordinary expenditures for the massive building projects, the homages to Caesar, and the many impressive benefactions for foreign cities and imperial figures placed a heavy burden on the Jewish peasantry. But they also compounded what were already inordinately large demands for tithes, tribute, and taxes. A consideration of the politicoeconomic structure of imperial rule in Palestine once Herod was imposed as Roman client-king may help us appreciate the economic burden thus placed on Herod's subjects. In the ancient world the land and people controlled by a ruler such as a king or high priest was a basis of revenue (as can be seen from Caesar's allocation of Herod's territories among his heirs, as described in *Ant.* 14.317–20). But no account was taken for the overlapping claims of various levels of rulers. Under the Hasmonean high priesthood prior to 63 B.C.E., the principal demand for tithes and taxes was for the Temple and high-priestly governing apparatus. When Rome laid Jewish Palestine under tribute beginning in 63 B.C.E., an additional demand was thus placed upon the peasant producers. When Herod imposed his kingship, however, the high priesthood and temple apparatus were not removed, nor did the Romans remit their demand for tribute. Structurally there was thus a triple demand for tithes, tribute, and taxes. The latter, however, must have been a tremendous burden just by themselves because of Herod's vast expenditures: for court, army, multiple palaces, impregnable fortresses, building projects in Jerusalem such as the Temple, new and rebuilt cities in Palestine, gifts to imperial figures, and munificent benefactions to cities in Syria and Greece.[7]

Herod was in fact bleeding his country and people to death. Earlier in his reign, at least, Herod realized the effect this policy was having. Josephus reports that about 20 B.C.E., that is, after a number of years of massive construction activity on top of regular expenses, "Herod remitted to the people of his kingdom a third part of their taxes, under the pretext of letting them recover from a period of lack of crops" (*Ant.* 15.365). Nevertheless, "since he was involved in expenses greater than his means, he was compelled to be harsh toward his subjects, for the great number of things on which he spent money as gifts to some caused him to be the source of harm to [or: to seek new sources of income in] those from whom he took his revenues" (*Ant.* 16.154). The situation of the people was so desperate at the end of Herod's reign that the urban mob clamored for relief from his ostensible successor, Archelaus (*Ant.* 17.204–5). The high-level delegation to Rome complaining of Herod's tyranny claimed that "he had reduced the entire people to helpless poverty" (*Ant.* 17.307–8). By lavishing the lifeblood of the Jews on other communities, he had crippled the towns in his own realm and sunk the people into poverty (*War* 1.84–85).

Besides bleeding the people dry, Herod was flouting their sacred traditions with many of his building projects and certainly with his dedications to Caesar and his institution of Hellenistic-Roman "cultural" activities. The spectacles in the theater and amphitheater, such as the gymnastic games, and even more, forcing condemned men to battle wild beasts, offended traditional Jewish sensibilities. The inscriptions dedicated to Caesar and particularly the captured trophies of nations displayed around the theater were highly objectionable. The latter appeared to Palestinian Jews as a display of idols, directly contravening their prohibition against idolatry, an issue that later became the cause of a massive popular demonstration under the Roman governor Pontius Pilate (*Ant.* 15.272–76; cf. 18:55–59 and *War* 2.169–74).[8] That Herod's many dedications to Caesar and temples honoring Caesar were anathema to Jewish traditions, and that Herod knew it, is indicated precisely by the fact that he knew better than to build any of them on Jewish territory (*Ant.* 15.328, 339–40, 364–65). He did have the audacity, however, to erect a giant golden eagle over the great gate of the Temple, which was doubly objectionable as a symbol of Roman domination as well as a violation of the commandment against images (*Ant.* 17.151; *War* 1.650).

Herod's own royal ideology, linked as it was with Hellenistic-Roman imperial ideology, was also surely offensive to his Jewish subjects. He claimed to be king by the will of God and to have brought the long-awaited peace and prosperity. Indeed, he claimed that his glorious rebuilding of the Temple was a magnanimous act of piety making full return to God for the gift of his kingdom (*Ant.* 15.387). Herod may even have made messianic claims in his royal propaganda.[9] He certainly seems to have used the Temple as just another instrument of his own kingship and his own royal (and imperial) ideology. "Round about the entire Temple were fixed the spoils taken from the Gentiles" (in his own military campaigns). That Herod held custody of the High Priest's robe used when offering sacrifice on high holy days indictates that the Temple and high priests were subordinated to his authority (*Ant.* 15.402–3). Herod appointed and deposed the high priests as suited his own policies, propaganda purposes, or romantic whims, and his appointees were accused of injustices or impieties (e.g., *Ant.* 15.319–22; 17.78, 164–67, 207). Not only was there an elaborate celebration upon the completion of Herod's rebuilding of the Temple, but thereafter that day, which happened to coincide with the day of Herod's accession to the kingship, was celebrated as a glorious festival (*Ant.* 15.423). In the non-Jewish areas of his realm there were even statues erected in Herod's honor.[10]

Resistance and Repression

Herod "the king of the Jews" thus must have seemed to be the very paradigm of tyranny to his Jewish subjects. Besides having conquered the people with Roman troops, he impoverished them in order to finance gifts to alien cities and imperial officials that served only his own and Caesar's glory, and both of the latter went utterly against the traditional Jewish way of life, against the letter as well as the spirit of the Torah.

Resistance to Herod's tyranny did not altogether cease after his successful conquest of the countryside and Jerusalem. Early in his reign, apparently, there was a conspiracy to asssassinate the hated king (*Ant.* 15.280–84). Pharisees and certain other lawyers-teachers—who had surely undergone a diminution in their status and prestige insofar as Herod's largely Hellenistic bureaucracy now performed some of their former governmental functions as the clerks and officers of the now superseded Temple-state government— were never reconciled to Herod's rule. In what was surely not the only such act of protest, when Herod's health declined toward the end, two of the most revered teachers in Jerusalem inspired their students to cut down the golden Roman eagle from atop the gate of the Temple, in defense "of the law of our fathers!" (*War* 1.648–53; *Ant.* 17.149–59).[11] Josephus suggests that the Jews had long since been praying for Herod's death and were eager to revolt (*Ant.* 17.276; cf. 15.286, 365, etc.).

Little by way of effective resistance could get started, however, because Herod instituted a heavily repressive regime, replete with fortresses, secret police, informers, as well as intimidating brutality. Many treatments of Herod's tyranny focus on his utterly paranoid behavior, particularly his treatment of his sons, toward the end of his long reign. Indeed, he had become increasingly suspicious of any and every relative or intimate at his court as time wore on; and many were the intrigues. He finally ordered two sons who had until only recently been his intended successors executed. Augustus is reported to have quipped that it was better to be Herod's pig (*hus*) than his son (*huios*).[12] Also, just before his death, he had ordered that distinguished men from every village of the country be locked up in the hippodrome and slaughtered when he died "so that all Judea and every household will weep for me, whether they will or not!" (*War* 1.659–60; *Ant.* 17.174–79). Focusing on such enormities arising from his increasingly ugly mood toward the end of his life, however, should not be allowed to divert attention from the intensely repressive and brutal regime he instituted from the outset.[13]

"He decided to hem the people in on all sides lest their disaffection should become open rebellion," says Josephus (*Ant.* 15.291). His own security was foremost in his mind and was ensured by construction or improvement of a whole network of fortresses and fortified palaces directed "against the whole people." In Jerusalem itself his own palace and the impregnable Antonia provided security. He even had a tower built for himself in the Temple complex, accessible through a secret underground passage, "to protect himself if there should be a revolt of the people against its kings" (*Ant.* 15.242). Then at strategic points around the country he either rebuilt and strengthened older fortresses such as Alexandreion, Machaerus, and Masada or built entirely new fortresses with palaces, namely, Cypros and Herodion (e.g., *War* 1.265, 419–21; *Ant.* 14.419; 15.323–25; 16.143).[14] Herod depended mainly on foreign mercenaries such as Thracians, Germans, and Gauls, along with his own body-guard (*Ant.* 17.198). He also constructed Sabaste principally as a military base, which he believed would help him control affairs in Jerusalem as well as in the country, and placed cavalry bases in Galilee at Gaba and in Perea at Esebonitis (*Ant.* 15.293–94). Eventually, as he kept thinking up new security measures, "he placed garrisons throughout the entire nation so as to minimize the chance of [the Jews] taking things into their own hands" (*Ant.* 15.195).[15]

Herod, in fact, instituted what today would be called a police-state, complete with loyalty oaths, surveillance, informers, secret police, imprisonment, torture, and brutal retaliation against any serious dissent.

> No meeting of people was permitted, nor were walking together or being together permitted, and all their movements were observed. Those who were caught were punished severely, and many were taken, either openly or secretly, to the fortress of Hyrcania and there put to death. Both in the city and on the open roads there were men who spied upon those who met together.[16] . . . Those who obstinately refused to go along with his [new] practices he persecuted in all kinds of ways. As for the rest of the populace, he demanded that they submit to taking a loyalty oath, and he compelled them to make a sworn declaration that they would maintain a friendly attitude to his rule. Now most people yielded to his demand out of complaisance or fear, but those who showed some spirit and objected to compulsion he got rid of by every possible means. (*Ant.* 15.366–69)

Herod further imposed repressive laws that went far beyond anything in the Torah. Josephus singles out a law providing "that housebreakers should be sold [into slavery] and be deported from the kingdom—a punishment that not only weighed heavily upon those who suffered it but also involved a violation of the laws of the country." This law was viewed as the act of a tyrant who held the interests of his subjects in contempt (*Ant.* 16.1–5). The Torah explicitly forbade the selling of fellow Jews into slavery, particularly to aliens out of the country.

Herod's prisons were clearly kept busy with political prisoners and those accused by informers or suspected of disloyalty. One of the principal demands of the crowd after the death of the tyrant was "the release of the prisoners who had been put in chains by Herod—and there were many of these and they had been in prison for a long time" (*Ant.* 17.204) Many others had apparently simply been killed: "They were indignant at having been deprived of those dearest to them during Herod's lifetime" (sec. 211).

Retaliation against any serious resistance was swift and brutal. The revered Torah scholars and their students who had conspired to cut down the great golden eagle from over the Temple gate Herod had burned alive, and the remainder of those arrested in the incident handed over to his executioners (*War* 1.655). When a faithful old soldier expressed reservations to the king regarding Herod's imminent execution of his two sons, the soldier, his sons, and a barber were tortured and eventually executed along with three hundred other disaffected soldiers and military officers (*Ant.* 16.379–94). Again, such brutal reprisals for expressions of protest or dissension were hardly confined to Herod's last years. Perhaps the most dramatic illustration of how tyranny could touch off a spiral of resistance, repression, further frustrated resistance, and brutal retaliation is the conspiracy and the subsequent chain of events from earlier in Herod's reign. One of Herod's undercover agents discovered the plot, so that the security forces caught the would-be assassins virtually in the act. After being tortured, they were brutally put to death. But sympathizers with the conspiracy caught the informer, chopped him up, and threw him to the dogs. Herod then had the witnesses to the latter incident tortured. When the perpetrators were finally identified, Herod did not stop with them, but went after their entire families (*Ant.* 15.284–90).

Not surprisingly, the popular hatred and resentment held in check by such systematic control and repression had built up explosive pressure during Herod's long reign. Also not surprisingly, given the juxtaposition of Herod's own high pretensions with his tyranny and utter illegitimacy as "king of the Jews," when the explosions finally came they took messianic form. Some of the Pharisees, who had always refused to take the loyalty oath to Caesar and Herod, prophesied that the kingdom would be taken from Herod by a new king who would bring the restoration of wholeness, in some manner or form (*Ant.* 17.43–45).[17] The visionary Pharisees were executed, of course. When Herod finally died, besides the outcry of grievances by the urban crowd in Jerusalem itself, there were spontaneous insurrections in every major Jewish district of the realm—Galilee, Perea, and Judea. And in each case the form taken by the popular revolt was messianic, that is, the acclamation of one of their number as "king" by the rebels finally able to reclaim their liberty.[18]

The end of Herodian tyranny under Caesar's imperial rule was not yet at hand, however. The Roman armies eventually put down the rebellions led by the popularly acclaimed kings. And in Jerusalem itself Herod's son and successor as ruler of Judea quickly followed in his father's footsteps. When the mob clamoring for relief from taxes and tyranny was swelled by pilgrims coming into the city for the Passover festival and threatened to get out of hand, Archelaus set his entire army upon them. "The soldiers falling unexpectedly upon the various parties busy with their sacrifices slew about three thousand of them and dispersed the remainder among the neighboring hills" (*War* 2.10–13; *Ant.* 17.213–18).

Historical Verisimilitude

The story in Matthew 2 comes to life vividly against the background of Herodian exploitation and tyranny. After suffering military conquest, economic impoverishment, destruction and violation of their traditional way of life, and strictly repressive control of their lives under the utterly illegitimate "king of the Jews" appointed by Rome, the people must have longed intensely for liberation. But the tyrant Herod, precisely because of his illegitimacy, offensive violation of the traditional life, and oppresive exploitation, was obsessive in his suspicion and tightly repressive in his stringent control of Jewish society. He in fact responded with brutality to any threat to his own rule. The people longed precisely for the birth of a liberator—the true, divinely designated king. And Herod's response would have been cunning investigation and systematically efficient military action. Nor would the death of Herod have ended the tyranny. As the sage Shemiah suggested, the appropriate stance in such a circumstance was to "love work and hate mastery—and make not thyself known to the government" (*Avot* 1.10). It is precisely against this background of Herodian exploitation and tyranny that the pre-Matthean and Matthean stories of "the massacre of the innocents" in reaction to the birth of the newborn king of the Jews originated and was cultivated.

HIGH PRIESTS AND ALL JERUSALEM

In Matthew 2:3–5, "all Jerusalem" along with Herod is troubled or startled to hear that "the king of the Jews" had been born, and then the high priests and scribes compliantly advise Herod as to the scriptural traditions about where the messiah was supposed to be born. The mention of the high priests and scribes has been said to indicate that Matthew is thus indicating the responsibility of the Jewish people for rejecting the messiah, while the Gentiles (the Magi here) recognize the revelation.[19] Such an interpretation reflects and satisfies a certain unfortunate Christian theological tradition, but it is not rooted in the text itself. Some simple sociohistorical observations should clarify the general social relationships reflected in the story of Matthew 2:1–12, especially verses 3–5. Then we can pursue briefly some of the further connotations of Jerusalem, high priests, and scribes around the time of Jesus.

Ancient Judea was a traditional agrarian society. Such societies generally are headed politically and economically by a fortified city in which the rulers live, with the people who serve their needs for security, administration, or privileged life-style. In the case of ancient Judea, this society took the form of a Temple-state centered in Jerusalem headed by a priestly aristocracy and their "retainers" such as the scribes. Thus, besides being merely a tiny fraction of the Palestinian Jewish people, "all Jerusalem" would have been the ruling city that politically dominated and economically exploited the rest of the people by means of the institutions of Temple and high priesthood.[20]

Not long after the return of the deported Judean ruling class from the Babylonian exile, Judea was restored in the politicoreligious form of a temple-state subject to the Persian empire. "Second Temple" Judea retained the same form under the Hellenistic empires after the conquest by Alexander the Great. It may well be an indication of how ingrained this form had become for Judean society that the Hasmonean leaders of the Maccabean Revolt against the Hellenizing "Reform" of the Temple-state soon set themselves up in the same political-economic-religious form of high priesthood.[21] The original Hasmonean high priests may have been heroes of national liberation as well as of the restoration of traditional Temple forms, but within two generations the people were pelting the high priest Alexander Jannai with citrons at the Festival of Tabernacles, while Jannai himself made war on his subjects and even crucified some eight hundred of his opponents (*Ant.* 13.372–80).

The Roman imposition of Herod as "king of the Jews" in effect demoted the high-priestly aristocracy and government. Herod, moreover, was able to manipulate the high priesthood and its operation of the Temple apparatus as instruments of his own domination. Partly because of his insecurity about his own illegitimacy as king, he at first kept the aging and docile former high priest Hyrcanus,[22] whose granddaughter he had married, in a prominent position in Jerusalem. He also appointed Hyrcanus's grandson, his own brother-in-law, the youthful Aristobulus, as high priest. But his own insecurity and jealousy quickly led him to have the youth drowned and Hyrcanus executed. To avoid any threat to his own regime, Herod placed his own creatures in the high priesthood. He thus eliminated the Hasmoneans as the leading family in the Judean aristocracy and replaced it with foreign Jewish priestly families from Babylon (that of Hananel) and Egypt (beginning with Jesus son of Phiabi, then Simon son of Boethus) and Jerusalem priestly families that may not have been of legitimate high-priestly lineage (Matthias son of Theophilus).[23] The consequence was a weakened high priesthood, now subject to appointment by the imperial political authority and no longer hereditary in one family.

The result of Herod's imposition of his own creatures was that the completely new priestly aristocracy of four families came to dominate the Temple-state under the Roman governors in the first century C.E. All but two of the high priests between 6 and 66 C.E. came from these four families, who apparently also monopolized the other key offices of the Temple-state. While these families were usually no longer directly subject to a Herodian king, a Herodian ruler at times had power of appointment (e.g., Agrippa I, 41–44 C.E., and Agrippa II, 59–66 C.E.), and they were subject to the Roman governor in Judea. These high-priestly families thus still dominated life politically and economically in Jewish Palestine but were definitely client-rulers dependent on their collaboration with the Romans and subject to the whims or needs of imperial rule. Besides being responsible to the Romans for the collection and payment of the tribute, as we have noted above, they were held responsible by the Romans to maintain law and order in Judean society.

Because these families that dominated the high-priestly government under Herod and the Roman governors lacked legitimacy, were collaborating with the Herodian and imperial regimes, and were insecure in their own position, they resorted increasingly to violence to maintain their domination. This is indicated in a famous popular lament, which also suggests the intensity of popular resentment and opposition to their rule.

> Woe is me because of the house of Boethus,
>   Woe is me because of their staves. . . .
> Woe is me because of the house of Kathros,
>   Woe is me because of their pens.
> Woe is me because of the house of Ishmael ben Phiabi,
>   Woe is me because of their fists.
> For they are high priests, and their sons are treasurers,
>   and their sons-in-law are temple overseers,
>   and their servants beat the people with clubs.
>   (B. Pesahim, 57a; T. Menahoth 13.21)

By the mid-first century C.E., these powerful high-priestly families, like their allies (or rivals) the Herodian families, had resorted to gangs of hired ruffians, both to defend their special interests and to prey upon the people and hold them in check.[24] It is significant that, when widespread popular revolt finally erupted in 66 C.E., the people attacked the priestly aristocracy as well as the Roman garrison.

The story in Matthew 2:1–12 reflects exactly the situation toward the end of Herod's reign with regard to the position of the high priests and scribes and "official" Jerusalem. As the traditional ruling class, now dependent on Roman power and Herod's favor, the high priests and the scribes who worked for them in the Temple-state apparatus would have been "troubled," to say the least, at news of any nascent challenge to Herod's kingship. Assuming that "all Jerusalem" likely refers to official Jerusalem—that is, retainers who formed part of the Herodian regime or the Temple administration, and others directly dependent on either for their livelihood—then these people, who composed much of the city's population, would also have been startled at, as well as threatened by, the news of a new "king of the Jews." Moreover, the high priests, who were beholden to and dependent on Herod for their positions, as well as the ranking scribes who staffed the Temple administration, would have been compliant to Herod's anxious inquiries and investigations. In sum, the story reflects the Palestinian Jewish milieu in which the fundamental opposition was between the rulers in Jerusalem, both Herodian regime and high priesthood, and the bulk of people, whose restlessness they feared. The story presents the direct opposition of the newly born messiah and the imminent liberation he represents to the tyrannical and now threatened Herod and the oppressive system he heads.[25]

Those unfamiliar with these structural relations in Judean society might take the narrative in Luke 1–2 to suggest less of an opposition between the high priesthood and the birth of the messiah. The Temple complex is the setting for some of the actions, the sanctuary for Zechariah's vision, and the outer courtyard for Simeon's and Anna's meeting with the infant messiah. Moreover, Mary and Joseph bring to the Temple a sacrifice prescribed by the Torah (Luke 2:24; cf. Lev. 12:8).[26] If anything, however, the high priests are conspicuous by their absence from the Lukan nativity narrative. Any resistance or liberation movement in Jewish Palestine was necessarily also against the high priesthood and Temple government as well as against Romans and a Herodian regime. Assuming that Luke is responsible for virtually all of these stories, one could surmise that they are missing because by the time he was writing, after 70 C.E., the high priesthood had been eliminated. But the latter situation surely does not affect his version of Jesus' encounter with the high priests, scribes, and elders in Jerusalem. And he portrays Jesus' followers as involved in direct confrontation with the high-priestly government in the early chapters of Acts. If Luke is dependent on earlier material in chapters 1–2, then the high priesthood and Temple were still in existence when such material originated. To be sure, whereas Matthew's stories focus more closely on the opposition to Herod, with the corresponding explicit reference to the high priests and scribes, Luke has in broader focus the opposition that the birth of Jesus means to the Roman emperor and tribute. But one must wonder, particularly when the Temple provides the setting for significant incidents, whether the high priests are not conspicuous by their absence. The birth of the messiah, the horn of salvation for the redemption of Israel, was happening among the faithful people and ordinary priests, but the high priests were completely unaware of it.

THE MAGI

Concentrating recently on what the infancy stories mean at the level of Matthean theology, interpreters have found that the Magi are the representatives of pagan religion and wisdom who significantly here subject themselves to Christ and that they are "harbingers of the Gentiles who will be gathered into the church."[27] This interpretation of the Magi as pagans is even presented as part of a broader scheme in Matthew of revelation and acceptance by Gentiles and rejection by Jews. Receiving their initial revelation through nature (the star), but having to be more fully instructed of God's plan of salvation from Scripture, "the wise men of the Gentiles accept and pay homage," while the Jewish leaders reject.[28] But this interpretation simply ignores much that (we have reason to believe) Matthew himself knew, according to these same scholars. Of course, such interpretations are fully consistent with the modern view that biblical narratives are basically religious stories or that whatever their character, they have primarily religious or theological significance for us. Again with the Magi, as with Caesar, the census, and Herod, however, once we take into account who the Magi were and how they are portrayed in this story, it is impossible to ignore the political dimensions, which are inseparable from any others.

The term *magos* in Greek was often used in reference to a magician, who might be an astrologer or a dream interpreter. But the term often had a far more precise meaning in Hellenistic-Roman culture, as attested in many Greek and Roman writers. Indeed the Hellenistic-Roman world was fascinated with the *magoi*, who were originally a caste of highest ranking politicoreligious advisers or officers of the Median emperor, then in the Persian imperial court as well. The ancient churches understood the Magi who did obeisance to Christ in exactly these terms. Although Justin Martyr has them come from Arabia, most of the church fathers thought they were from Persia; and earliest Christian art portrays the Magi in the typical Persian or Parthian dress of trousers, belted tunics with full sleeves, and Phrygian caps.[29] It is understandable that biblical and religious scholars emphasize their apparently "religious" functions. But we must be fully aware that, in the ancient world, many of these functions were political as well, that the purpose of what may appear to us as a religious ritual was to maintain the divinely given imperial order.

In the Persian empire the Great King, or King of Kings, was the divine ruler on earth for the universal high god Ahura Mazdah. The Magi were the royal priestly assistants of the Great King, particularly in communication with and propitiation of the gods to ensure the productivity, safety, and welfare of the kingdom.

The Magi attend the Persian kings . . . guiding them in their relations with the gods. (Strabo 15.1.68)

The Magi interpret the will of the gods. . . . The college of Magi was instituted [by Cyrus] and he never failed to sing hymns to the gods at daybreak and to sacrifice daily to whatsoever deities the Magi directed. Thus the institutions established by him at that time have continued in force with each successive king even to this day. (Xenophon, *Cyropaedia* 4.5.51; 8.1.23–24; cf. 7.5.35)

The Magi were instrumental in divine revelation as the interpreters of royal dreaming or extraordinary natural phenomena. In the legendary story of Cyrus's infancy, they play a central role as interpreters of the Median king Astyages' dream and advisers on his subsequent course of action.[30] The way in which their interpretation of a heavenly phenomenon could affect international politics is exemplified in the following incident. When an eclipse of the sun occurred as Xerxes was about to begin an expedition against the Greeks, he "asked the Magi what the vision might signify. They declared to him that the god was showing to the Greeks the desolation of their cities; for the sun (they said) was the prophet of the Greeks, as the moon was theirs. Xerxes rejoiced exceedingly to hear that and kept on his march" (Herodotus 7.37). The Magi also both supervised and assisted with the royal sacrifices and chanted hymns appealing for divine favor in royal undertakings.[31] Besides advising the king, they were responsible for educating the royal children.[32]

The fact that they were at one point successful in revolting against and replacing the rule of the Persian king and the existence of Persis of a festival called The Slaughter of the Magi have been interpreted to mean that the Magi were legitimate Median (-Persian) rulers in their own right and something of a constant internal threat to the Persian ruler.[33] Thus it may not have been subsequent Christian imagination that elevated them into kings.[34] Tertullian, at the end of the second century, knows that "the East considers Magi almost as kings" (*Adv. Marc.* 3.13). In any case, they participated at the highest level as the sacred or priestly advisers of the Achaemenid kings.

Given their important role in divine revelation through visions and accurate seasonal and other natural calculations, it is understandable that the Magi could become known primarily as necromancers and astrologers. The portrayal of the "magicians" and "enchanters" at the Babylonian court in the tales in the Book of Daniel (1:20; 2:2; 4:7; 5:7) provides a familiar if pejorative description of a parallel phenomenon, or perhaps, rather, depicts the earlier Babylonian court in terms familiar from the more recent Jewish experience of the Persian court. The Magi would also have cultivated knowledge of the cosmic order and have taken special note of unusual occurrences in the heavens in connection with their central role of interpreting the divine will and order of things. They were indeed "wise and learned men" (Cicero, *Div.* 1.23.46). It should be noted that, despite periodic harrangues in some biblical literature against idolatry, even Palestinian Jewish culture had long since assimilated and utilized certain astrological lore.[35] The story in Matthew 2, moreover, contains not the slightest hint of criticism of the Magi's astrology; rather, the star is precisely the way they are led to the newborn king. We should note, finally, that as the highest officers and advisers of the Great King, the Magi were thoroughly familiar with "doing obeisance" (*proskynēsis*); the Persian king, held in almost godlike elevation and seclusion, was regularly honored by ceremonial acts of obeisance, as the Greeks eagerly pointed out.[36]

In their official duties the Magi may well have been stationed in outlying administrative centers of the Persian empire well before the conquest of Alexander the Great. In any case, in Hellenistic times they were settled in a wide variety of places, including Babylonia, Cappadocia and western Anatolia generally, and even Arabia and Egypt.[37] They were involved in attendance of the goddess Anahita (syncretized with Artemis) at Ephesus.[38] Thus Western knowledge of the Magi in Hellenistic-Roman times would not have been simply an exotic but fading historical memory.

While it has not been noted by biblical interpreters, the Magi may have been instrumental in opposing the Hellenistic imperial forces that conquered them and other ancient Near Eastern peoples.[39] The Greeks, of course, had long looked upon non-Greeks—barbarians—as inferior peoples, worthy of being enslaved. They viewed the Persians in particular as decadent and weak. Such attitudes carried over into the Macedonian conquest and Greek-staffed Hellenistic imperial rule of the East. We tend to think of the portrayal of Hellenistic imperial rule in Daniel 7 as far more brutal and ferocious than the earlier empires. Antiochus Epiphanes brought unprecedented repression upon the Jews because they refused to assimilate to Hellenistic culture like all the other areas subject to his rule. But apparently the Jews were not the only people to feel that Hellenistic rule was especially oppressive. Well before the crisis in Judea after 175 B.C.E. and the writing of the Book of Daniel (168–167 B.C.E.?), there were apparently prophecies and propaganda of resistance to Western rule. The scheme of an increasingly decadent or oppressive series of empires (from the Babylonian through the Median and Persian to the Hellenistic) followed by the intensely anticipated divine rule that appears in both Daniel 2 and 7 is in fact likely derived from a Persian source.[40] Besides this scheme of the four empires followed by restoration of the divine empire, other prophecies expressed a longing among eastern peoples for a restoration of the true, Persian (or other properly indigenous eastern) kingship.[41]

Because of their special stake in and attachment to the former Persian rule as *the* divinely ordained order and their wide dispersion under Hellenistic rule, the Magi are prime candidates to have been the originators or carriers of such prophetic resistance against western imperial domination.[42] Cicero recounts a famous and, for our purposes here, very revealing story: "Everybody knows that on the same night in which Olympias was delivered of Alexander the temple of Diana at Ephesus was burned, and that the Magi began to cry out as the day was breaking: 'Asia's deadly curse was born last night' " (*Div.* 1.23.47).

We have already noted above that, from early in the first century B.C.E. and throughout the first century C.E., there was a continuing confrontation if not outright war between the Romans and the Parthian empire to the East. It is not difficult to imagine that the Magi would have been associated with the eastern empire in opposition to Rome.

In 66 C.E., the same year that widespread popular revolt erupted in Jewish Palestine, there occurred a spectacularly staged political event that marked a temporary truce in the East-West conflict and sheds light on the role of, and Roman fascination with, the Magi.[43] Realizing that it could not maintain its own puppet on the throne in Armenia against Parthian power, Rome agreed to accept the Parthian candidate as king if he would receive his crown from the hands of the Roman emperor. Thus the Armenian king Tiridates, accompanied by the sons of three neighboring Parthian rulers, made a nine-month journey by horseback to visit Nero in Rome. With an entourage of relatives, servants, three thousand horsemen, and numerous Romans, and the expenses all underwritten by Rome, his triumphal procession was greeted with pomp and circumstance in various cities along the route. In Naples Tiridates did obeisance to Nero as master. Nero then received Tiridates and party in a lavishly decorated and festively excited Rome.

> The king of Armenia, whom Nero induced by great promises to come to Rome . . . [Nero] presented with the praetorian cohorts drawn up in full armor about the temples in the Forum, while he himself sat on the rostra in the attire of a triumphing general, surrounded by military ensigns and standards. As the king approached . . . the emperor at first let him fall at his feet, but then raised him with his right hand and kissed him. Then, while the king made supplication, Nero took the turban from his head and replaced it with a diadem. . . . From there the king was taken to the theater, and when he had again done obeisance, Nero gave him a seat at his right hand. Because of all this Nero was hailed as Imperator, and after depositing a laurel wreath in the Capitol, he closed the two doors of the temple of Janus, as a sign that no war was left anywhere. (Suetonius, *Nero,* 13)[44]

Besides calling Tiridates himself a Magus, Pliny says that Tiridates brought Magi with him and initiated Nero into their sacred banquets (*Nat. Hist.* 30.6.17). A fascinating event in its own right, Tiridates' journey with his Magi provides a revealing comparison and contrast with the journey of the Magi in Matthew 2. Perhaps most important, it indicates the international political context of such a journey and its political as well as religious implications. In particular, it shows both that the East-West conflict was still an important issue in the Roman empire in mid-first century C.E. and that the Magi were still thought of as royal advisers to Eastern kings.

There appear to be three obvious ways to account for the inclusion of the visit of the Magi in Matthew's story about Jesus birth in chapter 2. The widely known visit of Tiridates and company to Nero in 66 C.E. could have suggested to Matthew the inclusion of the Magi's visit and obeisance to the newborn "king of the Jews" in a story that otherwise features the standard motifs of the "myth of the birth of the hero."[45] Or perhaps the scholarly Matthew had in mind the important passage in Isaiah (44:24–45:25) about Cyrus as the messiah responsible for the restoration of Judea as he wrote about the birth of the newborn messiah Jesus and, aware of the key role the Magi had played in the famous legend of Cyrus's birth, embellished the significance of Christ's birth with their visit.[46]

The third possibility, of course, which does not exclude the influence of the Tiridates visit to Nero or the memory of Cyrus as the messiah and the role of the Magi at his legendary birth, is that Matthew used an already current tradition or story about the Magi's visit to the infant Jesus. Brown has carefully demonstrated that a number of problems in the Matthean narrative as it stands can be accounted for and the development of the principal stories or motifs also explained by postulating the existence of two different pre-Matthean narratives. The larger one was a sequence of three "angelic dream appearances" (in which both Joseph and Herod played key roles), rooted in patterns already familiar from biblical traditions, while the other (completely separable from the roles of Joseph or Herod and the Magi's coming first to Jerusalem) focused specifically on the journey of the Magi to pay homage to the child.[47] Considering the other layers of the material in Matthew such as the recapitulation of Israel's history by the infant Jesus, the special concerns of Matthew such as the christological apology (Bethlehem as expected, etc.) and the formula quotations, and the widespread knowledge of the Magi in the Hellenistic world, particularly in connection with the East-West conflict, Brown's reconstruction of a separate, pre-Matthean legend concerning the journey of the Magi is highly credible.

Now, after the birth of Jesus in Bethlehem of Judea, behold, magi from the East came to Judea saying, "Where is the newborn king of the Jews? For we have seen his star at its rising and have come to pay him homage." And behold, the star which they had seen at its rising went before them until it came to rest over the place where the child was. (When they saw the star they were greatly overjoyed.) And entering the house, they saw the child with Mary his mother; and they bowed down and paid him homage. Then they went away to their own country.[48]

Whether in such a pre-Matthean form or the final Matthean version, the story or motif of the Magi's visit places the birth of "the king of the Jews" in the context of the long-standing politicoreligious conflict between Rome (and Hellenism) and the East. At the very least, here are royal priests known far and wide as the most important advisers to the Persian King of Kings now seeking and doing obeisance to the newborn king of a small and insignificant people supposedly subject to Rome. But they also surely represented the longing among eastern peoples generally, not just the Jews, for a restoration of their own native rule over against the alien western imperial rule that had seemed so oppressive. Now here at last the long-awaited ruler has been born, and here are the Magi, *the* figures in the East who would have the necessary wisdom and divine revelation to know this, coming to do the appropriate obeisance to the new king of kings. When the Magi do obeisance to the child, it is an act of highest respect for, homage to, and submission to a king, a political ruler, not an act of worship of divinity,[49] further expressing the worldwide political import of what is happening here. Finally—and it is less certain from our sources that this feature was widely known because it would of necessity have been "underground"—the Magi may well have cultivated (and probably connoted to others) a tradition of resistance to western (Hellenistic-Roman) imperial rule and cultivation of hope for the restoration of true kingship in the East. Such connotations or implications of the Magi's visit fit nicely with, but also add another dimension to, the story of the birth of the king of the Jews, the basic thrust of which is direct opposition to the existing tyrannical kingship of Herod as part of Roman imperial rule.

One further and important dimension in our story that we might miss because it is more implicit than explicit is that, in the Magi, men of the highest station and most sacred status are here proclaiming, with their obeisance, that an ordinary child has been revealed as the new king. This dimension is rooted in the difference between the Jewish tradition of *popular* resistance to alien imperial domination and hopes for liberation, on the one hand, and the resistance to Western imperial rule by the *aristocracy* or former rulers elsewhere in the ancient Near East, such as in Persia, on the other. Matthew does not mention the humble circumstances of Jesus' birth explicitly. But the juxtaposition of Jesus as from the tiny towns of Bethlehem and Nazareth, along with the slaughter of the children in Bethlehem, and the established king Herod along with the high priests in the ruling city of Jerusalem suggests that, whatever their lineage (Matt. 1:2–16), Jesus and his parents were ordinary people. Once people had the stories from Luke in mind alongside the story of the Magi from Matthew, then the high aristocratic position of the Magi stood out in more explicit contrast with the humble origins of Jesus. Thus there is clearly another dimension in this story: far from the restoration of the great Persian kingship in all its splendor for which they had long propagandized, the Magi now take the initiative in revealing that the hoped-for liberation from foreign domination has begun in this birth in a little town in the tiny principality of Judea.

In connection with the Magi, finally, perhaps a word is in order also regarding the connotations of the star, or more precisely the religious and especially political implications of the appearance of such an extraordinary "natural" phenomenon. Especially in theologically educated circles we often come to such an issue with a particular contrast in mind: that between the apocalyptically oriented Palestinian Jewish culture, which would attempt to interpret such a star as a sign of important events, and the metaphysical Greco-Roman culture or the earlier mythic culture, both of which understood heavenly phenomena as parts of a divine natural order (cosmos). This contrast, of course, underlies the interpretations that find in the Magi's visit the breaking or subordination of the (false or idolatrous) pagan science and superstition. The more popular view among the ancients (including the intellectuals who wrote literature, of course), that heavenly signs marked the births of great figures, may be closer to the story in Matthew and indicates the political dimension involved.

Since this story is clearly growing from Palestinian Jewish (and thus Eastern) soil, however, we should attend more closely to the Jewish apocalyptic tradition. Josephus mentions among the things that motivated the Jews to fight so fiercely against the overwhelming might of the Roman armies besieging Jerusalem were "a star, resembling a sword, that stood over the city, and a comet which continued for a year" (*War* 6.289). We know from Jewish apocalyptic literature that such signs, like the recurrent collective visions of "chariots and armed battalions hurtling through the clouds throughout all parts of the country just before sunset" (*War* 6.298–99), were associated with the people's intense longing for liberation from alien rule. Hence they could also be associated with hopes for and (traditional biblical?) oracles concerning the emergence of a king who would lead liberation and restoration (*War* 6.312). It is clear from our investigations of the Magi that the Jews were not unique in their hopes for liberation from alien, Hellenistic-Roman domination, or in their interpretation of an unusual natural phenomenon as pertaining to historical events. The star in Matthew 2, in sum, fits perfectly with the politicohistorical thrust of the story of the birth of a liberating king revealed to and by the distinguished sacral-royal Magi, eager for such signs and such deliverance.

PART TWO

◆

The Infancy Narratives in Historical Context: The People

· 4 ·

"To All the People"

PIETY AND PEOPLE

The background to Luke 1–2 has been sought in what has come to be known as the piety of the *'anawim*. Brown argued that the supposition that "Jewish-Christian Anawim" are both the source of the canticles and an influence on Luke's presentation can account for three important facets of the material in Luke 1–2: the distinctively Jewish language and orientation of the canticles (esp. the Magnificat and the Benedictus); the upright and devout Jewish characters Zechariah, Elizabeth, Simeon, and Anna; and the apparent connection of religious piety and the Temple setting of some of these stories. There appear to be six key steps in his sketch of "the Anawim." First, although the term may originally have designated the physically poor, "it came to refer more widely to those who could not trust in their own strength but had to rely in utter confidence upon God"; that is, it came to express a certain attitude of mind. Second, in postexilic times "the Anawin regarded themselves as the ultimate narrowing down of the remnant of Israel." Third, the Qumran community, the author of whose "psalms" (1QH) frequently describes himself as a "poor one," originated from the Hasideans, or "pious ones," of the Maccabean revolt (1 Macc. 2:42; 7:9–16), hence was "a sectarian group of Anawim." Fourth, "very often, woven together with this piety of dependence on God was a 'Temple piety.' " Fifth, thus it is credible "that Luke got his canticles from a somewhat parallel community of Jewish Anawim who had been converted to Christianity . . . who continued to reverence the Temple." These Jewish-Christian Anawim and their "Temple piety" are described by Luke in Acts 2:43–47; 4:32–37. Finally, even the characters in Luke's narratives "embodied the piety of the Anawin."

On the face of it, this is a highly attractive hypothesis, particularly on the assumption that the nativity narratives are primarily or exclusively religious.

What might otherwise look like politicoeconomic implications in the stories or canticles can be understood rather as expressions of religious piety. And our intepretation of the narratives can remain within the traditional Christian religious or theological conceptuality, which allows interpreters to ferret out the appropriate soteriology and christology of Luke or his sources.

This sketch of the Anawim, however, depends upon highly questionable traditions of biblical interpretation and is uninformed by any critical socio-logical investigation or model of traditional agrarian society. Late-nineteenth-century commentaries on the Psalms suggested that the *'anawim* in the Psalms were a *party* of economically impoverished over against the rich and powerful (e.g., the Levites over against the Aaronic high priests).[1] Subsequent inves-tigations, rather, found among certain Israelites a special religious orientation toward God as their sole hope and defender, with the Hasideans of Maccabean times as the first real party of the poor. Notwithstanding certain objections from Scandinavian work on the Psalms, during the decades just before and after the Second World War (and prior to Vatican II), attention had shifted to an " *'anawim* piety" in which biblical expressions about "the poor" were understood in purely spiritual terms.[2] Most of these interpretations, however, were uninformed by any adequate sense of, or even any attention to, concrete social structure and historical context. A completely new investigation is needed of the biblical literature that includes reference to *'anawim,* and any consideration of psalms in this connection must take into account the concrete institutional setting. In any case, it is inherently unlikely that the *'anawim* psalms are expressions either of private individual piety or of some socially disembodied Jewish spirituality.[3]

Brown's sketch of the Anawim, of course, includes the social dimension. But throughout his discussion he simply *assumes* the existence of some sort of group of people that were or can be designated appropriately by "the Anawim," and the social bases suggested by Brown are all problematic when one comes to look for solid evidence. With regard to the second step in Brown's sketch, "the remnant" has been a prominent theme in biblical inter-pretation, but it has not been notably connected with the *'anawim,* much less with historical developments of early second-Temple social structure and social conflict. Recent critical analysis of "the hasideans" in 1 Maccabees would lead more toward the conclusion that the term refers to all those who were resisting the Hellenizing reform and imperial military suppression.[4] There is no evi-dence, moreover, associating the term *'anawim* with *hasideans.* Thus, with regard to Brown's third step, there is no special party or other group from which the Qumran community could have originated, only the faithful or pious ("hasidic") people generally who were resisting their foreign imperial and domestic high-priestly rulers.

At least the "Temple piety," the fourth step in Brown's portrait of the

Anawim, would appear to have a concrete social context. "The Lucan infancy narrative (and Acts) has a context of 'Temple-piety,' a quasi-technical term used to describe devout observation of the Law, coming to the Temple 'to see the face of God,' taking part in the cult, and the recitation of the psalms."[5] There is little evidence for any such special mode of religious devotion, however, much less that it was very often "woven together with" the *'anawim* piety of dependence on God. The textual evidence consists of several verses in a handful of psalms (e.g., 42; 43; 63).[6] One can imagine that priests and Levites who served in the Temple more frequently than most (see further below on priests) might develop a special piety. Ironically, the best evidence for the hypothetical existence of some sort of special "Temple-piety" might be certain Dead Sea Scrolls, namely, expressions of those who had alienated themselves from the Temple because of the "wicked priests" who controlled the Temple apparatus.

For the existence of a group of "Jewish-Christian Anawim," the fifth step in Brown's sketch, there is no more evidence than there is for "the Anawim from whom they would supposedly have "converted." The very concept, of course, may be an anachronism, since there was no such thing as "Christianity" to which the early Palestinian Jewish followers of Jesus could convert. They were still involved in Palestinian Jewish communities. Luke's nostalgic descriptions of the earliest followers of Jesus in Jerusalem (e.g., Acts 2:43–47; 3:1–9; 5:42) has them spending time in the Temple courtyard, apparently preaching and healing and generally attempting to spread their movement.[7] Luke's descriptions leave no doubt, however, that anything that might be described as piety was dissolved into their excitement over the fulfillment they were experiencing and the corresponding *esprit de corps* of their joyous meals together. The locus of the latter, moreover, was their homes. They did, however, find themselves quickly locked in conflict with the high-priestly government, who headed the Temple apparatus. In Luke's descriptions the early followers of Jesus in Jerusalem see themselves as standing with the ordinary people—indeed, "having great favor with all the people"—over against the high-priestly authorities.

It becomes difficult, therefore, to discern how the characters in Luke 1–2 exemplify *'anawim* piety. There seems to be little direct connection between the righteousness and devotion of the characters in Luke 1–2 and the Temple. The Temple functions as the setting for Zechariah's vision. It is the place where he can be in the presence of the Lord, almost certainly dependent on the tradition Luke or the pre-Lucan story is following from Daniel 9, where Gabriel appears to "Daniel" in the Temple. It is surely reading into the text to suggest that Zechariah was a "Temple priest."[8] He was an ordinary priest who lived in the hill country of Judah, and such ordinary priests served in the Temple only two weeks each year (and perhaps during the principal festivals). The Temple court is the setting for the circumcision and presentation of the infant Jesus and the place where Simeon met and embraced the child. But the emphasis in the story is on following the stipulations of the Torah and on Simeon's guidance by the Holy Spirit, not on anything to do with the Temple.[9]

The only suggestion that devout expressions of piety were somehow connected specifically with the Temple is in the sketch of the elderly prophetess, Anna. There may be some significance, particularly for Luke's overall literary project, in Anna's close association with the Temple courts (see chap. 5 below). At this point, however, it should be noted that, as with Zechariah, the Temple is primarily the setting for Anna's continuous "fasting and praying." There is nothing in the narrative to suggest that she was participating in special Temple rites, certainly not those conducted in the sanctuary (a woman was not permitted beyond the courtyard). As with the entire "twelve tribes" of Israel, whom Luke characterizes as "earnestly worshiping night and day" in hopes of fulfillment of the promise to the ancestors, so Anna's "not departing from the Temple courtyard, worshiping night and day" is likely Lucan hyperbole. Brown even suggests that, in his portrayal of Anna, Luke may even be "creating a type of Anawim piety," in which case the Temple court clearly serves as the obvious setting, and Anna is not there to represent some already current Jewish "Temple-piety."

It is thus difficult to identify what "the piety of the Anawim" might be that Simeon and Anna would embody.[10] "The Amawin" have been difficult to locate socially. And beyond the supposedly interwoven "Temple piety," the distinctive characteristics of "the piety of the Anawim" other than dependency on God have not been identified. Simeon is described as righteous and devout. His righteousness, like that of Zechariah and Elizabeth, refers to his faithful observance of the Torah, something that would not have been distinctive to a special category of *'anawim*. Luke uses the term *devout* also in the Pentecost narrative for the Jews "from every nation under heaven" who were resident in Jerusalem at the time; hence "devout" would hardly be distinctive of the *'anawim* for Luke. It is difficult to find anything in the narrative, other than the "devout," that could be a characterization of his piety. The two noteworthy features of Simeon in the narrative, apart from his blessing and prophecy, are his guidance by the Spirit and his "looking for the consolation of Israel." He is not an embodiment of piety but a paradigmatic man of the people who has been longing intensely for the people's deliverance.

Anna is more credible as an embodiment of " *'anawim* piety," for widows, like orphans, were typical examples of "the poor." "Prayer and fasting,' however, would hardly have been distinctive of "the ideals of the Anawim." The combination of her widowhood, age, and habitual praying in Luke, who "mentions widows more than all the other gospels combined," could more likely be understood somewhat in parallel with the strikingly similar description of widows in 1 Timothy 5:3–16.[11] The most noteworthy and the highly distinctive feature of Anna, however, is her identification as a prophetess. Very few–and highly significant–women were so identified in biblical tradition. Perhaps the most remembered of the prophetesses, Miriam and Deborah, sang songs celebrating God's deliverance of the people from their enemies. Parallel to the Spirit-guided Simeon, who is paired with her in the narrative, Anna fills the prophetic role in the narrative of indicating the significance of Jesus "to all who were looking for the redemption of Israel." Her age and persistence in fasting and prayer further dramatize the longing of the people whom she represents. If her advanced age and widowhood are modeled after Judith as well (another famous heroic woman who sang a song),[12] then even more clearly the figure of Anna suggests, not Temple piety or the *'anawim,* but the memory of and longing for God's liberation of the subjected people from their alien rulers.

Many of the very psalms that were used to argue for the existence of *'anawim* piety, however, point toward an alternative to Brown's suggestion for the milieu reflected by the characters and canticles in Luke 1–2. A cursory reexamination of some of the so-called *'anawim* Psalms may be suggestive.[13] Many of the psalms often listed in connection with the *'anawim* do express a self-image similar to what is called *'anawim* piety in the secondary literature (Pss. 25, 34–35, 40–41, 86, 109, 140). But many of the psalms claimed for the *'anawim* appeal to God/Yahweh as the defender or refuge of the poor, oppressed *people of Israel/Judah* against the oppressive *foreign or domestic rulers:* Pss 9–10, 14, 147, 149 (cf. Pss. 82, 102–103, 113, 146). Thus one usage of "the poor" was for the people, that is, the people in general over against their rulers, foreign or domestic. These particular psalms tend to be late. Specially interesting is the parallelism of terms for the people, over against the enemy rulers, in Psalm 149: "Sing . . . in the assembly of the faithful [*ḥasidim*]. . . . For the LORD takes pleasure in his people; he adorns the humble with victory" (vv. 1, 4). The Qumran community had the same or a similar understanding of itself, namely, as "the poor"—the people, or Israel proper, over against oppressive and wicked domestic high-priestly or foreign rulers. Thus the usage of the term *'anawim* itself in the Psalms, along with the lack of evidence for any particular group that could appropriately be labeled "the Anawim," leads us to the Palestinian Jewish people generally (over against their own and alien rulers) as those who were "the poor" or "the lowly."

That the lowly or humble as the people of Israel in general, and not a particular group's piety, is the social reality and context reflected in the infancy narratives is of course exactly what is indicated in the Lucan text, particularly in the annunciation and the canticles. The conceptions and births of John and Jesus are declared repeatedly to be for the salvation, deliverance, or joy of the people (1:17, 68, 77; 2:10, 25, 32), of Israel (1:16, 33, 54; 2:25, 32). And clearly it is the people of Israel generally that is meant by "the lowly" and "the hungry" in 1:52–53. Correspondingly, the proud, mighty, and rich of verses 51–53, parallel to the enemies of verses 71, 74, are those from whom the people must be delivered. The actors/speakers involved in the narratives, moreover, are individually and collectively members and representatives of this poor and lowly people. In our usual reconstructions of history, including standard handbooks in New Testament studies, we seldom devote much attention to the common people. Those who make history, or so we assume, are the Caesars and the Herods. It is thus all the more important, therefore, to ferret out aspects of the situation and concerns of the ordinary people who are the object of God's deliverance in the infancy narratives. We can focus in particular on the actors in the narratives as representatives of the people. Thus after inquiring in this chapter into the situation of the Palestinian Jewish peasantry generally, we explore in succession the particular situations of Palestinian Jewish women, ordinary priests, and shepherds (chap. 5). Because peasants generally, women, the often illiterate lower clergy, and shepherds have left little by way of direct documentation of their lives and concerns, it is necessary to utilize cross-cultural comparative material and what may be reflections of popular memories and concerns in Jewish biblical traditions as part of our limited and fragmentary evidence.

PEASANTS

"The whole people" who would derive great joy from the good news of the birth of the savior/messiah were predominantly peasants, and that meant *poor*. In any traditional agrarian society the peasantry composed 90 percent or more of the population and included all those living in towns or villages and engaged in working the soil or related activities, in contrast to the rulers, their retainers, supporting artisans, merchants, and so on, who lived in the cities. Under the Hellenistic empires left in the wake of Alexander the Great's conquest, many cities had been founded along the coast and in the Decapolis, just south and southeast of the Sea of Galilee. But lest we have any doubts that Jewish Palestine was a relatively self-contained traditional agrarian society composed almost completely of peasants in villages and towns, Josephus's descriptions clarify the situation.

> Ours is not a maritime country; neither commerce nor the intercourse which it promotes with the outside world has any attraction for us. Our cities are built inland, remote from the sea; and we devote ourselves to the cultivation of the productive country with which we are blessed. (*Apion* 1.60)

> [In Galilee all] devote themselves to agriculture. In fact, every inch of the soil has been cultivated by the inhabitants. . . . The towns, too, are thickly distributed, and even the villages . . . are densely populated. . . . Perea is entirely under cultivation. . . . [Samaria and Judea] both consist of hills and plains, yield a light and fertile soil for agriculture . . . [and] have a dense population. (*War* 3.42–44, 48–50)

Not only the high-priestly government and Temple apparatus in Jerusalem, but the extensive Herodian governmental apparatus and elaborate development projects and the tribute taken by the Romans as well were all dependent on what was produced by the Palestinian Jewish peasantry, as noted in the previous chapters. Wolf's often-quoted definition of peasants fits the ancient Palestinian situation well: "Peasants are rural cultivators whose surpluses are transferred to a dominant group of rulers that uses the surpluses both to underwrite its own standard of living and to distribute the remainder to groups in society that do not farm but must be fed for their specific goods and services in turn."[14] Most peasants are economically marginal. After the demands for rents and taxes, most peasants are left with a minimal, subsistence living. The peasants' own needs for survival often conflict with the demands of their rulers. Their own consumption obviously cannot be curtailed below the caloric minimum needed to maintain human life. And production cannot be increased if the soil will not sustain higher yields or if there is not sufficient land to support the peasant population as well as the rulers' demands. Given the structure of politicoeconomic domination in Palestine at the time of Jesus' birth, with a double or triple layer of rulers' demands to be met, it is clear that the vast majority of the people would have been poor. Even Herod knew that his heavy demands on his subjects were becoming counterproductive and were simply killing his peasant producers.[15]

Debts and Displacement

Peasants unable to meet the heavy demands for tithes, taxes, and tribute would be driven increasingly into debt and might eventually be disinherited and displaced. A number of factors indicate that many Jewish peasants were indebted or displaced already during Herod's reign and that the problems of debt and displacement became steadily worse during the first century C.E. The devastation, slaughter, and enslavement involved in a generation of conquest and civil war, from 63 to 37 B.C.E., would have depleted or decimated some families and villages. On a lesser scale but nevertheless serious in its impact, when Herod sent raiding parties out into the countryside to commandeer provisions for the Roman troops, some families or whole villages would have been left destitute. Then the structure of the imperial situation would have forced many to borrow in order to make it through to the next harvest after rendering to Temple and Herod as well as to Caesar. There was a severe drought and famine near the midpoint of Herod's long reign, with its obvious consequences for farmers already at the subsistence level. It is not surprising that the people clamored for reduction of taxes (*War* 2.4; *Ant.* 17.204). But it is clear from the large numbers of workers utilized on reconstruction of the Temple and others of Herod's vast building projects that many had already been displaced from the land during his reign.

The escalating banditry and large numbers of people ready to abandon their homes and lands to join one of the popular prophetic movements at mid-first century C.E. are telling indicators that the economic (and hence social) viability of many peasants was in serious jeopardy. The severe drought and famine in the late 40s exacerbated the situation. Peasant indebtedness, of course, only further aggravated their already difficult situation—and further facilitated the flow of wealth to the creditors, some of them probably wealthy priestly families and Herodians in Jerusalem. The grain and oil for which the peasants were desperate was loaned at high interest rates (against the stipulations of the Torah), thus adding to their already impossible burdens of payment. Not surprisingly, one of the first acts of the rebels who took control of Jerusalem in the summer of 66 C.E. was to burn the public archives where the debt records were kept (*War* 2.427).[16]

The parables of Jesus portray just such a situation. It was apparently typical that peasants would owe a hundred measures of wheat (having borrowed eighty) or a hundred measures of oil (having borrowed fifty) to a wealthy creditor and absentee landowner (Luke 16:1–7), or that a peasant might owe a huge sum to a royal official, for nonpayment of which he could be imprisoned (Matt. 18:23–30) or his family members end up in debt slavery. The dominant form of land tenure was likely still independent family or lineage holdings. But large estates farmed by tenants and administered by stewards had become familiar (Mark 12:1–9; Luke 16:1–7). And those who had either lost their land or were desperate for supplementary employment were in great abundance, awaiting any opportunity to work in the fields of a prosperous landowner (Matt. 20:1–16). Jesus' message and practice of the kingdom of God was directed primarily to the poor, the Jewish peasantry whose life and livelihood in their family inheritance was threatened by indebtedness or displacement. "Blessed are you poor, for yours in the kingdom of God. Blessed are you that hunger now, for you shall be satisfied" (Luke 6. 20–21). It is surely significant that the prayer for the kingdom that he taught his disciples focuses on release from debts and satisfaction of hunger: "Give us today the bread of tomorrow (or: Give us our bread of subsistence). . . . Forgive us our debts."[17]

Once we are more familiar with the general situation of the Jewish peasantry, we can appreciate the likely reflection of that situation in the infancy narratives.

How little we have actually understood about the concrete structure of ancient Palestinian Jewish socioeconomic life is indicated by the fact that even recent interpreters still ponder why (in Luke) Mary and Joseph would be going from Galilee, where they lived under the client-king Antipas, to Bethlehem in Judea, where the census was being conducted.[18] We must clearly take more seriously the concrete as well as the christological implications of Luke 2:4: "And Joseph also went up . . . to Judea, to the city of David, which is called Bethlehem, because he was of the house and lineage of David, to be enrolled with Mary, his betrothed." Although evidence on census and taxation is extremely fragmentary from Palestine, papyri from Egypt provide information relevant to this aspect of Luke's narrative. For the census conducted in Egypt in 103 C.E., the prefect had issued the following decree:

> The house by house census having begun, it is necessary that all persons who for any reason whatsoever are absent from their home districts be alerted to return to their own hearths, so that they may complete the customary formalities of registration and apply themselves to the farming for which they are responsible. . . . Those who show their presence to be necessary [in the city of Alexandria] will receive signed permits. . . . All others are to return home within thirty days. Anyone who thereafter is found lacking a permit will be punished without moderation. (P. London, 904)

We can probably assume that Palestine was not as closely regulated as Egypt. But this papyrus indicates clearly how the enrollment for (and by implication, the payment of) tribute assumed that people remained tied to and responsible for producing within their traditional ancestral "house." Numerous other papyri and other sources from Egypt indicate that large numbers of peasants left their home villages, partly or largely because of the pressures of taxation. They simply could not both raise the tribute and support themselves at the same time. The Roman government, however, held them responsible for their portion of the local assessment and took stern measures to round up fugitives and force them back into productive labor in their ancestral villages.

Thus, instead of pondering why the Romans would be expecting people such as Joseph to go from their obvious place of residence to the place of their ancestral origins, we should perhaps inquire why Joseph was no longer in his ancestral town in the first place. In Jewish Palestine, as in any traditional agrarian society, the vast majority of the peasants would have been working their ancestral lands and supporting the ruling groups with a portion of their produce. How did it happen that Joseph now lives nearly a hundred miles from his "house and family" of origin and even in a different district of Palestine? Tradition has it that Joseph was a "carpenter." How did a carpenter make a living, especially in a village such as Nazareth? Was he perhaps a wage laborer in a nearby town such as Sepphoris? How did people become carpenters or wage laborers in the first place? Almost certainly because of some displacement from their ancestral land, because of debts, famine, war, and so forth. Thus Joseph and Mary represent the thousands of rootless people in ancient Jewish Palestine cut loose from their ancestral lands and villages by the Roman conquest or by indebtedness resulting from the intensive economic exploitation by Herod that compounded the demands for Temple dues and Roman tribute.

As noted in chapter 2, Caesar's decree of the census provides far more than an occasion for a christological shift of scene from Nazareth to Bethlehem. The Romans' demand for tribute was a heavily contributing factor to the intense economic pressures on the peasantry, which caused many of them to become refugees displaced from their ancestral land and laborers far from home. Having found some means of livelihood elsewhere, people such as Joseph and Mary were then forced to return to their "homes" to be enrolled for the tribute required by their conquerors. In the case of Mary, the imperial decree comes at the least opportune moment, during the final days of pregnancy. But this is exactly what life was like for the vast majority of people under the "peace" wrought by Caesar. And whether we have in mind the (hypothetical) "Joseph and Mary" of Jesus' own family of origin or the many urban residents who found their way into churches such as Luke's, many would have known firsthand the experiences of displacement from ancestral homes, relocation in a distant town or city, and then the necessity of meeting the imperial demands for tribute or labor requiring further disruption of their lives.

The flight into Egypt by Joseph and Mary with the child (told in Matthew) can also be seen to reflect the social relationships and political conditions that prevailed in Jewish Palestine under Roman and Herodian rule. This does not mean that the story of the flight into Egypt reports or reflects an actual event. The story perhaps originated as part of a legend showing how Jesus recapitulated the key events in the origin of the people as a whole (descent into Egypt, etc.). It is at least possible that Matthew is reponsible for the sequence of incidents in the narrative of Matthew 2. Nevertheless, the story reflects the historical situation in which, whether because of the steady impact of economic pressures or because of the direct effect of political-military actions, many people were forced to flee their homes if they wanted to avoid being killed.

The Roman and Herodian troops would have created refugees, often hundreds and thousands at once, virtually every time they took military action to maintain or reassert their domination in a given area. As we have seen in the previous chapter, both used death and destruction as means of terrorizing and intimidating the subjected people. In 4 B.C.E., or supposedly right about the time Jesus was born, the Romans were particularly brutal in the areas where the movements led by the popularly acclaimed kings had been active, burning the towns and enslaving the inhabitants after reconquering the towns and villages. But not all inhabitants waited to be killed or enslaved. Josephus says explicitly about Emmaus, for example, that its people had fled before the Roman devastation of the town (*War* 2.71; *Ant.* 17.291). Nor would such flight have been merely a temporary necessity, for the Roman general Varus then dispatched part of his army to search the nearby countryside for rebels and eventually crucified two thousand of those caught (*War* 2.75; *Ant.* 17.295).

The same situation of thousands of refugees prevailed again in the wake of the Roman reconquest of Palestine following the great Jewish revolt of 66, or about the time any pre-Matthean stories would have arisen and within memory of Matthew's contemporaries. Josephus describes at length implementation and effects of the typical Roman scorched-earth policy in the reconquest of Perea, Judea, and Idumea (*War* 4.410–90). The Roman troops would storm village after village, slaughtering and burning as they went. As Josephus writes curtly more than once: "The helpless were slaughtered wholesale, the more able-bodied fled, and the soldiers rifled the houses and then set the village alight" (*War* 4:430; cf. sec. 489). As the Romans advanced on Jericho, the mass of the population fled "into the hill country over against Jerusalem" (*War* 4.451). South of Bethlehem, Vespasian, "having taken two villages right in the heart of Idumea, Betabris and Caphartoba, he put upwards of ten thousand inhabitants to death, made prisoners of over a thousand, expelled the remainder and stationed in the district a large division of his own troops, who overran and devastated the whole of the hill country" (*War* 4.448). Some of those able-bodied fugitives or those expelled from these Judean or Idumean villages surely fled to Jerusalem and became anti-Roman combatants. The vast majority, however, would clearly have remained homeless refugees for some time to come.

Even without a war of reconquest, however, the Roman imperial system was creating fugitives and refugees aplenty. Simply because of the steady economic pressures, peasants who could no longer eke out a subsistence living from the soil would have fled the land. As indicated from papyri discovered in Egypt, there was a steady flow of fugitives from the land, many of whom must have sought their fortune in the cities. Records of the Arsinoite village of Philadelphia indicate that, during the first years of Nero's reign, one out of every seven or eight men were fugitives.[19] Although the scale of this flight from the countryside to the cities may not have been as great in Jewish Palestine and elsewhere in the eastern Mediterranean as in Egypt, the flow was a steady one. In Palestine the dramatic increase in banditry after the acute famine in the late 40s suggests that many peasants were leaving the land to join bands of brigands.[20] The Jewish and Roman ruling groups understood precisely the direct relationship between heavy taxation, insufficient food, and escalating banditry. As the Jewish peasants persisted in their massive strike protesting Gaius's egomaniacal plan to place his statue in the Jerusalem Temple, Herodians and other Jewish officials argued to the Roman legate Petronius (according to Josephus) that, "since the land was unsown, there would be a harvest of banditry, because the requirement of tribute could not be met" (*Ant.* 18.274).[21]

Popular Resistance Rooted in Memory and Expectation

In contrast to most such peasant societies and, in particular, to most other peoples subjected to the *pax Romana,* the Jewish people were not docile or passive. They apparently did not simply accept their situation under Roman, Herodian, and high-priestly rule. Resistance took a variety of forms, and we have evidence both for the general roots of that resistance and in particular for the forms it took in the very areas featured in the nativity narratives— the villages around Sepphoris such as Nazareth, and the Judean countryside around Jerusalem, such as "the hill country" and Bethlehem. Stories about the birth of the new "king of the Jews," or the savior whose birth was good news for the Jewish people in particular, as opposed to the savior whose birthday the rest of the Roman empire celebrated as the primal origins of the cosmos, obviously must be understood in this context of Jewish resistance to the Roman-imposed peace.

The various ruling groups provided plenty of "encouragement" for the Jewish people to submit. The Roman imperial policy and practice of conquest included brutal means to terrorize the subjected peoples, as noted above. Destruction of towns, enslavement of the people, and crucifixion of resisters was intended as intimidation for the rest of those subjected.[22] Peasants in northwestern Judea, for example, surely remembered what had happened to the people in the four main district towns of Gophna, Emmaus, Lydda, and Thamna when they had been somewhat slow in rendering up the special levy of taxes to Cassius (44 B.C.E., *War* 1.218–22; see chap. 2 above). As sketched above, Herod set up an elaborate security force along with his network of fortresses perhaps because he already knew how recalcitrant the Jewish people could be.

The people's motivation to send up their dues to the Temple and high priests was supposedly positive, not negative. That is, the various sacrifices, offerings, and other dues were supposedly an obligation to God as specified in the Torah. The new incumbents of the high priesthood, however, all creatures of Herod, must have held little legitimacy in the eyes of the people. The structure of the imperial situation was such that the high-priestly government in Jerusalem was, by definition, in collaboration with Roman rule of Palestine. Whatever the reason may have been, there is evidence from later rabbinic literature that the peasantry, particularly in Galilee, was resistant to payment of their dues.[23] There was clearly resistance to payment of the half-shekel tax due to the Temple from all adult males, a tax not mentioned in the Torah. The declaration of Jesus in Matthew 17:24–26 appears to mean what it says: "The sons are free" (of paying the tax).[24] Thus while certain divine sanctions were set forth in the official theocratic doctrine as motivations for the Jewish peasants to pay their Temple and priestly dues, we should not be naive regarding the effectiveness of those sanctions.

The persistent popular Jewish resistance to their situation despite Roman terror, Herodian repression, and religious sanctions thus requires some appreciation of the roots of their resilience. Much of the discussion of the Magnificat and other canticles in chapter 6 is directly pertinent to this question. At this point we should observe the importance of the people's memories of past liberation and longings for future deliverance, in particular those suggested by a few seemingly incidental motifs as well as by central themes in the nativity narratives.

Most prominent in the nativity narratives are the themes of the exodus of Israel from Egypt and the birth of the messiah as the son of David. In both cases the people's memory of past liberation in fact has informed their longings in a paradigmatic way. In Matthew 2, the implicit structure of the whole is a sequence of events by which the newborn "king of the Jews" recapitulates his people's formative history of descent into Egypt, being called out of Egypt, and coming back into the people's land still occupied by hostile rulers. This formative history of the people that Jesus recapitulates in Matthew 2 would have been immediately on the surface of the people's consciousness during the time of Jesus and the formation of gospel traditions. The original liberation of Israel from bondage in Egypt was celebrated annually in the great pilgrimage feast of Passover. We know from the reports of Josephus (as well as from the Christian Gospels) that this festival was frequently a time of heightened tension between the Jews celebrating their liberation from Egypt and the occupying Roman forces. In fact, the Roman governors ordinarily made a highly visible (and perhaps provocative) show of force by posting soldiers along the porticoes of the Temple during Passover "so as to quell any uprising that might occur" (*Ant.* 20.106–7). We shall see that the formative history of Israel also served as paradigm for certain movements in the Jerusalem area with an intense anticipation of God's new acts of deliverance.

To approach the memory of and longing for a Davidic messiah requries us either simply to abandon or to disentangle the highly synthetic, theologically determined concepts of "the messiah" and "messianic expectations." There was no standard or widespread concept or expectation of the messiah in first-

century Jewish Palestine. Indeed, occurrences of the term *messiah* are strikingly
rare in Jewish literature of any kind prior to the time of Jesus. From its
absence in earlier second-Temple Jewish literature, we must conclude that
there was little or no expectation of a messiah, at least among literate circles.
The limited occurrences of the term in late-second-Temple literature such as
Psalms of Solomon 17 and some of the Dead Sea Scrolls indicated that different literate groups had different expectations. In none of this literature,
moreover, is there any indication that any of the known Jewish groups focused
its expectations of future deliverance primarily on *a* or *the* messiah. Nevertheless, the dramatic appeal in Psalms of Solomon 17 for God to raise up
the king, the son of David, who is to be the lord messiah, indicates that, at
least among some literate circles, there was some expectation of such a figure.

The striking lack of literary evidence for messianic expectations at the time
of Jesus makes all the more important the occurrence among the Jewish peasantry of large social movements headed by popularly acclaimed kings. The
obvious explanation for why social unrest took this particular social form,
rather than some other, is that the tradition of popular kingship, in which
figures such as Saul, David, or Jehu were acclaimed or "anointed" by the
Israelites as their king, was still (or again) alive in the memories of the Jewish
peasants.[25] The statements about Jesus of Nazareth as the messiah, the son
of David, the son of the Most High, and so forth, in their present form in
the nativity narratives or elsewhere in the Gospels, are the result of a generation
or two of early Christians' reflection on the significance of Jesus. But the
memories and longings out of which the people would have responded to
Jesus and out of which traditions grew that stand behind the nativity narratives
can be most appropriately approached by comparison with the concrete
movements led by popularly recognized kings.

Memory and expectation of an anointed king would surely have been part
of a broader hope for the liberation of the people from oppressive alien and
domestic rule. Precisely such a hope is indicated in both the characterization
of Simeon as looking for "the consolation of Israel" and of Anna as speaking
of Jesus to all who were looking for "the redemption of Jerusalem" (Luke
2:25, 38). That these phrases are synonymous, virtual equivalents, and that
they refer to the liberation of the people from subjection to alien rule is clear
from so-called Second Isaiah (Isa. 40–55; see esp. 40:1, 9–11; 61:2) in general
and from Isaiah 52:9 in particular: "Break forth together into singing . . .
for the LORD has comforted his people, he has redeemed Jerusalem" (and
not the related language of good news, peace, and salvation, e.g., in verse
7). Some interpreters have sought to avoid or blunt the obvious political
implications of such expressions of Jewish longings for liberation, for example,
by shifting attention to the "revelation to the Gentiles" in Simeon's speech
(Luke 2:31–32).[26] But no more than in Isaiah 40—55 does the mention of

benefit to the Gentiles in Luke 2 divert attention from, much less eliminate, the focus on deliverance of Israel. Also there is nothing in either Isaiah or Luke 2 to indicate that such phrases referred to an eschatological redemption. Rather, they reflect the "actual aspirations of Palestinian Jews of the time."[27] That meaning is clearly indicated from the time of the second great revolt against Rome, in 132–35 B.C.E., in documents dated to "year one" or "year two" of "the Redemption of Israel" or of "the Freedom of Jerusalem."[28] As we shall see, there is further expression of this longing for the concrete consolation/redemption of Israel in the songs sung by Mary, Zechariah, and Simeon.

Two additional motifs in Luke's narrative provide further indications of the same or similar memories and expectations among the people of divine deliverance. The "messenger of the Lord" who appears to Zechariah in Luke 1:11 is named explicitly as Gabriel in verse 19. The name *Gabriel* means "God is my hero/warrior."[29] Gabriel appeared earlier in the context of revelatory visions that encouraged the people to persist in their traditional covenantal commitment and resist their imperial oppressors because God was sure to vindicate them and bring an end to their domination soon. In Luke 2:13, a "heavenly army" appears to the shepherds. Now this could be explained as simply the "heavenly host" or as merely the traditional fixtures of visions (e.g., 1 Kgs. 22:19). But it is difficult to avoid the connotations of the battalions of angels who fought (with the divine warrior) for Israel against the enemy forces, a long-standing biblical tradition.[30] Such heavenly armies appear in 2 Maccabees 5:1–4 (and 10:29–32) and are indicated as a widespread popular vision during the great revolt by Josephus: "Before sunset throughout all parts of the country chariots were seen in the air and armed battalions hurtling through the air and encompassing cities" (*War* 6.298–99). The saying of Jesus in the arrest scene (Matt. 26:53) would appear to refer to the same sense among the Jewish people that the heavenly armies would fight for their liberation.

Forms of Popular Resistance near Nazareth and Bethlehem

Because the nativity narratives revolve around Nazareth and Bethlehem, it would seem appropriate to examine the Jewish resistance that would have been associated with those respective areas from around the time of Jesus' birth as well as later, when some of the traditions of the nativity were taking shape. Nazareth was one of the many villages near Sepphoris, the principal city of Galilee until Herod Antipas built Tiberias. Sepphoris had apparently been a district capital and/or fortress under the Hasmoneans, which would help explain why the Romans made it one of the district capitals in the re-organization under Gabinius around 55 B.C.E. (*Ant.* 13.338; 14.91). The royal palace or arsenal there suggests that it was a principal center of Herod's rule and taxation of Galilee. When people erupted in revolt after the death of the hated tyrant, they attacked the royal arsenal and perhaps even took control of the city, which would better explain Varus's brutal retaliation in suppressing the rebellion. Whether it was punishment of the actual rebels or simply a means of terrorizing the people of the area, Varus burned the city and enslaved its inhabitants, according to both of Josephus's reports (*War* 2.5., 66; *Ant.* 17.271, 289). The particular social form taken by the uprising that attacked the royal palace in Sepphoris was that of a popular messianic movement, in this case led by Judas, son of the bandit chieftain Hezekiah, whom Herod had murdered a generation earlier. Thus within a short time after Jesus was born (according to Matthew), there was a movement in the immediate area of Nazareth led by one whom his followers acclaimed as "king." And people in villages such as Nazareth would have witnessed the Roman destruction of the city and enslavement of people in the area.

Sepphoris was rebuilt as a Greek-speaking city, and Herod Antipas then "fortified Sepphoris to be the ornament of all Galilee, and called it Imperial City" (Autocratoris, *Ant.* 18.27). There would thus have been major reconstruction underway during the time of Jesus' youth, supposedly in Nazareth— construction in an alien Hellenistic style of a city that would again have dominated the surrounding area. If what happened in the revolt of 66 is any indication, then the tensions between the city and the surrounding villages must have remained intense. Sepphoris remained loyal to the Romans midst widespread revolt in the surrounding area (*Life*, 104, 123, 232, 346, 373–75, 379; *War* 2.511). Thus, when Josephus arrived to take command of Galilee, he "found the inhabitants of Sepphoris in great distress concerning their native place, which the Galileans had decided to pillage because of their leanings toward the Romans" (*Life*, 30). And later, when he was leading an attack against the city, "the Galileans, seizing this opportunity . . . of venting their hatred on one of the cities which they detested, rushed forward, with the intention of exterminating the population, aliens and all" (*Life*, 375).

Bethlehem was only six or seven miles south of Jerusalem. It is impossible to isolate struggles that may have been rooted primarily in the villages near Jerusalem from the countrywide conflicts that also tended to focus on the ruling city. Because it was so near the city where conflicts tended to center, however, the people in Bethlehem and in villages of the hill country of Judea were probably also affected by those wider struggles and conflicts originating in the city as well as the local tensions between Jerusalem and its satellite villages. The escalation of tension and then hostilities in 4 B.C.E. would appear to be a vivid example. The entry into the city of Passover crowds, many of whom would have been from nearby villages, swelled the ranks of the mob demanding reduction of taxes and release of prisoners after Herod's death. A panicked Archelaus set his troops upon them. Those not slain escaped into the neighboring hills. Not surprisingly, at the Pentecost festival several weeks later, large crowds flocked into Jerusalem from all over the country, "but it was the native population of Judea itself which, both in numbers and ardor, was preeminent," as the aroused Jewish peasantry besieged the Roman garrison (*War* 2.10–13, 42–43).

Meanwhile in the Judean countryside, as in the vicinity of Sepphoris, the rebellion took the form of a popular messianic movement, led by the shepherd Athronges, as noted above. Those who were following Athronges as king fought against both Roman and Herodian troops, apparently quite successfully. As in Sepphoris, the Romans retaliated sharply for their defeat of a Roman supply train by destroying the district town of Emmaus (whose inhabitants had been enslaved a generation earlier). In addition, they crucified two thousand of the rebels whom they eventually caught, apparently in the Judean hills (*Ant.* 17.291, 295). Josephus reveals that it was some time before Archelaus's troops could root out Athronges and his followers, indicating that popular kingship could effectively achieve independent rule for the people, at least for a few years, although only by constant vigilance and guerrilla warfare (*Ant.* 17.283). One can imagine that such a successful movement, and probably the Roman reconquest as well, would have left a lasting impression on the people of the Judean hills.

Continuing resistance or protest in the area near Jerusalem around mid-first century took a form more directly relevant to prophetic figures in the Lucan narrative (Ann, as well as John). Theudas, like a new Moses announcing a new exodus from alien rule, must have drawn his followers from villages near Jerusalem such as Bethlehem (*Ant.* 20.97–98). Similarly, it would likely have been peasants from "the countryside" of no great distance from the city that the "Egyptian," like a new Joshua, led around Jerusalem in the anticipation that the walls would collapse and the alien rulers disappear (*Ant.* 20.169–71; *War* 2.261–63).[31] However fantastic their expectations of deliverance may have been, these two movements in the immediate area around Jerusalem indicate that biblical traditions of God's great acts of liberation were very much alive among the people, so much so that, when liberation movements emerged, they were patterned after these formative biblical prototypes.

People in villages such as Bethlehem and those in the Judean hill country would surely have been aware of, if not involved in, the escalating tensions with both their own high-priestly rulers and the Roman governors in the 60s C.E., as conflicts escalated toward the outbreak of the extensive revolt. Most of the early excitement and actual fighting occurred in the city itself. But as the high priests were able to persuade the people to acquiesce in their provisional government of the country (while they secretly negotiated an arrangement with the Romans), a fairly extensive movement began to coalesce in Judea, particularly the southern area toward Hebron, where David had initially been "anointed" by the people as king of Judah. This was yet another messianic movement, centered on Simon bar Giora as "king" (noted in the previous chapter), the one eventually executed ceremonially in Rome as the leader of the conquered enemy ("king of the Jews"?). Among the many significant aspects of Simon's kingship was his proclamation of "freedom for slaves and rewards for the free," suggesting that his movement was clearly seeking socioeconomic liberation from debts and debt slavery as well as deliverance from foreign domination (*War* 4.507–13, 529–34).[32] As in 4 B.C.E. in the Judean hill country as well as in Galilee near Sepphoris, so again in southern Judea in 67–69 C.E., the social form taken by the actual historical movements of resistance among the Jewish peasantry was that of popular kingship. And that social form was clearly informed by the biblical tradition of popular kingship, the great prototype of which was David. Perhaps some deliberation is called for regarding the possible parallels with the nascent liberation movement reflected in the Gospel infancy narratives that proclaim the birth of Jesus as the anointed king of the Jews.

·5·

"A People Prepared"

The actors in the infancy narratives include the parents of John the Baptist, who are both of priestly descent, a band of shepherds as the first to receive the good news of the child's birth, and no less than three women in prominent roles, including Mary, who is the principal agent of deliverance in Luke's narratives. While the shepherds have been overinterpreted, the women have received less attention in interpretation than that they have in the narratives, and the fact that John the Baptist and his parents, Elizabeth and Zechariah, are of priestly lineage has been virtually ignored. To attend more closely to the situations and roles of women, priests, and shepherds in Jewish Palestine may open up a greater appreciation of the social structure and dynamics reflected in the stories of the messiah's birth.

WOMEN

Women play prominent roles in the infancy narratives. This might not appear to be the case in Matthew 1–2, where the angel always communicates to Joseph, even in the "annunciation," and not to Mary. But in contrast to the uninterrupted patrilineal genealogy in Luke 3:23–38, tracing Jesus, son of Joseph, back even to Adam, *son of God,* Matthew's genealogy is interrupted four times in 1:2–6 with the insertion of foreign women known in biblical tradition for their unusual actions: Tamar, who seduced her father-in-law, Rahab the prostitute, Ruth the Moabitess, and the unnamed "wife of Uriah" (Bathsheba). In Luke 1–2, not only does the angel communicate with Mary instead of Joseph in the annunciation, but Mary sings the militant Magnificat and is joined by two other women in the narrative—Elizabeth her cousin and Anna the prophetess. Moreover, Mary is the one to whom Simeon directs his prophecy (2:34–35); her unique role and relationship with God are articulated by both Gabriel and Elizabeth (1:28, 30, 42–45); and Mary is portrayed in an intimate personal manner as troubled or as actively pondering the significance of Jesus' identity (1:29; 2:19).

The prominent position and roles of women in these narratives must be understood against the background not only of the androcentric attitudes and assumptions of modern and ancient culture, including those in the narratives themselves, but against the context of patriarchal social systems (that are at once political, economic, and religious) "in which a few men have power over other men, women, children, slaves, and colonialized people."[1] Moreover, our investigation here must attend to Israelite-Jewish traditions of leadership by women, particularly in situations of crises in partiarchal institutions, traditions that were carried in, while implicitly critical of, biblical literature produced by and supportive of a patriarchal society. Furthermore, since virtually all of our sources are products of patriarchal presuppositions, some of them even explicitly concerned to reinforce patriarchal control of women, we should be critically aware that they likely do not reflect actual social relations accurately, but rather the interests of the literate and well-situated male authors.

Women's Leadership in the Jesus Movement and in Biblical Tradition

As in virtually all traditional agrarian societies, so in ancient Jewish Palestine, the fundamental social unit of production as well as reproduction was the patriarchal family. As illustrated by its name *bet-av*, "father's house," the head of each family was the "patriarch," in whose name the family inheritance was held and whose line it was essential to perpetuate in connection with that inheritance, which was the basis of economic livelihood and social position. Women had a place in the society only under the authority of a man, either her father or, moving to a different family and inheritance, her husband ("lord"). In such a system women and children appear as virtually the property of the male head of the family. Local patriarchal authority in the family and lineage or village was reinforced as well as reduplicated by patriarchal authority at the higher, governing levels of the society—in this case, the priesthood and high priesthood and the scribes who assisted the priestly aristocracy in teaching, applying, and enforcing the traditional customs and laws.

Within the local patriarchal forms, however, the division of labor and roles was by no means highly developed. The women were obviously responsible for reproductive labor. But women fully shared the responsibility for productive labor in the agricultural cycle of planting and harvesting. Old and young, men, women, and children—all worked the fields, as depicted in the Book of Ruth. As in other traditional agrarian societies, the division of labor among the Israelite-Jewish peasantry would have been more egalitarian and less sex-based than in the ruling class and their scribal or military retainers, where the men governed or studied or fought, while the women were confined to the domestic sphere.

In circumstances of imperial subjection such as prevailed at the time of Jesus, alien political-military rule and compounded economic exploitation intensified patriarchal domination. As the lowest in status, women received the brunt of the pressures passed down along the chain of domination. Jewish men, who were experiencing humiliation and frustration under the effects of Roman rule, would have reacted by demeaning their own women.[2] And the "authorities" responsible for maintaining the integrity and boundaries of the society would have sharpened and intensified their concern with the ordinances governing the proper behavior of their women.

Besides sharpening patriarchal authority, imperial subjection also effectively caused local patriarchal forms to disintegrate under the pressure of intensified economic exploitation and relativized native authority. A family left without enough food to sustain itself until the next harvest, after rendering up tribute, taxes, and tithes, would fall into debt. Heavy indebtedness, however, might lead a father to send a daughter out as a debt slave. Severe indebtedness would lead to loss of the family's inheritance. Given the pressures, such a head of family would have proved incapable of responsibility for his daughter, then utterly impotent to maintain the family. At the village level, similarly, the "elders," or principal heads of families, were incapable of protecting the welfare and integrity of the village community. And at a regional or societywide level, the patriarchal authorities who were attempting to intensify societal discipline found their authority relativized by higher competing layers of government. At one or several levels the traditional patriarchal authorities and institutions thus proved incapable of preserving the welfare and continuity of the people in its basic forms of family and village (or lineage). The patriarchs and patriarchal forms had failed.

In such circumstances it is not surprising that women should emerge in leadership roles. That women were prominent and instrumental in the Jesus movement in Galilee can now finally be seen from the careful and sophisticated analysis by Schüssler Fiorenza.[3] Some of these women disciples must have been important in the movement already during Jesus' Galilean ministry. It is highly significant that the first witnesses of the resurrection of Jesus are some of these Galilean women—Mary of Magdala, Mary mother of James, and Salome, according to the pre-Markan tradition in Mark 16:1–6, 8a, a tradition that was somehow unknown or suppressed in another tradition cited by Paul in 1 Corinthians 15:3–7. The prominence of women in the infancy narratives, with Anna the elderly widow and *prophetess* announcing the new salvation and Elizabeth playing important roles alongside both Zechariah and Mary, thus parallels and reflects the importance of women in the Jesus movement. The women, moreover, are involved in action as well as in revelation. As should become increasingly evident from the rest of this discussion, Elizabeth and especially Mary are presented in Luke 1 as active agents of their people's deliverance.

Women's prominence and assumption of leadership in the Jesus movement and in the infancy narratives are prefigured and almost certainly informed by long-standing traditions of women prominent in the redemption of the people in times of crisis. The resistance to the Egyptian Pharaoh's oppression and the exodus movement had begun not with Moses but with the Hebrew midwives, who subtly but nonetheless effectively disobeyed Pharaoh's orders to kill the babies. The very fact that their names were pointedly remembered indicates Shiphrah's and Puah's importance in the tradition of redemption.[4]

At points of crisis throughout biblical history, women emerged as inspired liberators or prophetesses to lead the people. King Josiah and his advisers looked to Huldah the prophetess as *the* authority who could verify whether the law book discovered in the Temple was genuine Mosaic covenantal tradition (2 Kgs. 22). The earlier prophetess Deborah, like her male counterparts, had inspired the disintegrating and despondent people to resist the advances of the Canaanite kings and to reestablish their independent covenantal life under Yahweh (Judg. 4–5). The three great songs of deliverance embedded in the historical narratives were all sung by and named after women: the Song of Miriam (also a prophetess [Exod. 15]), the Song of Deborah (Judg. 5), and the Song of Hannah (1 Sam. 2, which has strongly influenced the Magnificat). As noted above, the prophetess Anna in Luke's narrative stands in this long biblical tradition of inspired prophetesses.

The central role of women in traditions of the people's deliverance is most explicitly indicated in the story of Mary's visit with Elizabeth. The latter exclaims to Mary, "Blessed are you among women!" That greeting, or rather proclamation, is clearly a direct allusion to Jael in the Song of Deborah and possibly to Judith as well. The Song of Deborah, Judges 5, paralleled by a prose account in Judges 4, recounted the struggle of early Israelite tribes to maintain their independence against a coalition of Canaanite kings. Deborah was the prophetess who rallied the Israelite peasantry to resist the threatened domination by the Canaanite kings. Jael the Kenite woman was the heroine of the people's actual battle against the overwhelming military superiority of the Canaanites with their war chariots.[5] As the one who killed the enemy general after he fled the battle on foot, Jael is singled out in the Song of Deborah as the principal agent in the liberation of the people:

> Most blessed of women be Jael . . .
> she struck Sisera a blow . . .
> He sank, he fell,
>   he lay still at her feet;

at her feet he sank, he fell;
where he sank, there he fell dead.
(Judg. 5:24–27)

Also significant in the Song of Deborah is the clear consciousness of class difference, manifested in the juxtaposition of Sisera's upper-class mother with the tent-dwelling Jael. The epic poem mockingly depicts the courtly lady as looking through her palace window awaiting her warrior son's return—with spoil that would presumably include a captured "maiden or two for every man . . . and dyed work embroidered for my neck" (Judg. 5:28–30). The Song of Deborah expresses a popular tradition of Israelite peasants struggling against domination by foreign kings whose women live in finery and whose military conquests mean sexual abuse for the Israelite women.

Elizabeth's exclamation to Mary may also be an allusion to the beautiful widow Judith, who also struck the head of an enemy general threatening to subject the people: "O daughter, you are blessed by the Most High God above all women on earth" (Jdt. 13:18). As in the case of Jael, the reason for this blessing is that she has been the agent of deliverance for the people, as articulated in the song in the final chapter: "For she took off her widow's mourning to exalt the oppressed in Israel" (16:8). Judith is described in the story as a prosperous widow (and not a male steward, but her "maid . . . was in charge of her possessions" [8:10]). But she is clearly distinguished from the ruling circles in Jerusalem. Indeed, the established patriarchal authorities, both the high priest and senate in Jerusalem and the elders in her own town of Bethulia, are portrayed in the story as utterly incapable of making effective resistance to the impending imperial subjugation.

A number of other women were remembered for their crucial roles in the deliverance of the people, but for actions less militant than the slaying of the enemy general. The interruptions in the patriarchal genealogy in Matthew 1:2–6 recall four such women.[6] They may all have been sinners, but that is clearly not why they are remembered in biblical and other Jewish traditions. They were also all foreigners, yet that is not a focal factor in itself, but merely one that highlights their action or role.

After God slew Er for his wickedness, Judah ordered his second son, Onan, to "go in to" Er's wife Tamar in order to raise up offspring for his brother (Gen. 38). When God slew Onan for spilling his semen on the ground, the fearful Judah attempted to get rid of Tamar by sending her back as a widow in her father's house until his third son should grow up. When it became clear that Judah was simply trying to get rid of her, Tamar seduced Judah unawares and then embarrassed him by presenting his pledges to her when, as the patriarchal authority, he judged that she should be burned for her harlotry. Judah acknowledged his greater injustice in not having given her his third son, Shelah, and Tamar produced twin boys, Perez and Zerah, replacing the two sons in the lineage of Judah who had died without issue. It is clear in the narrative of Genesis 38 that Judah and his sons wrongly fear the womanly power of Tamar (instead of God) and that Tamar is wrongly blamed as well as unjustly treated and condemned. By her initiative to claim her own rightful position in the patriarchal order, she enabled the all-important lineage of Judah to continue.

Although there is no biblical or other evidence that Rahab was linked with the Abrahamic or Davidic lineage (e.g., that she was mother of Boaz by Salmon), she played an instrumental role in Israel's taking possession of the land from the Canaanite kings who had previously controlled it. According to biblical traditions in Joshua 2 and 6, by collaborating with the Israelite spies, Rahab had enabled the Israelites to take the fortified city of Jericho.

The Moabite woman Ruth was left a widow after her Bethlehemite husband as well as father-in-law died, following a crisis of famine and migration in search of sustenance. But rather than seek another husband among the Moabites, Ruth, in close collaboration with her mother-in-law, Naomi, deliberately and skillfully took the initiatives that led to a patriarchal next-of-kin redeeming her father-in-law's heritage, which included marrying her (Ruth 2–3). The story of Ruth is a critique of patriarchal forms; throughout the two women take the initiative, not especially to restore men's names or heritage, but in the pursuit of "life for the living."[7] Yet, because of the initiative Ruth took, the lineage of Israel through Judah and Tamar was able to survive the threat of extinction because of the famine (and the death of the men in the lineage)— and two generations later to produce David (4:10–12, 18–22).

Now it is surely evident in virtually all of these cases where women played prominent roles in the people's deliverance from oppression or other crises that they did not exert leadership in a traditionally masculine role. Indeed, with the possible exception of prophecy, women exerted their leadership through traditional feminine roles or techniques. And that generalization includes both Jael and Judith, who, although they utilized a mallet and sword respectively, used their women's roles to bring the enemy generals into fatally vulnerable positions. In the case of Tamar and Ruth, what they did to bring about deliverance was precisely to rescue and restore the central lineage of Israel—by being more faithful to it or more effective in perpetuating it than the principal males through whom the lineage was supposed to be sustained. The tradition that remembers these prominent women as leaders is patriarchal, and notwithstanding the critique of patriarchal structures inherent in their stories and actions, they are remembered because they contributed mightily to the perpetuation of that same tradition.

Challenges to Patriarchal Forms

It might be expected, therefore, that the infancy narratives, which stand in this same patriarchal tradition, would simply reaffirm and uncritically perpetuate traditional social forms. In the Jesus movement from which the infancy narratives originated, however, we find a clear challenge to those patriarchal forms. In exploring that challenge, we cannot separate the issues of patriarchal structures and poverty or socioeconomic oppression, precisely because the patriarchal family and village were the fundamental socioeconomic forms of life, both reinforced and exploited by the patriarchal ruling structures. Any attempt to divide the issue of patriarchal culture and social structures from the economic issue "tends to overlook the reality that in the first century—as today—the majority of the poor and starving were women, especially those women" whose links with the basic patriarchal socioeconomic units had been broken. "In antiquity widows and orphans were the prime paradigms of the poor and exploited."[8]

In circumstances of widespread disintegration of traditional patriarchal institutions, particularly the patriarchal family but also the ruling mechanisms of Temple and Torah-enforcement through the "scribes and Pharisees," Jesus and his movement appear to have fostered alternative nonpatriarchal but familial communities.[9] The true family is now constituted not by physical kinship or blood relationships, but "whoever does the will of God is my brother, and sister, and mother" (Mark 3:35). Far from being some general abstract ethical relationship, however, that "kinship" means concrete socioeconomic local community, *already,* now in this time, *with lands* (10:29–30). Within the new, egalitarian familial community, moreover the followers of Jesus were to "call no one father, for you have one father (and you are all siblings)" (Matt. 23:9).[10] Similarly, besides criticizing the higher patriarchal authorities such as the scribes and Pharisees, Jesus insisted that such "rabbis" not be allowed to arise in the egalitarian communities of his disciples (v. 8).

If Matthew understood the Jesus traditions he utilized in Jesus' discourse against the scribes and Pharisees in Matthew 23, he appears not to have heeded them in his composition of chapters 1–2. There, as noted at the outset of this section, he has the angel consistently communicate to Joseph, who, after taking Mary under his protection, takes the lead through the rest of the narrative, while Mary never even speaks or is spoken to. Moreover, while the genealogy features the four irregularities of women who are instrumental in the continuation of the line, the overall framework is clearly patriarchal. Perhaps it can be discerned, however, that in foreshadowing Mary, the four irregular women prepare the reader "for a woman's irregular production of the Messiah outside of ordinary patriarchal norms."[11] In those irregular links in the genealogical chain of Abraham and David, moreover, the patriarchs had been unfaithful, unjust, or simply incapable of sustaining the welfare or continuity of the people or its representative head. In those circumstances, insofar as the biblical traditions behind Matthew's genealogy are any guide, not God's initiatives but women's actions proved the means by which the people or its leadership were delivered.[12] In that sense, at least, even the Matthean infancy narrative would appear to undermine as well as defend patriarchal structures.[13]

Luke's infancy narratives appear to be more appreciative of the importance of women in both current and historical redemption. In contrast with Matthew, Luke features Mary's role, and Joseph is merely there. Of the two recipients of annuciations, the male Zechariah is incredulous, for which he is struck dumb, while Mary is responsive. Although Zechariah receives the annunciation of John's birth and the Benedictus is placed in his mouth (for symmetry with Mary's Magnificat?), Elizabeth is the active figure of the couple, in conceiving, giving birth, and speaking (Luke 1:24, 42–45, 57, 60). One wonders if the sketch of Mary and Elizabeth together does not even portray, in however tentative a manner, women identified as women in solidarity with other women.[14]

Most important, particularly in contrast with Matthew 1–2, is Luke's portrayal of Mary. Much more completely and deliberately than Matthew, Luke has used the traditional biblical pattern of annunciation of the birth of a son, a narrative pattern that has been discussed extensively in recent years.[15] A relatively consistent form of an annunciation by an angel of the conception or birth of a son can be found in the stories about Ishmael (Gen. 16.7–13), Isaac (17:1–21; 18:1–15), and Samson (Judg. 13:3–23), which can then be the pattern for evaluating the stories about John the Baptist (Luke 1:11–20) and Jesus (1:26–37; Matt. 1:20–21).[16] It may be far more significant, however, to observe how a standard traditional pattern is adapted and utilized in new and original ways.[17]

Schaberg makes the highly significant observation that, in all of the biblical texts that have been considered in connection with this traditional pattern, "the annunciations occur as a response to the plight of a woman." Often the plight is barrenness, even into elderly years, which is a source of reproach and self-blame, as in the cases of Hannah (1 Sam. 1:1–11) and Elizabeth (Luke 1:7, 25; and note Luke's assurance, in v. 6, that both she and Zechariah were utterly righteous and blameless). Schaberg suggests, furthermore, in connection with Isaiah's annunciation to Kind Ahaz of the conception and birth of Immanuel, that beyond or underlying the plight of the prospective mother lies a crisis situation for the people, or the promises to Abraham, or the royal leadership. These broader crises are sometimes explicitly stated in the preceding literary context (e.g., Judg. 13:1) and are sometimes implicit in the narrative of the annunciation and its circumstances (e.g., 1 Sam. 1–2).

In Matthew 1, the immediate problem is the plight of Mary, who is found to be pregnant but not by her betrothed, but the preceding and succeeding sections of the narrative, as well as the names announced in the annunciation itself, indicate that there is also a crisis of the people needing deliverance. How the plight of the pregnant Mary is dealt with—that is, in the annunciation and Joseph's response—is then also the solution to the crisis for the people as a whole. (And, although Mary is not the active figure in Matt. 1, there is thus otherwise a certain parallelism between what happens through her and what happened at least through two of the women in the genealogy: i.e., in taking initiative to deal with their own plight, Tamar and Ruth also delivered the key lineage in the people of Israel from its crisis.)

In Luke 1, Elizabeth is fitted into the more precise pattern of angelic annunciation that an elderly woman who is suffering reproach because she is barren will bear a son. Her story is almost certainly modeled after those of Sarah and Hannah. But what is Mary's plight? Since barrenness was not always the particular plight of the potential mother, we should not seize upon either the supposed parallel or contrast to the traditional pattern offered by Mary's virginity as the plight. As a supposed parallel it would be absurd, for virginity was surely neither a problem for a needed pregnancy nor a source of reproach. And it is difficult to imagine how her virginity could be problematic as a contrast to the barrenness of the traditional pattern. Could it be that in the case of Mary, her own plight, her "lowliness" (v. 48) is representative of that of the people in general? Such would appear to be exactly what is articulated in the words of Gabriel and in the hymns that Mary and Zechariah sing.

Yet another observation by Schaberg must be taken into account in this connection, namely, that in the account of Gabriel's appearance to Mary, Luke has fused the form of annunciation with that of a prophetic commission, which is similar in most regards anyhow.[18] The call or commissioning of Mary in Luke 1:26–38 is thus strikingly similar to those of Moses and Gideon, two of the most prominent prototypical liberators of the people (Exod. 3:2–6, 10–12; Judg. 6:11–24).[19] The annunciation that tells her of her impending motherhood is also a prophetic call or commissioning of Mary as a deliverer of the people in a long tradition of prophets and liberators such as Moses and Gideon.

Such an understanding of Luke's portrayal of Mary fits better with other aspects of that portrayal already or about to be noted, such as Elizabeth's proclamation, which alludes clearly to the militant figures of Jael and Judith, and the contents of Mary's own song, the Magnificat (see next chapter), in which the lowly are exalted and the mighty pulled down from their thrones.

Schaberg points out that Mary's consent to the annunciation is unusual, a Lucan innovation in the traditional pattern. And she points out that "Luke's Mary voices here more than her consent to motherhood."[20] In accepting her role as mother of the one who will eventually be given the throne of David and will rule Israel, Mary is also accepting the distinctive role of a prophetic deliverer commissioned by God. In the Magnificat she herself articulates more precisely the substance of the deliverance in which she has accepted the key inaugurating role.

Is not Mary's consent to her role(s), particularly her self-acknowledgment as a "servant" (*doulē*) of the Lord, not simply a way of "setting her up as a model, *the* model, for submissive feminine behavior, and of articulating an acceptance of patriarchal belief in female inferiority, dependency, and help-lessness?"[21] The overall framework and presuppositions of Luke's narrative are still patriarchal.[22] Moreover, in Hellenistic-Roman culture generally, *douloi* were slaves believed to exist on a lower level of humanity, and a *doulē* or "slave-girl," was even subject to sexual abuse by her master.

This is not the connotation of "servant," however, in the context of biblical literature in general or of an annunciation or commissioning against the background of biblical traditions in particular. In Hebrew biblical culture, as in the ancient Near East in general, everyone in the society was a servant of god(s) or of the king. In biblical tradition Israel as a whole, like Israelites individually, was a servant of the Lord (see Luke 1:54). But there were also very special servants of God or of the Lord, the principal leaders of the people such as Moses, Joshua, or David (e.g., Mal. 4:4; Josh. 24:29; Judg. 2:8; Ezek. 34:23; 37:24). Obviously the two usages overlap. If we take our cue from the devout prayer of Hannah in 1 Samuel 1:11, then Mary would be a paradigmatic Israelite in her faithful acceptance of God's will. Once we recognize that the broader context of Mary as servant in Luke 1:38 is her call as a deliverer of the people, then she is also a special servant of the Lord like Moses, Joshua, and Deborah before her.

Thus it appears that, far from presenting Mary as a model of submissive feminine behavior, Luke presents her as specially commissioned as the principal agent of deliverance in the infancy narratives. The annunciation and Mary's consent does not simply portray something done to her ("the Holy Spirit will come upon you") but also points to the action she will take (carrying, giving birth to, and raising the child) in bringing about the people's liberation. In contrast with Matthew's account, Luke's Joseph simply hovers in the back-ground, acquiescing in what Mary is called to do. Mary is portrayed in terms of her relationship with God, not her relationship with her husband.[23] In contrast with Tamar or Ruth, Luke's Mary does not integrate herself back into the established patriarchal structures as she acts in the redemption of the people. But like them and like Jael and Judith, with whom she is allusively compared by Elizabeth, she does not step outside of traditional women's roles in her principal act of deliverance—giving birth to the anointed king. However critical the Lucan infancy narratives may be of patriarchal structures, the overall framework of the narratives is still patriarchal. It is evident elsewhere in the Gospel and particularly in Acts that Luke has participated in the general androcentric tendency of obscuring the prominence and importance of women in the leadership of the early churches.[24] But in the course of his infancy narratives, Luke also has presented stories, and alluded to memories, of women who threatened to break through patriarchal social structures and worldviews.

PRIESTS

After reading the opening incident in the Gospel of Luke, we might have the impression that we are in for a story featuring priests and centered in the Jerusalem Temple. Besides Zechariah's being identified explicitly as a priest belonging to the division of Abijah, Elizabeth his wife is identified as coming from a priestly family (Luke 1:5). Then the special duty of Zechariah in the sanctuary of the Temple becomes the scene for the point of the incident, his vision of Gabriel, the messenger of the Lord, who announces the birth of a son (vv. 8–13). The incident then reaches closure "when the time of his priestly service was completed" (v. 23).

The explicit statement of Zechariah's and Elizabeth's priestly descent, however, carries no special import, either in the nativity narrative or in the Gospel as a whole. This is particularly striking in the infancy narratives. The story of John the Baptist's birth is surely included as a parallel to the story of Jesus' birth, in connection with which the Davidic lineage of Jesus' parents is of utmost significance. The fact that even scholarly commentators find little or no importance in the priestly descent of John and his parents surely reflects its lack of emphasis in the narrative itself.

We could attempt to explain the priestly descent of Zechariah and Elizabeth as either a literary device or a piece of Luke's theology of history. The depiction of Zechariah as a priest in a particular division might serve primarily as a device to get him into a situation to have the vision. But in Daniel 9:21, which serves as the model for the appearance of Gabriel in a vision here, "Daniel" receives the vision without actually being in the sanctuary of the Temple. Perhaps Luke portrays Zechariah and Elizabeth as priests as part of his schematic presentation of salvation history, in which the message and events start in the Temple in Jerusalem and flow dynamically out to the whole world from there (see the ending of Luke and the first few chapters of Acts). But he would not need priestly characters for that sequence, any more than he required the apostles to be priests in Luke 24 or Acts 1–10. This analysis suggests, however, that the information about the priestly lineage of John and John's parents is a piece of early tradition that Luke included but did not exploit in any significant manner.

Immediately after declaring that "Luke makes nothing whatsoever" of John the Baptist as a priest, however, Brown finds considerable significance in the priestly origins and uprightness of Zechariah and Elizabeth. As representatives of "the institutions of Judaism" or "the Temple/priesthood," they are used to show that, despite the opposition that arose later, there was not "an inherent contradiction between Christianity and the cult of Israel."[25] However important that point may be in theological apologetics, it is a great oversimplification of the historical situation in the origins of the "Christian" movement, including the situation and events as portrayed in Luke-Acts. Historical phenomena that would match the modern concept of religion simply cannot be abstracted from the historical institutions of Jewish Palestine in the late-second-Temple period. Nor do either historical events or literature from the period such as the gospel tradition match the theologically determined scheme of a fundamental division between "Christian" and "Jewish." The principal divisions were within Jewish Palestine, including within "the priesthood" itself. Luke himself indicates that, simultaneous with the intensifying conflict between the nascent Christian movement and the high-priestly government in Jerusalem, many *priests* were becoming "obedient to the faith" (Acts 6:7). The opposition between the followers of Jesus and the high-priestly rulers seems to develop along the lines of the already existing fundamental conflict between the rulers in Jerusalem and their scribal and Pharisaic agents such as Saul, on the one hand, and the crowds of ordinary people on the other, as portrayed clearly in the Gospels and particularly in Luke. Nor is this reducible to a "religious" conflict. Thus to locate significance in John's priestly parents as representatives of the institutions of Judaism simply perpetuates an outmoded and historically ungrounded theological scheme.

The seemingly incidental information that John's parents were of priestly descent, however, might be significant in another respect, namely, the sociohistorical background and foreground of who stands where in the network of social relations presupposed and portrayed in these narratives. On the surface of things, it seems utterly incidental that John is born into a priestly family. Far more important are the tradition of resistance (Samson, Samuel, Elijah) and the revolutionary model (the spirit and power of Elijah) after which John the prophet is to restore Israel. Exploration of the social context, however, can perhaps lead us to an important point in the social dimension of the narrative: priests such as Zechariah and Elizabeth and John belonged with the people, as opposed to the high-priestly rulers, and may even have had a special sensitivity to and role in the fundamental conflict in Jewish Palestine under Roman rule.

Standard discussions of second-Temple Jewish society faithfully present information for which we have sufficient evidence on the distinctive facets of the Jewish priesthood. Thus we have some sense that the priesthood was hereditary, that it was divided into a number of "courses" that alternated in actual service in the Jerusalem Temple, and that the priests along with the Levites were supported by the tithes, although many had to supplement their income with other work. In order to appreciate literature such as the birth narratives, however, we need to explore more precisely the social relationships suggested by these distinctive aspects of the priesthood.

Ideally, Jewish society was a theocracy, in which the people living under the rule of God brought sacrifices and offerings which the priests were specially designated to handle, and the priests were supported in their special service by tithes from the people's produce. Both the social structure and the Temple in which the system was centered involved concentric circles of purity in which the ordinary peasants sent or brought offerings, the Levites attended to the temple courtyards, the priests attended to the service of God in the sanctuary itself, and only the high-priestly head of the society entered the holy of holies, once a year on the Day of Atonement. The purity of the priests, moreover, was maintained by patrilineal heredity, so that only the sons of priests could serve at the altar.

But this was also a system of power. Indeed, precisely because of their position at the center of the system religiously, the high priests dominated the whole society politically and economically as well. And this state of affairs was not only recognized but powerfully reinforced in the Persian, Hellenistic, and Roman imperial order. In effect, the significant division within Judean society came not between the priesthood as a whole and the people but between the ruling high priests and the people along with the ordinary priests. Josephus, in touting his own illustrious lineage, explains that nobility in Jewish society was based on priestly descent (*Life*, 1). That was absolutely true. But most priestly families, like the people generally, were dominated—and even abused—by the priestly "nobility."

The high-priestly domination was rooted in the control of the tithes and offerings as well as in the imperial politicoeconomic order. Historically, in the Torah, the tithes were to be given to the Levites in return for their service in the tent of meeting (Num. 18:21; cf. Josephus *Ant*. 4.68, 205), who then supposedly gave a tithe to the priests. In the postexilic restoration of Judea as a temple-state, however, not only were the tithes channeled to support the priests as well as the Levites, but the tithes and the various offerings came under the control of the officiating priests in the Temple. As was feasible in an initially small temple-state, collection and distribution of the dues, including the tithes, were centralized in the Jerusalem Temple.[26] The effectual centralization of taxation is clear, if subtly phrased, in the Book of Nehemiah, and is confirmed by Tobit's description of his own practice (Tob. 1:6–7).

> We obligate ourselves to bring the first fruits of our ground and the first fruits of all fruit of every tree, year by year, to the house of the LORD; also to bring to the house of our God, to the priests who minister in the house of our God, the first-born of our sons and of our cattle, as it is written in the law, and the firstlings of our herds and of our flocks; and to bring the first of our coarse meal, . . . the wine and the oil, to the priests, to the chambers of the house of our God. . . . And the priest, the son of Aaron, shall be with the Levites when the Levites receive the tithes. . . . For the people of Israel and the sons of Levi shall bring the contribution of grain, wine, and oil to the chambers. (Neh. 10:35–39)

After the expansion of territory subject to the Temple and high-priestly government by the Hasmonean conquest of much of the rest of Palestine, it would not have been feasible to collect all dues from outlying areas in Jerusalem itself. We simply do not know precisely how the revenues were managed—whether dues were given to priests, who were then more widely distributed throughout the predominantly Jewish districts, or whether dues were locally collected but then converted into revenues that could be utilized more flexibly. In Josephus's attempt to bring Galilee under control in 66 C.E., his priestly colleagues "amassed a large sum of money from the tithes which they accepted as their priestly due" (*Life*, 63), suggesting that at least some priests may have received their dues locally. But we have no idea whether the income of Josephus's colleagues in 66 C.E. was due to the breakdown of the usual system at the outbreak of the great revolt, or resulted from the use of their special authority under the provisional government in Jerusalem, or finally resulted from ad hoc relationships with particular elements in Galilee. Our general sense is that, while the tithes were indeed directed to the support of the priests and Levites, the collection and administration of dues was still centralized as much as possible once the territory dominated by the high priesthood in Jerusalem had expanded. The famous scene of "money-changing in the Temple" from the gospel tradition indicates that those who did come from a distance to give sacrifices and offerings in Jerusalem exchanged goods for coins locally and then exchanged coins for the appropriate goods to be offered at the Temple.

While collection and administration of dues were centralized in Jerusalem, only a small percentage of the priests could live in the city. (Pseudo-) Hecataeus in early Hellenistic times reports 1,500 priests there receiving the tithe of the produce and administering public affairs (Josephus, *Apion* 1.188; cf. Neh. 11:10–19). That number would be out of a total of roughly 8,000 priests and Levites. By the time of John and Jesus, the number of priests and Levites had expanded to around 18,000.[27] Thus at the time of John and Jesus, the number of priests living in an enlarged city of Jerusalem would surely have expanded, but the percentage there of the total would not have increased. And a substantial number of the priests who resided in the city would have been those of the principal high-priestly families and those who collaborated closely with them. Moreover, we have noted already in discussion of the high priests that some of these high-priestly families at the time of Jesus had recently come to Jerusalem from Egypt or Babylonia under Herod.

The vast majority of the priests lived in various towns and villages around the country. Many may have been located in the immediate environs of Jerusalem. And some villages may have been heavily or completely composed of priests. The Hasmonean family that provided the leadership of the Maccabean Revolt and the resultant new dynasty of high priests came from the village of Modein (1 Macc. 2:1). In the story of John the Baptist's birth, Zechariah and Elizabeth live in the hill country of Judea and return to their home village after Zechariah's service and vision. Bethphage was a whole village of priests, according to Origen (*Comment.* in Matt. 16–17). Jericho (roughly fifteen miles northeast of Jerusalem) had a large concentration of priests, as did the town of Gophna (in western Judea), where "eighty pairs of brothers (priests) married eighty pairs of sisters of priestly origin in one night."[28] Priests apparently lived in the villages of Zevaim, north of Lydda (western Judea), Mekoshesh, and Kefar Barkai (in northern Judea).[29] Besides being thus dispersed in villages and towns throughout Judea, however, priests also lived at places in Galilee as well, such as Shihin and Sepphoris.[30] Thus the majority of the ordinary priests lived outside Jerusalem in the villages and towns of Judea and even in Galilee.

Besides living among the people, the ordinary priests and Levites also apparently worked among them as well. As we have noted, the priests received tithes from the people. But this was not sufficient to support many thousands of priests and their families. Thus they had to have other means of support. Only a few families, such as that of Josephus (but principally the high priests), would have become wealthy landowners (probably by means of peasants' becoming indebted to them). Some priests served as scribes. Eliezer son of Zadok bought and sold oil, and Phineas son of Samuel—who, though a villager, belonged to a legitimate high-priestly lineage and was selected by lot as high priest by the Zealots proper in 68 C.E.—was a stonecutter.[31] Many priests, perhaps the majority, probably worked their own or others' fields alongside their nonpriestly village neighbors. It is assumed in Nehemiah (13:10) that "the Levites and the singers" had their own "fields," so we must assume that (in contrast to earlier Israelite history) priests and Levites in the second-Temple period not only could but did own or have access to fields and functioned economically very much as did nonpriestly peasants. It seems obvious that, if some villages were predominantly or completely settled with priests, then at least in those villages the priests were engaged in farming, like ordinary peasants.

In addition to living and, apparently in most cases, also working with the people in villages and towns, the ordinary priests had special responsibilities for service in the Temple that may have given them an unusual role in their society. The priests were divided into twenty-four "courses," or "divisions," each of which served two different weeks in the Jerusalem Temple (and perhaps at the special festival times as well).[32] Most of the priests thus lived year-round among their fellow villagers or townspeople but then also spent a week at least twice a year in Jerusalem.

This combination of village residence with periodic service in Jerusalem may be highly significant, for two interrelated reasons. First, by serving in the Temple in Jerusalem periodically, the priests, as the people most likely trained in and sensitive to the sacred covenantal traditions of the people, had occasion to experience the discrepancies between those sacred traditions and the actual state of affairs. Obviously the priests' training and practice concentrated most heavily on cultic observances stipulated in the Torah. But they would also have been the ones in the society, other than the scribes and other scholars, most exposed to the covenantal traditions that featured ideals of egalitarian socioeconomic relationships as well as of independent life under the direct rule of God. In Jerusalem, however, they had ample occasion to observe the lavish life-style of the high-priestly families as well as the splendor and alien forms of the Herodian court. The practice of offering twice-daily sacrifices for Rome and Caesar, which had become standard following Roman conquest, may have been particularly objectionable.[33]

Second, the priests provided a built-in network of communications between the dominant capital and the local towns and villages, something highly unusual in any traditional agrarian society. Indeed, social scientists attempting to understand how peasant revolts can be mobilized, sustained, and even successful in modern times have noted that it is essential but unusual and difficult in most such societies for a communication network to emerge. Native intellectuals or the popular clergy are often the basis for the emergence of such a communications network between the central urban area and the villages on the periphery.

There is every reason to believe that the priests would have been in an uneasy and threatened position in Roman Palestine. Following the Hasmonean period, during which the society was virtually independent of alien domination, their people, their Temple, and in effect the god they served in that Temple had been conquered by the Romans. The Romans and then Herod had defeated or executed the last of the Hasmonean high priests, to whom some may have felt considerable traditional loyalty or simply seen as an alternative to Roman rule. Herod had then elevated men of priestly families from abroad to the high priesthood. And of course the imposition of the Herodian kingship meant a demotion in power, prestige, and status for the whole Temple and high-priestly apparatus and, correspondingly, for the role of the ordinary priests and below them the Levites as well. It is conceivable also that the increased importance of scribes and scholars in the later second-Temple period was threatening to the status of ordinary priests, particularly as some of their own numbers had come to function in such capacities.

An incident from mid-first century provides us a window onto the anxieties of the Levites and priests about their roles and status. From the outset a hierarchical system such as that operating in a temple-state under an imperial regime involved a chain of domination and of differential status. Those at the bottom would be understandably eager to improve their standing and, correspondingly, those near the bottom would be therefore all the more anxious about their own position relative to both those lower and those higher. Also it should be clear that some alteration in title or attire, while providing an apparent gain in status symbolically, might well point to an actual slippage in status or perquisites in the dynamics of the system or situation as a whole. At the time of Nehemiah the term *Levites* does not appear to have included the "singers" and the "gatekeepers" (see, e.g., Neh. 11:15, 19; 13:10), whereas by late-second-Temple times it did. But there was still anxiety among both the singers and the lower-status Levitical servants in the Temple about their status relative to the priests—and thus surely anxiety among the latter as well, and on up to the wealthy priest Josephus, who heartily disapproves of the petitions about which he reports. "The Levites—this is one of our tribes— who were singers of hymns urged the king [Agrippa II] to convene the Sanhedrin and get them permission to wear linen robes on equal terms with the priest [which was done]. . . . A part of the tribe that served in the Temple were also permitted to learn the hymns by heart, as they requested" (*Ant.* 20.216–18). The importance of this incident lies not in the particular dispute involved but in how it illustrates the anxiety over their insecure status and role in the society that must have been increasingly operative among the priests and Levites at least since the Roman conquest and Herodian kingship.

Two matters reported by Josephus illustrate not only how the long-standing conflict between the ordinary priests and the high-priestly rulers in Roman-dominated Palestine had come to a head by mid-first century C.E. but also how the various aspects of the priests' network of social relationships were interrelated. The first matter Josephus describes in two, parallel reports, both implying that it was an ongoing problem in the late 50s C.E.:

> There was now enkindled mutual enmity and class warfare between
> the high priests, on the one hand, and the priests and the leaders
> of the populace of Jerusalem on the other. . . . Such was the shame-

lessness and effrontery which possessed the high priests that they actually were so brazen as to send servants to the threshing floors to receive the tithes that were due to the priests, with the result that the poorer priests starved to death. (*Ant.* 20.180–81)

[The high priest] Ananias had servants . . . who would go to the threshing floors and take by force the tithes of the presms; nor did they refrain from beating those who refused to give. The [other] high priests were guilty of the same practices as his [Ananias's] servants, and no one could stop them. So it happened at that time that those of the priests who in olden days were maintained by the tithes now starved to death. (*Ant.* 20.206–7)

Several points are indicated from these passages. The fundamental division is between the high priests, on the one hand, and the ordinary priests and the people (Jerusalemites and peasants at the threshing floors), on the other. This eruption of high-priestly violence was apparently rooted in a long-standing conflict. It was established tradition that the ordinary priests were to be supported by the tithes, which were not supposed to be taken from the threshing floors by the high priests. Rather, the ordinary priests were expected to take, or to be given, the tithes from the threshing floors, which suggests that they resided locally (transportation of heavy amounts of grain, etc., for any great distance would have been costly). Some of the peasants at the threshing floors apparently stood by the traditions or in defense of the rights of the ordinary priests. The high-priestly families, apparently no longer having any pretense of legitimacy and rapport with the populace, had long since gathered gangs of ruffians to use in terrorizing the priests and people. Even allowing for a little exaggeration by Josephus, who was no sympathizer with the poor, numbers of the ordinary priests lived in virtual poverty such that to be without their annual portion of the tithes would cause serious hunger and even starvation.

The second illustrative matter is more famous because it was the symbolic beginning of the massive popular revolt against the Romans and the Jewish high-priestly collaborators in the summer of 66 C.E.

Eleazar, son of Ananias the high priest . . . and then holding the position of [Temple] captain, persuaded those who officiated in the Temple services to accept no gift or sacrifice from a foreigner. This action laid the foundation of the war with the Romans; for the sacrifices offered on behalf of that nation and the emperor were in consequence rejected. The chief priests and the notables earnestly besought them not to abandon the customary offering for their rulers, but the priests remained obdurate. Their numbers gave them confidence, supported as they were by the stalwarts of the revolutionaries. . . . The notables [*dynatoi*] assembled with the chief priests and the most notable Pharisees . . . called the people together. . . . They produced priestly experts on the traditions, who declared that all their ancestors had accepted the sacrifices of aliens. But not one of the revolutionaries would listen to them; even those who served [*hoi leitourgoi*, i.e., in the Temple] failed to come to their support and were thus instrumental in bringing about the war. (*War* 2.409– 10, 417)

Again the fundamental division is between the high priests and other rulers, on the one hand, and the ordinary priests (in considerable numbers) and "the revolutionaries" among the people, on the other (although the daring young Temple captain has broken ranks with his father and the other high priests). The dispute is over what is ostensibly merely a "cultic" matter. But cultic matters were inseparable from politicoeconomic matters in ancient days, and both sides recognized the revolutionary implications of the cessation of sacrifices for Caesar and Rome. It is also clear that the issue in dispute was not a new one, with the high-priestly party attempting to fabricate precedents from tradition to counter the authentic tradition recognized, and now reverted to, by the priests (from the particular course?) actually serving in the Temple.

It should be clear by now that the ordinary priests (including Levites), many of whom lived and worked in the towns and villages, were basically part of the Jewish populace, over against the ruling high priests and client-kings. As those trained in, and specially devoted to and engaged in, the practice of the sacred traditions of the people, they would have an unusual sensitivity to the situation of subordination to foreign imperial rule. Indeed, in offering the sacrifices for Caesar and Rome, they were engaged in the symbolic cultic celebration of that subjection, hence regularly involved in a contradiction and dilemma.

That John the Baptist's parents were from priestly families thus does not set him apart from the people in any unusual or highly distinctive way. On the other hand, it is not surprising that one who assumed a distinctive prophetic role, one reminiscent of charismatic leaders of resistance to alien rule in biblical tradition, would come from a priestly family in the hill country of Judea. Such a family, involved in the network of social relations sketched above, would be unusually sensitive to the situation of the Jewish people under Roman rule. This awareness can be seen no more clearly than in the longings expressed by Zechariah in the Benedictus: "That we should be saved from our enemies . . . ; to perform the mercy promised to our fathers, and to remember his holy covenant, the oath which he swore to our father Abraham, to grant us that we, being delivered from the hand of our enemies, might serve him without fear, in holiness and righteousness before him all the days of our life" (Luke 1:71–75).

SHEPHERDS

The emphasis in Luke 2:1–20 is not so much on the actual birth of Jesus as on the announcement of its significance to the shepherds and their response to the good news. This is clear simply from the relative attention given in the narrative. We noted already above that Caesar's census receives far more narrative space (vv. 1–5) than the actual birth of Jesus (vv. 6–7); by comparison, the annunciation to and the response by the shepherds are clearly the center of attention (vv. 8–18, 20). Moreover, the shepherds are the representatives here of the whole people: they are receiving the "good news" which will prove jubilation for "the whole people" (v. 10). Moreover, the narrative clearly also emphasizes the *manger* in which the baby is lying, the trough or stall in which animals would be fed by such shepherds (vv. 7, 12, 16). That the baby will be found lying in the manger is the *sign* that the savior and messiah has been born, observing which the shepherds themselves proceed to proclaim the glorious event.

It is conceivable, of course, that the shepherds and the manger can simply be understood as bits of local color in the story. It was likely known that Bethlehem was in a relatively dry area where the herding of sheep and goats was as important as the cultivation of crops in the local economy. The statement in the Mishnah (Shekalim 7:4) that livestock between Jerusalem and the "tower of the flock" near Bethlehem were used for sacrifices in the Temple suggests that herding was prominent in the area. That the shepherds (along with the manger) have such a key role as recipients and proclaimers of the good news of the savior's birth, however, suggests that we should not simply dismiss them as local color. There would appear to be some more substantive significance in the story to the child's being laid down "in a feeding trough for domesticated animals" and the news of the birth of the messiah being made known (first) "not to religious or secular rulers of the land, but to lowly inhabitants of the area."[34] And the shepherds here of course cannot simply be dismissed as another example of Luke's own predilection for the lowly, since, because of the distinctively Semitic language and other stylistic features, it would be arbitrary to decide that Luke himself composed this story.[35]

Recent scholarly interpretation has found little or no significance in the shepherds as shepherds. The older search for meaning in Hellenistic bucolic literature for the shepherds as symbols of an ideal pastoral existence has been abandoned. Brown piles up passages by word association to support an argument that Luke has in mind a midrashic reflection on the "tower of the flock" (*migdal eder*), mentioned in Genesis 35:21 and Micah 4:8 and from which "the king messiah will be revealed at the end of days" (see the Targum Ps.-Jonathan of Gen. 35:21).[36] But the "tower of the flock" is parallel to Jerusalem/Zion, not Bethelehem, in Micah 4:8, and the Targum Pseudo-Jonathan is far too late and unlikely to have preserved a pre-Lucan tradition.[37]

Although he notes that shepherds are "lowly," in contrast with the rulers, to whom we might expect that such news should be first communicated, Fitzmyer then almost completely reverses the status symbolism of the birth scene. He finds allusions to biblical texts that use key terms in Luke 2:7 in associations virtually the opposite of lowly. Instead of the swaddling being "what any Palestinian mother would have done for a newborn babe," it becomes "a token of his regal condition" (supposedly suggested by "Solomon" in Wis. 7:4–5, though this text is late and written originally in Greek). There having been no room in the "lodging" (*katalyma*) and the baby's being laid in the animals' food trough turn out to symbolize rather that Jesus is born "not in a lodge like a stranger, but in the manger of the Lord, who is the sustainer of his people," by association with Jeremiah 14:8 and Isaiah 1:3. The shepherds themselves are "introduced by Luke into the story" simply because of the association of Jesus' birth with Bethlehem, which was "shepherd country."[38] It may be comforting theologically to be reassured, contrary to the appearances of the narrative, that the condition of the Christ-child was regal and secure. The role of the shepherds in Luke 2:7–20, however, seems like more than just a traditional feature of the Bethlehem landscape. Also, if the swaddling is really a token of "regal condition" and the child is really at home in the town of David (and secure in the manger of the Lord, who is the divine Shepherd of Israel, etc.), then such a description of the birth of Jesus would appear all the more political, an appearance that Fitzmyer is at pains to deny.[39]

If Luke was alluding to biblical passages that would suggest the child's "regal condition," then it is much more likely that he would have been referring to the traditional image of the (future) Davidic king as a shepherd of the people in Ezekiel 34:23 than to the "stranger in the lodging" of Jeremiah 14:8 or the "swaddling" of Solomon in Wisdom 7:4. Although Yahweh was occasionally described in the Hebrew Bible as "Shepherd" of Israel, and the image of shepherd and sheep is used generally for the ruler-people relationship elsewhere in official ancient Near Eastern ideologies of established kingship, biblical literature does not use the word *shepherd* as a title for the ruling king. Rather, in prophetic oracles from Jeremiah, unfaithful "shepherds" (= rulers) are condemned for scattering the sheep, in contrast to which a righteous branch or shoot for David would be raised up to execute justice (Jer. 23:1–5). Ezekiel, however, does utilize the standard image of established imperial monarchies. In Ezekiel 34:23–24, the new David (God's servant) is explicitly called the "one shepherd" who will feed the sheep as prince among them. Psalm of Solomon 17:40 picks up this same royal "shepherd" motif in description of the messiah, son of David, as the established and exalted king who will rid Jerusalem of foreign domination.

After the previous narrative in Luke 1, in which the baby to be born is clearly interpreted as the son of David who will rule in Israel and as the horn of salvation in the house of God's servant David (1:32–33, 69), the presentation in Luke 2 of Jesus' being born in the town of David among shepherds would suggest the "one shepherd" from Ezekiel 34:23–24. And that allusion might be confirmed by the angels' proclaiming "peace" on earth, since in the next verse in Ezekiel, God promises to make a "covenant of peace." There is no clear indication in the text of Luke 2, however, that such an allusion is present. In fact, it seems clear that the point in Luke 1 and 2 is not to present the new ruler of Israel, as opposition to the imperial Roman ruler, in similarly regal condition. Besides the opposition between saviors in Luke 2:1–20, there appears to be a stark contrast between Caesar's taking tribute and the humble circumstances of Jesus' birth as well.

Surely it is significant that the good news of the birth of the messiah is announced to the lowly, just as it is significant that the occasion for the birth of this new savior is a decree of tribute by the imperial savior. That the child is laid in a feeding trough for animals literally and socially places the messiah and savior on a level with the lowly shepherds, in complete contrast with Caesar Augustus.[40] The question to be explored is not whether the shepherds were lowly (and represented other lowly folk) but just how lowly they were, and thus what their relationship is to the messiah/savior whose birth they witness and proclaim.

It has been argued that, at the time of Jesus, "a whole series of trades were despised, and those who practiced them were . . . exposed to social degradation."[41] The lists of such occupations made by the rabbis included shepherds because they were viewed as dishonest; they led their herds onto other people's lands or pilfered the produce of the herd (esp. B. Sanh. 25b). The highly favorable portrayal of shepherds in Jesus' teaching is dismissed as "isolated" in comparison with the generally unfavorable references to shepherds in rabbinic literature. Practitioners of some of the trades were even deprived of rights (e.g., not allowed as witnesses). In any case, the herdsman was despised: "There is no more disreputable occupation than that of a shepherd" (Midrash Ps. 23:2).[42]

That picture of "despised trades" and of shepherds in particular is highly problematic, particularly with regard to the sources on which it is based and how the lists are interpreted. The texts from which the lists are taken are very late, hence not good evidence for the time of Jesus. Equally as important as the dating of evidence should be the social location of evidence. It is unlikely that rabbinic debates on who is ineligible to serve as witnesses in court provide good evidence for whether certain people were despised or hated "by the people." We would certainly have to take the rabbis' social status and attitudes into account. Thus we do not have here solid direct evidence that shepherds were a specially despised group of people in first-century Palestine.

We may have, however, a reflection of the suspicion in which shepherds were held by those in high status or an indication that shepherds had very low social status in certain Jewish areas in the fourth or fifth centuries C.E. And either of these interpretations suggest that the social status of shepherds may have been fairly low in earlier centuries as well. There does not appear to be evidence that shepherds were "despised by the people" at the time of Jesus. It seems clear in a story such as Luke 2:8–20 that they were understood as part of "the whole people." But their status in the society generally was probably very low. Urban dwellers of high status and aristocratic ideals surely thought so: "such pursuits [as the herding of sheep and goats] are held mean and inglorious . . . most of all in the eyes of kings" (Philo, *On Husbandry*, 61).

If Bethlehem and other places where there was insufficient rainfall to do extensive cultivation of the soil was "shepherd country," then the shepherds in such areas were the equivalent of the farmers or peasants elsewhere. About their particular socioeconomic situation, we can only speculate whether they owned their land and herds or were in the employ of large landowners. If much of the land in the environs of Jerusalem and nearby villages had come under the control of high priests in Jerusalem, as might be suggested by Mishna Shekalim 7:4, then shepherds around Bethlehem may well have been working on large estates supplying sacrificial animals. Heavy demands were placed on local Judean livestock production by the requirements of the Temple sacrificial system, and there is reason to believe that the high priests controlled the production of sacrificial animals.[43] While somewhat speculative, such a reconstruction of the situation would fit the other politicoeconomic circumstances. Of course, even if the shepherds owned their flock, they would still, like peasants and herdsmen generally, be economically marginal (i.e., poor)— unless they are to be conceived in analogy with a Nabal or Job (1 Sam. 25; Job 1).[44]

The shepherds in this story set in Bethlehem represent the ordinary people, the peasantry in the area. Crops were cultivated in the area, as we know from the Book of Ruth. But herding of flocks was probably very important also, given the local ecology. And in a story about the birth of the messiah from the lineage of David, who himself had been a shepherd when anointed king, it would naturally be shepherds who would receive the good news, witness the event, and proclaim it. Two points belong integrally together in the story: the messiah and savior has been born in the midst of and indeed as one of the ordinary people, and the shepherds as the obvious local representative of those ordinary people are called to witness and proclaim the good news of the eventual liberation the child represents.

Josephus reports a concrete social phenomenon in Judea contemporaneous with Jesus' birth that illustrates not only that shepherds were, in certain areas, an integral part of the peasantry but also that other common people looked to shepherds for distinctive leadership, even though they were despised by those of high status.

> And then there was Athronges, a man whose importance derived neither from the renown of his forefathers, nor from the superiority of his character, nor the extent of his means. He was an obscure shepherd, yet remarkable for his stature and strength. . . . He also had four brothers. . . . Each of them led an armed band, for a great throng had assembled around them. . . . Athronges held council on what was to be done. . . . He held power for a long time, having been designated king. (*Ant.* 17.278–81; cf. *War* 2.60–62)[45]

As this popular messianic movement in Judea illustrates, the common people, including shepherds, were ready to become involved in a movement directed against Roman and Herodian rule and led by a king from among their midst. This appears to be precisely what is announced to and by the shepherds in Luke 2:8–20, as well as celebrated in the songs in Luke 1 and 2, except that the army is a heavenly one in chapter 2, not one of Judean peasants as in the movement led by the popularly acclaimed king Athronges.

The manger in which the child was laid suggests and fits with the same interpretation, either by itself or understood in connection with Isaiah 1:3. The first principle of interpretation would be to work within the narrative rather than to search for biblical allusions. Indeed, in the first of its three occurrences within the narrative, there is even a causal clause indicating why Jesus is laid in a manger: "because [*dioti*] there was no place for them in the lodging [*katalyma*]" (Luke 2:7). It is somewhat unclear just what the *katalyma* means. It is not "inn"; for that, Luke uses the term *pandocheion* in the parable of the Good Samaritan (10:34). It could be "room," such as when Jesus seeks a room (*katalyma*) in Jerusalem in which to eat with his disciples (22:11). More likely it was a kind of caravansary or khan where several travelers might find shelter under one roof. Thus it would appear that, because there was no room in the place where the people would stay, Mary had to lay her child in the obvious place in the area for the animals, the feeding trough. The contrast between this savior, laid in the animal feeding trough while his parents were traveling an appreciable distance to be registered for their assessment of tribute, and the exalted position of Caesar, who could demand that tribute, seems clear.

That the child is laid in a manger then is declared to be the *sign* for the shepherds that the savior, the messiah and lord, has been born in the city of David (Luke 2:12). A sign in biblical history and literature is not simply an authenticating proof or token of a message or a promised future event but an occurrence that bears out or exemplifies a message or a future event. A sign, moreover, usually affects or is directly related to the people addressed in the message.[46] Now it might not seem so to urban and urbane intellectuals, who cultivate more sophisticated, higher levels of meaning, but the simple fact that Jesus is laid in a manger by itself could well be the sign in this case, as the narrative states. The exemplification that bears out the message that a savior and messiah has been born *for them* and *for the whole people* is that the child is right there in the manger in their midst, as one of them. The other figures that the Jewish common people themselves recognized as significant leaders of deliverance for themselves in this period—the popular kings and the popular prophets—were apparently from among the people themselves: Athronges, a lowly shepherd; Judas, son of Hezekiah the Galilean bandit chieftain; John the Baptist, child of ordinary priests from the hill country of Judea; Jesus son of Hananiah, a "crude peasant" (according to either Josephus or the Gospels). And such humble origins for the messiah would not have been in contrast to standard expectations, for we are finally realizing that there is precious little evidence that there were any standardized or generally held expectations of "the messiah" at this time in Jewish Palestine, let alone that a regal messiah was the standard expectation.

The implications of deliverance are also present in the manger, if we pursue the possible allusion to Isaiah 1:3: "The ox knows its owner, and the ass its master's manger. But Israel has not known me; my people has not understood me."[47] The manger is the only apparent link to this text, for the ox and ass do not appear in Luke 2. It is possible that the much later depiction of the manger scene as including an ox and an ass is dependent on this prophetic passage. In any case, if we are supposing that Luke himself was alluding to Isaiah 1:3 or that very early readers of the story found it there, then it still is not immediately clear that the manger in Luke 2 would be the manger of the Lord (i.e., of God). That reading would almost require two- or three-step deductive or analogical reflection: from the manger in Luke 2 to the ox and ass (whether in Isa. 1:3 or not); from the image of the manger of the donkey's lord in Isaiah 1:3 to a manger of the Lord (supplied from analogy; not in the text); and finally back to the manger in Luke 2 as being the Lord's. The *sign* for the shepherds could thus finally be that the child is laid in the Lord's manger, a symbol of God's sustenance of his people, by analogy with the donkey's manger in Isaiah 1:3. But then what would God's sustenance of his people be in the context of this story in Luke 2:1–20, as suggested by the allusion to Isaiah 1:3? Luke and his early readers probably would still have appreciated the covenantal denotations in Isaiah's language: the Lord's sustenance consisted in the great acts of righteousness or redemption, such as the exodus (and Israel's "knowing" should have been keeping covenantal righteousness or justice). The laying of the child in the manger of the Lord would thus have been the sign, that is, the exemplification that related directly to the shepherds, of the coming redemption or "deliverance from the hands of our enemies" (Luke 1:71, 73).

The preceding considerations suggest that the shepherds of Luke 2 should not be overinterpreted, whether in the older fashion as symbols of some idyllic pastoral life or in the more recent mode as representatives of the despised and ostracized in Jewish society. Shepherds were simply part of the peasantry in ancient Palestinian society. Peasants, almost by definition, were poor, and especially in relation to their rulers and certain other (but not all) urban dwellers were lowly in status. Shepherds, while not despised by the people, were apparently some of the lowliest of the lowly. Thus, in addition to shepherds being the obvious recipients of the message of the birth of the messiah/savior in the environs of the "Davidic" city of Bethlehem, for them to receive the message and visit the child dramatically portrays that the messiah has been born among the lowly ordinary people as the leader of their liberation. What the angel had announced and what Mary and Zechariah had sung about in Luke 1 has been inaugurated among the shepherds with the child laid in the manger.

·6·

Songs of Liberation

The Magnificat and other poems in the Lucan birth narratives are not so much pious prayers as they are revolutionary songs of salvation. This fact has been obscured in popular Christian piety by the emphasis on the meekness of the blessed virgin Mary, who obediently consents to be used for God's salvific purposes as the mother of the messiah and the vessel of the divine incarnation. Ironically, the traditional religious attachment to the Magnificat as Mary's song, reacting against the critical probings of biblical scholarship, fuels intensive debate concerning the authorship, attribution, and original language of the Magnificat and the related songs, and this debate also serves to divert attention from their content and significance.

In scholarly biblical interpretation the special concerns of modern theology have obscured the more revolutionary thrust of these victory songs. Scholars have acknowledged the relative lack of christology in the Magnificat and the other canticles in Luke's birth narratives.[1] Yet, Christian biblical theologians have been concerned to understand salvation as individual and spiritual, to stress the universal over against the specific significance of Christ, and to set Christianity off from its Jewish heritage. Correspondingly, they have neglected the collective and concrete sociopolitical dimensions of the victory songs and their rootage in the particular history and biblical heritage of ancient Palestinian Jewish society.

The songs now embedded in Luke's infancy narrative may be some of the earliest expressions we have from the Jesus movement. The Magnificat (Luke 1:46–55), the Benedictus (vv. 68–79), and the Nunc Dimittis (2:29–32) are clearly separable from their literary context as poetic psalms that interrupt the flow of the stories. One can move from Luke 1:45 to verse 56, or from verse 66 to verse 80, or even from 2:28 to verse 34 or 36 without missing the now intervening poetic material. In fact, there are even certain tensions or seeming conflicts between the statements in the songs and the information

in the narratives. Moreover, the language in these songs is more highly Semiticized than that in the surrounding narrative—which is already noticeably
Semiticized by comparison with the rest of Luke's writing. Furthermore, the
poems are full of terms and phrases familiar from biblical literature, particularly
the Psalms and other hymnic material, never directly quoting, but clearly
directly dependent on the biblical. Besides their traditional biblical-psalmic
language, these songs fit generally into the traditional structure of the declarative psalm of praise (imperative word of praise, followed by statement of
the reason for praise, namely, that God has acted). As we shall see in connection with the Magnificat in particular, the hymns now embedded in Luke's
infancy narrative stand in the same tradition as the great songs of liberation
such as the Song of Miriam (Exod. 15), the song of Deborah (Judg. 5), and
the Song of Judith (Jud. 6). The closest parallels to these songs in Luke 1–
2, in concern, forms, and thought world, are with other Jewish hymns from
late-second-Temple times, such as the psalms in 1 Maccabees, Judith, 2 Baruch,
4 Ezra, the Psalms of Solomon, and the Qumran *Hodayoth* and War Scroll.

It is thus generally recognized that these songs are pre-Lucan, although
Luke probably inserted 1:48 into the Magnificat and verses 76–77 into the
Benedictus in order to adapt them somewhat to the narrative context. Many
Christian commentaries on Luke have insisted that these songs were composed
in Greek, even though they also posited a "Jewish-Christian" origin. Recent
studies of these songs, individually or together, have returned to the judgment
of scholars of biblical psalmody from earlier in the century, such as Gunkel
and Mowinckel, who believed that they were originally in Hebrew.[2] The
many similarities with Septuagint language can be accounted for as the influence of the translator, who would have been familiar with the Bible in
Greek.

Sociologically considered, a Hebrew original for these songs is intrinsically
very likely. There is a good deal of evidence that Greek was spoken in Jewish
Palestine. But much of that evidence is for Jerusalem and other cities and
would fit literate strata, probably people of high status in the society. It is
generally accepted that most people, certainly the ordinary people, would
have spoken Aramaic. But besides there being inscriptional and other evidence
for the use of Hebrew, ordinary people's knowledge of psalms and other
poetic material from biblical tradition would have been in Hebrew (in oral
form, even if they were not literate). In any case, ordinary Palestinian Jews
would hardly have carried on their traditional way of life in Greek, much less
sung their psalms in Greek.

The recent scholarly analysis of the language and form of these songs in
comparison with contemporary Palestinian Jewish hymns can perhaps take
us even a further step into the milieu from which the Magnificat, the Benedictus, and the Nunc Dimittis originated. Although these songs fit generally

into the traditional form of declarative psalms of praise, they do not fall more precisely into any particular type of psalm. The authors of late-second-Temple psalms such as those in Sirach, the Qumran *Hodayoth,* and Judith 16 still appear to follow particular traditional patterns of Hebrew psalm composition.[3] Ben Sira and the Qumran authors were clearly well educated and, literarily, highly productive "sages" or "scribes." A comparison of their well-formed psalms with the songs in Luke 1–2 suggests that the latter were produced by less educated people. Three further observations of literary criticism confirm such a conclusion.[4] First, in the psalms embedded in Luke 1–2 there is "no sign of self-conscious art" and "none of the new features that we find in post-exilic psalmody, revealing the purpose of the psalm." More particularly, second, there is "no didactic or reflective element, no discussion of general truths, no attempt at theodicy," in contrast to more learned near-contemporary psalmody. Instead, third, the psalms in Luke 1–2 celebrate "the fulfilment of the old," and "art is forgotten in preoccupation with the mighty acts of God." It would apear that, in comparison with other, near-contemporary psalms, with which they share many features of language and theme, the songs in Luke 1–2 were produced and used in a less learned, more popular milieu.

Finally, because these songs speak joyously of a salvation that has already happened, that is already a reality for which God is to be praised, a search has been made for some obvious event of salvation to which they were a response. However, the suggestions made, such as the victory of the Mac-cabean revolt or the crucifixion and resurrection of Jesus,[5] have been largely determined by the Christian and the Jewish *canons* of historical events. We are increasingly aware now that there was a much greater diversity of events and movements than have been included in that canonized history. Clearly not all followers of Jesus focused in Pauline fashion on the crucifixion and resurrection. Or, as noted above, the popularly acclaimed "kings" of 4 B.C.E. all had sizable followings. If for no other purpose than to open ourselves to the historical possibilities, particularly in the life-situation of ordinary people in first-century Palestine, we might consider that the songs in Luke 1–2 could fit the shepherd-king Athronges as easily as they fit Jesus of Nazareth. In attempting to hear these songs of liberation, it is important to remain open to the different emphases and sensitivities that a popular Palestinian messianic movement focused on Jesus would have had, in contrast to Pauline, Petrine, or later orthodox Christian theology.

This exploration of the likely origins of these songs of deliverance is intended to open us to the possible milieu from and in which they should be heard rather than to place heavy emphasis on the question of origins itself. Our interest is fundamentally in the meaning of the songs to the concrete groups of people who used them. In this connection, given their probable popular Palestinian Jewish origins, it is all the more significant that they were preserved and utilized by a sophisticated Greek writer called Luke. The songs must have been of considerable importance to some communities in the "Jesus movement" to have been translated from Hebrew to Greek (prior to or by Luke himself). And Luke himself must have deemed them either of such importance that they should be preserved for their own sake or eminently suitable to express the significance of Jesus' birth. Use and meaning of these songs has varied and shifted over the generations. But perhaps we can attempt to free ourselves of this theological overlay in order to hear them afresh.

MARY'S SONG

It is understandable that Christian religious or theological concerns would influence interpretation of songs that have held such an important place in established patterns of worship and piety. With respect to the Magnificat in particular, God's regard for Mary is extolled as a sign of "God's eschatological act for the world," and the gift of the child as an image of "God's eternal purpose."[6] Interpretations of particular terms or phrases often reflect the peculiar modern assumption that the spiritual aspect is somehow separable from the socioeconomic and political aspects of life,[7] an assumption not shared historically by people in more traditional societies. References in the text to God's "deeds" or "salvation" are left unexplicated in specific terms. It is proposed rather that "originally the hymn (Magnificat) referred to a general salvation in Jesus Christ given by God to Jews who had become Christians."[8] But even a cursory reading of the Magnificat reveals that none of these interpretative categories is contained in or indicated by the text itself.

Simply attending to the language and style of the Magnificat, however, should be sufficient to indicate that this song portrays intense conflict. Strong verbs of action dominate both strophes, verses 46–50 and 51–55. Indeed, in the Greek text those verbs usually stood first in their respective lines, and both the conjunctions and the articles were eliminated, thus giving greater prominence to the action verbs.[9] In the second strophe, verses 51–55, the parallelism of poetic lines changes from synonymous and synthetic to antithetic, articulating sharp contrasts and conflict.

The language and style accord with the subject of the song: God's revolutionary overthrow of the established governing authorities ("the mighty from their thrones") on behalf of Israel. The words and phrases used throughout the Magificat are taken from and vividly recall the whole tradition of victory songs and hymns of praise celebrating God's victorious liberation of the people of Israel from their oppressive enemies. The dependence on and allusion to the Song of Hannah, 1 Samuel 2:1–10, and to God's paradigmatic "mighty acts" of deliverance of Israel from bondage in Egypt are particularly striking, but there are a number of parallels and reminiscences of other Old Testament hymns of praise as well.[10] The closest parallels in style and in praise of or appeal to God for liberation from enemies are significantly in Jewish hymns from the period of intense conflict with and resistance to Hellenistic and Roman imperialism, such as those in Judith, 1 Maccabees, the Psalms and War Scroll from Qumran, and the apocalypses of 2 Baruch and 4 Ezra. By attending to the ways in which the Magnificat resonates with the rich biblical traditions that celebrate God's liberation or the ways it parallels contemporary hymns, we can more adequately discern the meaning of Mary's song of salvation.

"The Lord . . . God my Savior" of Luke 1:46–47 is identified more precisely as "the mighty one" in verse 49. This is clearly the divine warrior, champion of Israel who saves the people from their enemy oppressors, as in Zephaniah 3:17.[11] "He has shown strength with his arm" is similarly a reference to the divine warrior, who, in Psalm 89:13, 10, has "a mighty arm," with which he "scattered his enemies." The "great things" done by the mighty one refer to events of liberation, as in Deuteronomy 10:21 and Psalm 105, and "holy is his name" similarly refers to God's redemption of and provision of land and food for his people, as in Psalm 111, which is echoed also in the Benedictus (Luke 1:68). The hymn thus focuses on praise of God as the champion of the people and evokes a long and deep memory of God's great acts of deliverance such as the exodus from Egypt and of prophetic promises of renewed redemption.[12]

The objective of God's salvation in the Magnificat is clearly the liberation of the people of Israel, as stated explicitly in verse 54. The designation of Israel there as "servant" has parallels in contemporary psalms of deliverance, the one being an appeal to God to send the anointed king as agent of the people's liberation and restoration (Pss. Sol. 12:7; 17:21). In biblical, particularly psalmic, language, moreover, "the poor/humble/lowly" (*tapeinoi*/*'anawim*) in verse 52 is a clear reference to the people of Israel, usually in conditions of domination, oppression, and affliction (e.g., see Deut. 26:7; Ps. 136:23, including the contexts). As noted at the beginning of chapter 4, it has been argued on the basis of the use of *'anawim* in certain Psalms that "the lowly" here refers rather to those who possess a certain spiritual humility, even to a community of humble righteous ones within Jewish society, some of whom must now have converted to Christianity and produced this hymn.[13] But most passages concerning "the lowly" refer to concrete socioeconomic and political conditions, not primarily spiritual humility, and the term often refers to the people generally, not to some community or remnant within the overall society.[14]

Mary, in her "low estate," or humility (Luke 1:48), is thus a representative of the people, "the lowly" generally. "He has regarded the low estate of his handmaiden" may well be an allusion to Hannah's vow to dedicate her son,

Samuel, to God's service in 1 Samuel 1:11. But the connotations of lowliness in Luke 1:48 and the recurrence of the cognate "the lowly" as being exalted in verse 52 indicate the representative relationship. The "great things" that "the mighty one" is doing through or to her are the liberation and salvation for the lowly, the people of Israel. She is the representative voice praising God the savior as well as the instrument or means by which the salvation is being effected.

God accomplishes the liberation of his people by "scattering the proud" and "putting down the mighty from their thrones" (Luke 1:51–52). "The proud" are indeed spiritually arrogant. But more concretely they are the enemies of God, either alien or domestic rulers, as can be seen in the tradition of songs praising God's redemption (Pss. 18:27; 89:10). Thus on "the day of the Lord," in which the warrior-champion of Israel will deliver the people from domination, God will decisively humble the proud and exalted (Isa. 2:11–12; 13:11). Perhaps the most striking parallel to the Magnificat in this respect is a near-contemporary messianic psalm in which both the illegitimate and oppressive domestic rulers (the Hasmoneans) and foreign conquerors (the Romans) are called "proud" (Ps. Sol. 17:8, 15, 26; cf. Ps. Sol. 2:1–2, 25, 28–31). A passage from the Qumran War Scroll, while a good deal more militant than the Magnificat, parallels the sense of sharp conflict between the poor and the mighty foreign rulers: "For Thou wilt deliver into the hands of the poor the enemies from all the lands, to humble the mighty of the peoples by the hand of those bent to the dust" (1QM 11:13).

But if God "scatters the proud" and "topples the mighty from their thrones," this is clearly a political liberation of the people from concrete political enemies (and not simply some vague and indefinite "salvific intervention in Israel's history").[15] The new liberation for which God is praised in the Magnificat is surely no less specific and concrete than the previous great historical acts of deliverance to which it alludes, the redemption from bondage in Egypt, the rescue from the Canaanite kings, and the defense against the Philistines— and Mary is leading the hymns of praise to God the savior of the people, as had Miriam, Deborah, and David of old (Exod. 15; Judg. 5; Ps. 18 = 2 Sam. 22).

Besides resonating with the traditional psalms of praise of God's historical acts of liberation ("his mercy is from generation to generation"), the Magnificat also proclaims that God's new act of liberation is the fulfillment of the ancient promises to Israel: "in remembrance of his mercy, as he spoke to our fathers, to Abraham and to his posterity forever" (vv. 54–55). Thus the new act of salvation is decisive, being God's fulfillment of the historical promises to the people's ancestors that they would become a great people, have land to live on, and be the channel of blessings to all peoples of the earth (see Gen. 12:1–3; 17:1–8).

In addition to constituting a liberation of the people from arrogant rulers, the deliverance praised in the Magnificat is also a social revolution, the termination of the seemingly endless class conflict with the deliverance of the lowly and the provision of food for the hungry. As noted, "lowliness/the lowly" refers to those who have suffered exploitation, oppression, and affliction by the wealthy and powerful ruling groups. The perpetual class conflict in which the arrogant, sinful rulers perpetuated systematic injustice for the poor is regularly portrayed in precisely the terms used in the Magnificat (e.g., Sir. 10:7, 12–13). God's concern for, and defense or liberation of, the lowly from arrogant rulers is a prominent theme, particularly in prophetic oracles and stories as well as in the tradition of hymnic celebration of God's deliverance in which the Magnificat stands (e.g., Ps. 18:27; Isa. 2:11–12; Ps. Sol. 17:26, 46; and cf. wisdom teaching such as Sir. 10:14–17). It may not be accidental that the descriptions of the arrogance of the oppressive rulers alternates between alien nations or imperial rulers and the rulers of Jewish society itself. In the very structure of the imperial situation, imperial regimes ruled through local aristocracies and client-kings, and the latter were dependent on the imperial regime for the maintenance of their privileged position at the head of their own people. Thus liberation of the people from the arrogant rulers would have meant the toppling of both local and alien rulers from their thrones. In order to assert the only true, divine rule, God had to put down pretentious human rulers. But the revolution described in the Magnificat is not simply "political." It is social as well; for the poor, marginal peasantry, heretofore exploited to the point that they went hungry themselves in order to render up the tribute and taxation demanded by their local and imperial rulers, are being "filled with good things." A new social order of justice and plenty is at hand.

The social revolutionary message of the Magnificat is often blunted by current scholarly interpretation of the toppling of the rulers and the exaltation of the lowly in terms of "eschatological reversal."[16] But there is nothing in the Lucan context to suggest that God's redemptive actions here are eschatological.[17] And in the Magnificat itself God's overthrow of the rulers and exaltation of the lowly is portrayed in much the same way as the typical historical actions of God in near-contemporary poetry such as Sirach 10:14 and the War Scroll from Qumran ("You have raised the fallen by your strength, and have cut down the high and mighty" [1QM 14:10–11]).[18] Having discerned that God's revolutionary action proclaimed in the Magnificat refers to historical and not eschatological deliverance, we should be careful not to let it be dissolved into a Pauline theology. There is nothing in the Magnificat itself to suggest that God's "definite action" in "scattering the proud" and so forth refers to "the salvation brought about through the death and resurrection of Jesus."[19] Indeed, Luke's use of the song in the birth narratives at the beginning of the Gospel would suggest just the opposite. That is, the definite action of God to which the Magnificat refers is not the death and resurrection of Jesus but that manifest in the overall ministry of Jesus and begun already in his birth.[20]

Hellenistic philosophers such as the Stoics and Cynics did indeed discuss such theoretical issues as whether "wealth and power" were "real values." But the Magnificat deals in the concrete and specific. It hymns God's liberation of the lowly, the people of Israel generally, the vast majority of whom were poor peasants, by overthrowing their arrogant rulers, both alien and domestic. The results were new life-possibilities for the lowly, the hungry who would now be "filled with good things." The message of the Magnificat has thus rightly been compared with the blessings (and woes) Jesus proclaimed for the lowly:[21]

> Blessed are you poor, for yours is the kingdom of God.
> Blessed are you that hunger now, for you shall be satisfied.
> Blessed are you that weep now, for you shall laugh.
> (Luke 6:20–21)

It is generally recognized that Matthew has spiritualized the blessing for the poor in his parallel to Luke 6:20—"blessed are the poor *in spirit*" (Matt. 5:3)—the original tradition having been more concretely socioeconomic as well as spiritual. But there is nothing in the text of the Magnificat to suggest that "the poverty and hunger of the oppressed...are primarily spiritual."[22] Like the blessings Jesus proclaims for the poor and hungry, so the salvation hymned in the Magnificent involves concrete socioeconomic transformations. Mary's song praises God for effecting dramatic social and revolutionary changes.

ZECHARIAH'S SONG

As with the Magnificat, perhaps our principal difficulties in attempting to hear the Benedictus and its message are to strip away the Christian christological concepts and concerns that are simply not in the biblical text and to cut through the peculiar modern assumption that biblical literature and its message are somehow primarily "religious," and not politicoeconomic as well. The song here placed in the mouth of Zechariah is literarily completely separable from its narrative context. One could move from Luke 1:66 to verse 80 without noticing that anything was missing—in fact, the story would flow more smoothly without being interrupted by the song. The song, moreover, is not primarily focused on the significance of John the Baptist. Only verses 76–77, usually viewed as a Lucan insertion by those who recognize the rest of the song as a pre-Lucan "Jewish(-Christian)" hymn, connect it with its narrative context and finally, as it were, answer the question all were asking: "What then will this child be" (v. 66). But the song is not therefore christological.[23] The song itself does not refer to Jesus by name. Only from the context of the Lucan infancy narrative as a whole do we understand that "the horn of salvation in the house of David" refers to the child who was announced to Mary and is about to be born. Throughout the song, however, "the description of deliverance is in Jewish terms which bear no trace of the highly developed christology of the later NT."[24] Furthermore, there is nothing in the song itself to suggest that the salvation for which it praises God is primarily religious and not also politicoeconomic in character, as we shall see in closer examination of the song itself against the background of traditional and contemporary Palestinian praise of God.

In form the Benedictus is a declarative psalm of praise with a simple two-part structure: word of praise followed by statement of the reason for praise, namely, that God has acted. The song praises God for act(s) of salvation already accomplished. The blessing with which the Benedictus begins is not found as an opening praise in the Psalter, but this blessing does end four of the five books of the biblical Psalms.[25] Significantly, the contemporary Qumranites used this same blessing formula at the opening of the "Hymn of Return" (from the War Scroll, 1QM 14:4), in which they praised God for their deliverance after the divine warrior's victorious battle against their oppressors.

God is blessed because he has "visited and redeemed his people" (Luke 1:68). The idiom of God's having "visited" his people is not a distinctive "religious sense of the verb" (*episkeptesthai* in Greek) used to render the Hebrew *paqad*.[26] The idiom is used in the Septuagint for very concrete deliverance, such as the imminent exodus from bondage in Egypt (Exod. 4:31), sufficient crops and food following a devastating famine (Ruth 1:6), and what is clearly politicoeconomic care or rescue of the people with the memory of the exodus in mind (Pss. 80:14; 106:4). "Made redemption" is a Semiticism (an awkward Greek rendering of what must have been a Hebrew phrase). There is no indication whatever that it refers to something spiritual; *lutrōsis* and related words are not used in the Gospels with sins or in a cultic sense (cf. Heb. 9:12). In the closest parallel in the Psalms, "sent redemption" stands parallel to the sociopolitical "commanded his covenant" and such "mighty works" of God as provision of food and land (Ps. 111:9, cf. vv. 5–6). The phrase refers to God's *ransom* or *release* of his people, apparently from their enemies, judging from the immediate context. Luke uses the term again significantly for the politicoeconomic redemption of the people, namely, of "Jerusalem" or of "Israel" (2:38; 24:21).

That God "has raised up a horn of salvation for us in the house of his servant David" is a bold political statement. It is difficult not to find christological significance in "the horn of salvation." But the term does not even *necessarily* refer to a Davidic king, much less *the* messiah. The phrase may allude to the saving power of God, as in Psalm 18:2, where God is the "horn of salvation" as well as fortress, rock, deliverer, and so forth. In Ezekiel 29:21, God raises a horn "to the house of Israel." The phrase is at least messianic in the minimal sense of referring to some divinely chosen figure when Hannah sings that God will exalt the horn (power) of his anointed one (1 Sam. 2:10). And in a psalm that proclaims God's covenant with David, he "will make a horn to sprout for David" (Ps. 132:17).

The statement in Luke 1:69 obviously makes explicit that this horn of salvation is raised up in the house of David, thus recalling memories of the vigorous leadership David provided in establishing the independence of Israel and evoking whatever hopes may have focused on new Davidic leadership. But it is unwarranted, on the other hand, to find here some supposedly standardized "Jewish expectation of a triumphant Messiah king from the House of David."[27] We have little contemporary textual evidence for expectation of such a triumphal Davidic messiah, other than the Psalms of Solomon (17), which provide evidence only for one, probably scholarly-scribal group. The image in the Benedictus is more of relief than of royal triumph. The tone is more like the petition in the Fifteenth Benediction of the *Shemoneh Esreh*, a text that represents popular Jewish prayers of the first century C.E.: "Let the shoot of David [Your servant] speedily spring up and raise his horn in Your Salvation. . . . May you be blessed, O Lord, who lets the horn of salvation flourish." That the image and tone are less triumphal and exalted and more of rescue from threatened domination and disintegration of the people is indicated also by the verb *egeirein* (raise). Whereas in the Septuagint the horn is "exalted" or "lifted on high," in the Benedictus God "raised up" the horn of salvation. That verb, of course, stems from the biblical tradition of God's having "raised up deliverers" or "liberators" from among the people when they were threatened with subjection, as in Judges 2:16, 18; 3:9, 15 (cf. the sequence of popular leaders, climaxed by David, who was "raised up" as king, in Acts 13:16–22).

Luke 1:71 and 74 would appear to specify that the people's salvation is more particularly and concretely from their political enemies. Ironically, while most recent biblical interpreters simply assume that when Jesus says "love your enemies" he has the Romans in mind, they want to avoid or soften the clear political reference here.[28] But there is nothing in these traditional stereotyped phrases ("the hand of our enemies; those who hate us") in the Psalms to indicate that only pagans or personal enemies are meant, or in the Benedictus itself to suggest that, at the Lucan level, it could be narrowed to those who resist "the new form of God's salvation-history."[29] To find in these phrases a completely vague and general reference "to all the forms that hostility to the chosen people took over the ages"[30] would open us toward the biblical tradition, so full of cases in which God liberated his people from foreign domination (from Egyptian and Canaanite kings, Philistines, Babylonians, etc.), but it would also tend to make the song as a whole vacuous. In David's psalm, Psalm 18:17 = 2 Samuel 22:18, and in Psalm 106:10 the enemies are concrete, domestic or alien, political foes—in the latter case, the Egyptians. As in those close parallels or psalmic prototypes, so in the Benedictus itself. "Our enemies/those who hate us," however far-ranging the broader connotations may be, refers to particular political enemies. To specify them as Israel's national enemies may be somewhat misleading, or perhaps rather an imposition of modern assumptions about international politics. The concrete enemies meant in the Benedictus would have been clear from the historical context in which the song was sung. And in first-century Palestine, "enemies" could have meant the heads of the Jewish Temple-state as well as the Roman rulers.

Verses 72–75 also have a *politico*religious and not merely a religious reference. The covenant and oath that God swore to Abraham included possession of land and a prosperous independent life of their own for the Israelite people as well as blessings for other peoples. Nothing in the Benedictus indicates that the biblical precedent is broadened or narrowed, much less deserted, for example, in the direction of some supposed "Temple piety."[31] Rather, the Benedictus appears to have the biblical history of the exodus latently in mind. "Holiness" does not necessarily mean cultic or temple holiness but has a socioethical reference. What modern scholarship understands as two different covenants, that to Abraham and that through Moses, ancient Jews would have understood as one. And the term *latreuein* (v. 74) simply cannot be narrowed to mean cultic "worship." It means to serve in a more comprehensive way, in the entire way of life of a people. In the exodus the people of Israel are called to leave Egypt to serve God. Once they were delivered from Egyptian bondage, they contracted to serve God in covenantal justice or righteousness. These lines in the Benedictus are a close parallel: the covenant or oath that God swore to Abraham "that we, being delivered from the hand of our enemies, might serve him without fear, in holiness and righteousness" (vv. 74–75).

The final lines of the song, verses 78–79, recapitulate the statements of verses 68–75 (which originally they may have followed directly), while sensitively characterizing both "the tender mercy" of the divine savior and the desperate and demoralized circumstances of the people. God is intensely compassionate in the mercy (v. 72) shown in his deliverance. The term *anatolē*, which most versions translate as "dawn" or "dayspring" or "rising light," is the same as that in "his star at its rising/in the East" in Matthew 2:2. But this word is used in the Septuagint to render the "shoot" (hence "scion") in

Jeremiah 23:5 and in Zechariah 3:8; 6:12 that refers to a Davidic heir. The "shoot" or "scion" of David appears significantly also in Qumran literature (e.g., 4QPBless 3; 4QFlor 1:11). A Hebrew original of the Benedictus thus may have had a "shoot from on high" as synonymous with the "horn of salvation in the house of David" (v. 68). In Greek the meaning is pulled toward the "dawn" or "rising light" from on high because of the situation of the people "who sit in darkness and in the shadow of death," another idiomatic biblical characterization of people in need, as seen from Isaiah 9:2 or Psalm 107:9–10. Having their "feet guided on the way of peace" (v. 79), finally, would be much the same as "serving God in holiness and righteousness," that is, societal or community life according to the will of God for justice and wholeness.

Even the Lucan addition of verses 76–77 fits well into the rest of the Benedictus. The description of John here more closely parallels that later in Luke (3:3–4; 7:26) than the one in the infancy narrative context itself (1:16–17, in the annunciation to Zechariah).[32] But the role of John here fits the features of God's salvation stated in the rest of the Benedictus. The child (John) is to have the role of the prophet preparing "the way of the Lord" (Mal. 3:1, 23; and Isa. 40:3. which is "new exodus"). "Knowledge of salvation" has the sense of *experience* in a Palestinian Jewish thought context such as this.[33] That the experience of salvation consists in "the forgiveness of sins" does not lessen the sociopolitical character or increase the spiritual aspect of the deliverance.[34] The context has been clearly stated in verses 73–75 as the covenantal service of God in just social relations. Just as in the "baptism of repentance for the forgiveness of sins" that John eventually practices (3:3) and the "release of debts" in the Matthean parallel to Luke's "Lord's Prayer," so here in the Benedictus the "forgiveness of sins" provides a new beginning for the people in living covenantal righteousness.

In sum, the Benedictus is a song about God's liberation of his people from subjection to their Roman and domestic rulers so that, as God fulfills the covenant to Abraham, they can serve God by maintaining covenantal justice among the people. In order to illustrate how this song could have expressed the concrete experience of Palestinian Jewish followers of Jesus who were convinced that God had delivered the people and made present the saving "reign of God," we can compare the expressions of a contemporary Jewish community from which we now have abundant sources. Utilizing many of the same phrases or idioms, though with somewhat different combinations and emphases, two passages from the Qumran community state a similar combination of God's visiting and redeeming the people, saving them from their enemies, raising up a leader, keeping the covenant with the ancestors, and leading the people in the covenantal way of life.

> Blessed be the God of Israel
>   who keeps mercy towards His Covenant,
> and the appointed times of salvation
>   with the people He has delivered!
>   (1QM 14:4–5)

Remembering the Covenant of the forefathers, . . . He visited them, and He caused a plant root to spring from Israel and Aaron to inherit His Land and to prosper on the good things of His earth. . . And He raised for them a Teacher of Righteousness to guide them in the way of His heart. (CD 1:5–12)

Contrary to established Christian theological interpretations, the Benedictus is not noticeably christological. This song, rather, celebrates God's salvation of the people in a comprehensive sense, the sociopolitical dimensions being inseparable from the religious. The occasion for the song is God's "raising up" of "a horn of salvation in the house of David" as the agent of deliverance. But far from focusing only on the agent of redemption, the song declares in broad terms that God is both liberating the people *from* domination by their enemies and freeing them *for* the service to God in their own covenantally ordered social relations.

SIMEON'S SONG

The song opens with a special sensitivity. The verb translated "depart" is a euphemism for "die." Thus the psalmist here is an elderly man who had apparently longed for God's deliverance and had been promised that he would "see" it before he died. The singer is thus also a symbolic elderly representative of the people generally, who have been hoping and waiting for deliverance.[35]

The language of the phrases such as "seeing (God's) salvation" made ready "in the presence/sight of all the peoples" and "a light for revelation to the Gentiles" are clearly reminiscent of psalms such as Psalm 98:1–3 ("The Lord . . . has revealed his vindication in the sight of the nations . . . [who] have seen the victory of our God") and particularly of Second Isaiah. In the "servant songs" there, faithful Israel itself is "a light to the nations" (Isa. 42:6; 49:6). Especially striking in connection with Simeon looking for "the consolation of Israel" and others for "the redemption of Jerusalem" in the narrative context of the song is Isaiah 52:9–10: "The LORD has comforted his people, he has redeemed Jerusalem. . . . [B]efore the eyes of all the nations [they] shall see the salvation of our God."

The principal question in interpretation of this short song, as well as in the Isaiah passages behind it, "is whether the Gentiles are to be participants in the salvation of Israel or merely witnesses of it."[36] Again we must cut through our Christian presuppositions. In a process that began with other New Testament literature, Christians have understood the "servant of the Lord'" passages in Isaiah as referring to Jesus Christ, particularly his expiatory death on the cross. Moreover, Christian theological interpretation of the New Testament often presupposes a scheme, not particularly grounded in New Testament literature itself, that Jesus Christ was rejected by his own people generally, while accepted by the Gentiles. In Second Isaiah one of the effects, even purposes, of Israel's faithful maintenance of covenantal justice is to be "a light to the nations," and Israel is finally vindicated in the eyes of the nations, who recognize the benefits they have gained (Isa. 52:13–53:9). But the emphasis, the main conclusion of the prophetic drama, is that the people special to God—Israel—would finally be returned to prosperity, even exalted (52:13; 53:12). Simeon's song, where God's salvation means "revelation to the Gentiles" but "glory for thy people Israel," would appear to give Israel a clear priority.[37] Thus while the nations are beneficiaries, and not simply witnesses, God's salvation is focused on—indeed is—the redemption of Israel.

That the focus is clearly on salvation of the Jewish people in Simeon's song, while also including revelation to the nations, is confirmed by two other factors. Simeon's song is followed by an oracle: "Behold, this child is set for the fall and rising of many in Israel" (Luke 2:34) All four lines in the oracle carry the same theme: a judgment that divides. And "many in Israel" suggests the wide-ranging effects on the whole Jewish society.[38] There is nothing in the text, however, that indicates that Jesus' own people, "the Jews" as a whole, are here announced as rejecting him.[39] The child is to cause "the fall and rising" of many within Jewish society itself. Indeed, the rest of the Gospel of Luke portrays how the people generally respond to Jesus, while the ruling authorities oppose him. The final indication that the focus in Simeon's song is on the salvation of Israel, the Jewish *people,* whatever the revelatory benefits for the nations, lies in the narrative context of the song. The song celebrating the final presence of salvation is framed by those who are looking for "the consolation of Israel" and its equivalent, "the redemption of Jerusalem."

The principal point to be realized is that the focus of Simeon's song is not on those other peoples "out there" somewhere but on "these" people "right here," the people involved in the dramatic and exciting events of liberation now happening in their midst. Their lack of self-aggrandizement and their broader, almost universalistic perspective are impressive and provide an admirable basis for subsequent Christian developments. But the focus of their song is their own liberation.

LIBERATION OF ISRAEL AND THE GOSPEL

That the infancy narratives in general and the Lucan canticles in particular
deal with politicoeconomic as well as religious liberation and focus on the
liberation of Israel places them in conflict with commonly held views about
the early Christian gospel in general and the thrust of Luke-Acts in particular.
Jesus and early Christianity have been understood as basically apolitical, and
the evangelists interpreted as offering a political apology in their presentation
of Jesus' ministry and crucifixion. Israel has been understood to have rejected
Jesus and the gospel, in response to which God supposedly rejected Israel
and opened salvation to the Gentiles.

We are beginning to recognize, however, that these previously common
conceptions were misconceptions. The rule of God preached by Jesus stood
in conflict with, even in judgment upon, the rule of Caesar and Herod. The
charges leveled against Jesus at his trial were not spurious but true. Luke
clearly portrays Jesus, for example, as claiming a kingdom, stirring up the
people, and prophesying against Jerusalem and its rulers (e.g., Luke 3:21–
22; 9:20; 13:34–35; 19:37–38, 41–44, 47–48; 20:9–19). In Acts the followers of Jesus are consistently portrayed as in conflict with the high-priestly
rulers in Jerusalem (e.g., Acts 5:27–32; 9:1–2). The gospel and the activities
of Jesus and his followers were inseparably religious *and* political.

There is no evidence in early Christian literature, moreover, that the people
of Israel as a whole rejected Jesus and the gospel. Despite apparently sweeping
statements in Acts (13:46; 18:6; 28:28), Luke portrays diverse responses by
Jews to Jesus and the aggressive preaching and organizing by his followers.
The Jewish authorities are hostile and repressive. But large numbers of Jews
respond positively and join the movement, both in the Gospel (e.g., Luke
5:1–3, 15; 19:47–48) and at points throughout Acts (2:21; 4:4; 5:14; 6:7;
9:42; 13:43; 14:1; 17:10–12; 21:20). And one has the impression that Luke
is presenting the Jews who respond to the gospel and join the movement as
the ones truly faithful to the heritage of Israel.[40]

These misconceptions of Jesus and his followers as being apolitical and of
Israel as having rejected Jesus and the gospel are rooted in a failure to read
the Gospels and Acts historically. In New Testament literature itself it is difficult to find the dramatic break between Judaism and Chrisitianity that subsequent Christian theological interpretation often assumes. With regard to
Luke-Acts in particular, David Tiede has shown how the narrative as a whole
must be understood in the context of first-century Jewish history as well as
that of the nascent "Christian" church(es).[41] Indeed, the history of Israel is
the presupposition and context within which the Jesus movement, as well as
Jesus himself, is presented. Luke, like other New Testament writers, under-

stands and presents Jesus and his movement in terms of the fulfillment of God's promises to Abraham. The blessings promised to the Gentiles were to come through Israel. Fulfillment of the promises would mean the renewal of Israel, followed by the extension of salvation to other peoples. Such is Paul's assumption about history, as indicated in his reflections in Romans 9–11 that God had somewhat altered the original plan. This view is also behind the way Matthew presents Jesus and the gospel: Jesus himself and his disciples go first "only to the lost sheep of the house of Israel," and then, following the crucifixion and vindication, the resurrected Jesus commands the mission to "all nations" (Matt. 28:19–20). The same assumption that fulfillment came as renewal of Israel followed by the extension of salvation to other peoples underlies Luke's two-volume history. Jesus' mission to the people of Israel and the people's renewal are the very presupposition and basis of salvation being taken to the Gentiles.

The fulfillment of the promises, however, is not simply a scheme according to which Luke or others *interpret* history. The fulfillment is understood to be actually happening historically in the events of Jesus' birth, ministry, crucifixion and resurrection and of his followers' mission. Perhaps one reason it is so difficult for us to take this seriously historically is that we are accustomed to understanding history as the glorious achievements of the victors, whereas the Jesus movement portrayed by Luke and Matthew was at the time insignificant. The promised messiah had been executed, Jerusalem had been destroyed, and Jesus' followers were periodically being persecuted. Luke and Matthew and others who understood the events that they were experiencing as the fulfillment of God's promises, however, understood history as struggle— in particular, the history of the fulfillment of those promises as involving struggle for themselves.

Thus, far from standing in tension with the rest of the Gospels and the early Christian gospel, the infancy narratives, with their focus on the deliverance of Israel and the distinctively Palestinian Jewish milieu that they portray, provide the crucial first step in Matthew's and Luke's gospel history. That, with the birth of Jesus, the people of Israel is finally being liberated was not only historically given but was necessary, according to the biblical understanding in terms of promise and fulfillment. That the context and character in the infancy narratives are distinctively Palestinian Jewish is historically given and biblically to be expected. And however legendary the stories themselves may be, they portray the conflicts of which the history of the deliverance of Israel, hence also of other peoples as well, was made, according to Matthew, Luke, and other "Christians." The historical situation and relationships portrayed, moreover, are precisely and typically those involved in the history of fulfillment of those promises. Caesar and the census and Herod and the high priests (the enemies) constituted the problem from which the liberation initiated in the birth of Jesus was God's solution. Once deliverance was in-augurated, there was no middle ground, no neutral position from which to avoid (or "observe") the now-engaged historical conflict. While the keynote throughout Luke 1–2 is relief and rejoicing, Matthew 2 depicts the often brutal repressive implications for the very people to whom deliverance had supposedly come. Simeon's oracle points prophetically to the judgment en-tailed for those who oppose the divine deliverance. The realization of God's salvation of the people in concrete historical circumstances is the message of the infancy narratives.

That Luke and Matthew incorporated the birth stories and (in Luke's case) the canticles into their Gospels as the integral first step in the history of fulfillment indicates how seriously they took the origins of the Jesus movement among the Palestinian Jewish common people. In making use of the (pre-Matthean and pre-Lucan) stories and hymns stemming from popular circles in Palestine, they also incorporated and preserved some distinctive early wit-nesses to the significance of Jesus as the leader of their liberation. These tra-ditions should not simply be assimilated into later or more cosmopolitan theological frameworks. It is important to hear directly from the Magnificat, the Benedictus, and the infancy stories, preserved and retold in Luke and Matthew, their representation of the political-economic-religious conflict en-tailed in God's initiation of salvation in Jesus' birth.

PART THREE

◆

Analogy and Critical Understanding

· 7 ·

A Modern Analogy

From the very beginning, "Americans" have understood themselves in biblical terms. Puritans and other Protestant groups in northern Europe saw their own persecution as similar to that of the early Christians. In Plymouth and Boston and numerous other places in New England, the earliest English settlers set up covenant communities patterned after that of early Israel. Later the thirteen colonies struggled under the Pharaoh-like bondage imposed by George III and eventually gained their liberation as "God's new Israel." Jefferson thought that the Great Seal of the United States should depict Moses leading the Israelites through the Red Sea. And in 1787, sermons preached before state legislatures called to ratify the newly written Constitution compared it explicitly with Israel's covenant given on Sinai. Little thought was given to the displacement and killing of the Indian "savages." After all, Israel has carried out a conquest of the promised land.

The great early American theologian, Jonathan Edwards, was far from alone in considering the wondrous new society now taking shape in the New World as nothing less than another "coming" of Christ. The scores of canvases by the early American painter Edward Hicks of "The Peaceable Kingdom," with "the wolf lying down with the lamb," portrayed the widespread feeling that the American experiment was surely the fulfillment of Old Testament prophecies of the perfect age. It has been realized for some time that the apocalyptic spirit in late prophetic books and the New Testament is an important source of the American sense of "manifest destiny." Of course, to Africans who were brought to the New World in chains and were then taught their masters' Bible stories, their own enslavement was the new bondage in Egypt and white American slaveholders were the Pharaohs whom Moses had to tell again to "let my people go." Nevertheless, the consciousness of being the continuation of, or the new, biblical people pervaded the (dominant Protestant white) American self-image in a society in which, not too many generations ago,

127

most children learned to read from the Bible stories reprinted in McGuffy's Reader. Thus when contemporary Americans approach "the Christmas story," the infancy narratives in Matthew 1–2 and Luke 1–2, they understandably identify with Mary and Joseph or with the shepherds, certainly with the people of Israel to whom Christ has been born as the messiah and savior.

Assuming that North Americans do not have a monopoly on the Bible, however, it would be entirely legitimate and understandable for other peoples of the world, when they hear or read biblical narratives, to identify with the biblical people of God. Because of the popularity of reggae music in the last decade or so, numerous North Americans have become aware that many Caribbean blacks understand their experience as another "Babylonian captivity," in terms of the prototypical captivity of the Jews in Babylon.[1] More recently still, because of increased awareness in the United States of events in Central America, including the emergence of "basic Christian communities," many North Americans have become aware of how Latin Americans find their own experiences mirrored in biblical narratives. The collection and publication of group discussions of weekly Gospel passages after mass by the famous poet-priest Ernesto Cardenal made such views easily accessible to North American readers.[2] According to those who have worked in Latin American communities, these discussions in Solentiname, which took place in the early 1970s, prior to the Nicaraguan Revolution, express typical views. It is instructive to note how this largely peasant group sees its own situation and experience as parallel to those portrayed in the Gospel infancy narratives.

The peasants of Solentiname immediately and consistently identify with the ordinary people in the infancy stories such as the shepherds, and particularly with Mary herself. Moreover, they see themselves in and as "the nation of Israel" that God was/is delivering, as expressed in such passages as the Magnificat. "That nation of Israel that she speaks about is the new people that Jesus formed, and we are this people."[3] Mary calls herself a "slave"; the equivalent today would be themselves, the peasants (campesinos). When the angel congratulates Mary that she is to be the mother of the messiah, "he congratulates all of us because he means that the savior is not going to be born among the rich but right here among us, the poor people."[4]

Their interpretation, however, is by no means abstract or hypothetical but directly from their own life situation. "That angel was being subversive just by announcing that [i.e., 'you will name him "Jesus,"' which means 'salvation']. It's as though someone here in Somoza's Nicaragua was announcing a liberator." Another adds, "And Mary joins the ranks of the subversives, too, just by receiving that message."[5] The social situation in the infancy stories is seen to reflect their own: "We are the shepherds of the rich people because we work for them. We support them with our work, and a liberator has to come to help us too. We are *campesinos* and woodcutters. . . . Maybe right now when we're reading this and hearing these words the angel is coming to give us the news."[6] Indeed, similar to the way in which North Americans have seen their Revolution as a new exodus, analogous to the liberation of Israel from Egypt, the people of Solentiname see the birth of their own critical consciousness as analogous to the birth of Christ-child. "That Jesus who was born in a manger, like a child is born here . . . in a farmhouse, is the liberation that's being born here, in a humble form." "The revolutionary consciousness in these countries is still a child, it's still tiny. And they persecute it so that it won't grow."[7]

Just as New England preachers in the 1770s viewed George III as a new Pharaoh, so the people of Solentiname in the 1970s identified their own dictator, Somoza, as the equivalent of Herod. "The wise men [messed] things up when they went to Herod asking about the liberator. It would be like someone going to Somoza now to ask him where's the man who's going to liberate Nicaragua."[8] Moreover, "all Jerusalem" suggests "the big shots, like the Somoza crowd. . . . The powerful people knew that the Messiah had to be against them."[9] The chief priests with whom Herod consults are just like their own higher clergy who support the Somoza regime.[10] The people of Solentiname do not seem surprised at the slaughter of the children by Herod, "the Somoza of that region. . . . As soon as they glimpse a sprig of liberation anywhere they do what Herod did." Except perhaps that "Herod was less cruel than these people."[11] Even once Herod died, it was obviously necessary for Joseph, Mary, and Jesus to stay in hiding, for it was "just as if a Somoza dies and somebody else is in power, you're still always afraid."[12] As it happened, early in the morning before the Sunday Mass at which they had read Matthew 2:12–23, a National Guard patrol had come to inspect their houses. By the early 1970s, such a passage resonated with the Nicaraguan experience. As one of the girls said, "The same thing happened up north when Catalino appeared: Since they didn't know him well or even which one he was, they killed all the farmers around there."[13]

The section about Caesar Augustus's decreeing that the world should be taxed is left out of the passage in Luke 2 discussed at Solentiname, which may account for the lack of more than a passing reference to the contemporary analogy of Caesar. The people there, however, are well aware that the Somoza government was "set up by the empire." And they know about the activity of the "green berets" in Nicaragua, which they compare to the Roman soldiers that occupied Palestine in the Gospel narratives.[14] That is, North Americans may still identify with Israel and the people of God for whom the Christ-child was born. But the people of Solentiname view them as more analogous to Caesar and the Romans.

For some time now, professional biblical interpreters have been aware that their preunderstandings influence how they read and interpret Scripture. From numerous hermeneutical debates there has emerged a virtual consensus that the interpreter's own life situation and interests play a major role in determining his or her understanding of biblical texts and that bringing these factors critically into consideration is important in order for the texts to address the interpreter more adequately. Many of those discussions, however, concentrate on the modern interpreter's intellectual presuppositions, with little or no attention to the social or political position—which, ironically enough, has often been excluded by definition precisely by the interpreter's intellectual presuppositions. Yet it would seem fairly obvious that taking one's own life situation and interests more fully into account would open up additional dimensions of potential significance in the interaction between interpreter and biblical text. By including the national and international relations implicit in our own life situation, moreover, we would be merely attempting to have the scope of critical consideration of the interpreter's life situation match that which is explicitly represented in biblical narratives to be interpreted.

The inclusion of such a broad political dimension in biblical interpretation is nothing new among international church bodies and in certain circles of clerical and lay biblical study. Established biblical studies, however, have not yet developed any well-defined guidelines and techniques for comprehensive consideration of the interpreter's social situation. The principle of procedure by analogy, however, is long familiar. Perhaps it would be useful to extend that principle at least into exploration of the broad parallels that have been discerned between the network of sociopolitical relations in the Gospel infancy narratives and that in contemporary Central America. Such a procedure would by no means indicate any definitive meaning of the infancy narratives. But it might open up or bring into focus some possible implications of the Christmas story. The following, therefore, is simply an attempt to delineate briefly and document minimally the analogy discerned by Central Americans between the structure of their situation and the sociopolitical relationships they read about in the infancy narratives.

THE UNITED STATES AND ITS CLIENT-REGIMES IN CENTRAL AMERICA

Like the Romans in the eastern Mediterranean, the United States established its domination in Central America and the Caribbean by force of arms, taking over from declining imperial powers, and driven to maintain its control in opposition to the ostensible threat of a rival empire. Also like Rome, the U.S. maintained its control through indigenous rulers. Both Rome and the U.S. engaged in heavy economic exploitation of the subjected peoples, although the form of economic exploitation differed considerably. The Romans took tribute from the subjected peoples that was gathered by the indigenous rulers, with whom they collaborated closely in the rule and exploitation of the peasant producers. In the modern capitalist economic system, exploitation works through such means as investment in agribusiness or industry and return on the investment, control of resources (such as minerals, oil, land, and cheap labor), markets for manufactured goods, loans at interest, and generally integrating the subordinate country's economy into the metropolitan economy and its needs. The client-regimes serve to protect foreign economic interests as well as the position of the indigenous oligarchies. Thus, just as the "peace" established by the imperial "savior" meant politicoeconomic subjection for the peoples under Roman rule, so the "freedom" and "democracy" maintained abroad by U.S. economic and military power mean politico-economic subjection for Central American and other peoples.

North American Economic and Political Domination

The United States' domination of Central America under the *pax Americana* has developed in stages over the last century.[15] Toward the end of the nineteenth century, U.S. imperialism in Central America and the Caribbean took the forms primarily of investment in and occasional policing of the subject countries, apart from some initial military actions by which U.S. power displaced the Spanish in the area. It seemed obvious to many Americans that, as Senator Beveridge proclaimed in 1898: "Fate has written our policy . . . the trade of the world must and can be ours. . . . We will cover the ocean with our merchant marine. We will build a navy to the measure of our greatness. Great colonies, governing themselves, flying our flag, and trading with us, will grow about our ports of trade. Our institutions will follow. . . . And American law, American order, American civilization and the American flag will plant themselves on [other, bright] shores."[16]

In the early twentieth century the U.S. tended toward military intervention and even occupation in the area to protect and encourage private investment.[17] Looking back over his thirty-four-year career in the marines, often as head of military interventions in Central America and the Caribbean, Gen. Smedley Butler observed that he had "spent most of my time being a high-class muscle man for Big Business, for Wall Street, and for the bankers. . . . I helped purify Nicaragua for the international banking house of Brown Brothers in 1909–1912. . . . I helped make Honduras 'right' for American fruit companies in 1903."[18]

Coinciding with the depression in the 1930s, however, the U.S. learned that it could exert its control just as well by training indigenous "National Guards," who would keep order in each country.[19] The natural corollary, of course, was military dictatorships. The military strongmen who seized power, such as Somoza in Nicaragua and Ubico in Guatemala (1931–44), thus maintained order and protected private property—that is, that of North

American investors as well as the indigenous oligarchy. One new development of Roosevelt's Good Neighbor policy was that now U.S. government agencies as well as giant corporations such as United Fruit guided "development" in Central America in ways that enhanced opportunities for North American capital, trade, and expertise and that further integrated Central American export agriculture into the North American economic system.

Concerned to keep Latin America safely under U.S. control in the East-West conflict that emerged after the Second World War, Washington moved steadily to tighten its client-states' military dependency.[20] Fearful that behind any move for reform or unrest stood a communist threat, anxious U.S. policymakers declared that "we should not hesitate before police repression by the local government. . . . It is better to have a strong regime in power than a liberal government if it is indulgent and relaxed and penetrated by Communists."[21] The U.S. established the School of the Americas in the Canal Zone to train Latin American officers in anticommunist ideology and techniques of military control.[22] This tighter military dependency, however, began to work both ways, so that, while Central American military governments now depended on the U.S. for training, direction, funding and now-standardized (U.S.) equipment, Washington also depended on its creatures for protection of North American economic and political interests. In cases where legitimate, democratically elected governments attempted to make reforms on behalf of their people, of course, the CIA, in collaboration with United Fruit or the great banks and the local, U.S.-trained army, engineered their overthrow, as in Guatemala in 1954.

Under the Alliance for Progress in the 1960s, the U.S. sponsored "development," but it included little or no willingness to make any serious changes in the system by which Central America was already dominated by the coalition of foreign investment and indigenous oligarchies and armies.[23] The emphasis on private North American investments of course simply exacerbated the already glaring economic imbalances and further subordinated economic activites in Central American countries to U.S. economic interests. Meanwhile, as underlying unrest began to surface, particularly in the light of the Cuban Revolution and the escalating involvement of U.S. forces in Vietnam, the U.S. government began emphasizing "counterinsurgency" in its increased military aid to and direction of Central American armies.[24]

Besides the high stakes involved for U.S. investment, of course, the North American public generally had a stake in avoiding any serious adjustment in the economic and political system that had evolved. "Within Latin America, a dualistic society provides the basically cheap labor that is a requisite to keeping prices on export items low. . . . There is no getting around this simple relationship, and no amount of diplomatic good will can alter the basic structural relationship that keeps Latin America in a subordinate position."[25] Thus despite good will among the people of the United States, increasingly vocal cricitism of U.S. policy and practices in academic and church circles, pressures from other countries and international agencies, there has been little or no organized public pressure to restrain the steps taken by powerful economic institutions and the U.S. government to deepen and strengthen the system.

We should note some of the obvious differences between the politico-economic system by which the United States dominates Central America and the analogous Roman domination of Jewish Palestine. Perhaps most immediately obvious are the ideals shared by many, perhaps the majority, in the United States that are opposed to the U.S. government and corporation practices. Such are the source of the many outcries and political demonstrations that protest and the relief projects that attempt to mitigate the human degradation wrought by economic exploitation or military repression. There was little Roman criticism of Roman imperial practices. Also, because of such ideals shared by the American public and other peoples, the U.S. government and corporations do not have the same free hand in their domination of subjected countries that the Romans had but must finesse things and avoid too much public attention. The Romans had their propaganda, such as worship of Caesar the savior, but they did not have to worry about the phenomenon known as the "mass media," so that public opinion did not unduly limit a course of action.

Another principal difference is that the U.S. domination of Central America is far more pervasive and disintegrative of the very fabric of the subject societies. Ancient Roman domination left the subject society more or less intact, except for those slain or enslaved in the course of conquest. The Palestinian peasant village, the fundamental social form, was also the basis of economic expolitation, and the collaborative Jewish priestly aristocracy provided the political means. U.S. economic and political domination, however, has fundamentally uprooted the subject Central American peoples and transformed those societies, as we shall explore further below.

Client-Regimes and Political Repression

Just as Rome worked through native kings and aristocracies, such as Herod and the Jewish high priests, so the U.S. has been relying upon Central American military regimes and oligarchies. Like Herod of old, only more systematically and thoroughly, Central American military governments maintain order through tight military security, including secret police, informers, and security checks. In recent decades, however, the U.S. client-regimes in Central America have systematized and escalated the intimidation and outright massacre of their subjects far beyond anything conceived of by the prototypical tyrant Herod.

The Somoza regime in Nicaragua constituted almost a caricature of U.S.-

backed dictatorship and displayed striking parallels even to the particulars of Herod's rule and relations with Rome. The U.S. placed the elder Anastasio Somoza at the head of the National Guard as the marines withdrew from Nicaragua early in 1934. Within three years Somoza had overthrown the nominal president and had himself elected instead. A crucial step along the way was the assassination of Sandino, popular leader of the guerrilla forces that had been fighting the U.S. marines for years. After having him ambushed, Somoza sent the National Guard out to the areas of former guerrilla activity, where they slaughtered hundreds of men, women, and children.[26]

Somoza the elder and his two sons after him secured control of the country by dominating the National Guard and isolating it from the people. Command was kept in the family. Virtually all officers of the Somoza National Guard spent a year or more training at the School of the Americas. U.S. military advisers regularly worked with Somoza forces, and the Pentagon provided a healthy share of their defense budget. When their civilian power base eventually evaporated, the Somozas relied more and more on a network of spies and informers, such as telephone operators, cab drivers, and corner grocers.

While Herod had brought new families into the high-priestly aristocracy, Somoza simply dominated or coopted the Nicaraguan oligarchy.[27] His close associates among the Liberals became relatively more wealthy and powerful under his rule, while he made various deals with the Conservatives of the older oligarchy. Until the late 1970s, the Somoza family was consistently supported and legitimated by the Catholic hierarchy.[28]

The Somozas always followed the U.S. lead internationally and always maintained the closest relations with Washington. Just as Herod had cultivated key Roman leaders, the Somozas cultivated key leaders in the U.S.[29] Similarly, just as Herod had his sons raised in Rome, the elder Somoza, himself educated in the U.S., dutifully sent his two sons to be educated there as well, one at West Point.

Like Herod, the Somozas sponsored "development," with emphasis on export agriculture and the creation of an economic infrastructure. As the elder Somoza himself commented, they treated Nicaragua as their own farm, and its National Bank as their own private account to be looted at will.[30] U.S. aid and private investment flooded steadily into Nicaragua, further enriching the Somozas, the Guard officers, and the oligarchy.

While the younger Anastasio Somoza fully shared Herod's greed, brutality, and obsequiousness toward his imperial patrons, he apparently had none of Herod's prudence. Like Herod, Somoza came to control most of the land and wealth of his country: five million acres (roughly the area of El Salvador) and the twenty-six largest businesses.[31] When serious drought and famine struck Palestine, Herod had used some of the wealth he had accumulated to relieve the distress, at least in Jerusalem. On the contrary, in the wake of the Christmas earthquake of 1972 that devastated much of Managua and other cities and killed thousands, Somoza channeled international relief funds into his own accounts and businesses and allowed the Guard to steal and sell international relief materials.

To any opposition Somoza retaliated by turning loose the National Guard in extensive pillage, torture, and mass executions. By the mid-1970s, Somoza had achieved international notoriety for his atrocities, which were finally being reported, for example, by priests, and investigated by Amnesty International and U.S. Congressional hearings.[32] Despite the atrocities and the widespread outcry over them even within the U.S., Somoza's many friends in Washington defended him, and the Carter administration attempted to prop him up virtually to the end with military aid and the facilitation of loans.[33] It is estimated that the Somozas and the U.S.-trained officers of the National Guard presided over the killing of some thirty thousand Nicaraguans during the four decades of their dictatorship.

Guatemala may provide a better illustration of the structural analogy between ancient Roman and modern U.S. client-rulers precisely because there is no single Herod-like figure or family involved. The U.S.-engineered overthrow of the democratically elected Arbenz government in Guatemala has become a classic case of the heavy-handed North American domination of Central American affairs.[34] The huge United Fruit Company, which had come to own 42 percent of Guatemala's land, was nervous about Arbenz's plans for land reform.[35] United Fruit mounted an extensive propaganda and lobbying campaign in the U.S., raising the spectre of Soviet menace and communist takeover. Following the CIA-organized coup in 1954, the army again ruled the country. By 1963, the army, reorganized and modernized, with extensive internal intelligence set up by CIA operatives, had simply taken over virtually all areas of the government.[36] With the escalating war in Vietnam and the outbreak of guerrilla activity in Guatemala itself in the mid-1960s, the U.S. military placed special emphasis on counterinsurgency methods and training. At the instigation of U.S. military advisers, the Guatemalan army developed paramilitary bands of vigilantes instructed in techniques of counterterror to help intimidate and force peasants and others into compliance with the government's wishes.[37]

"The most intense and brutal military repression in Guatemala's long history of political violence occurred in the 1980s," with thousands killed, some four hundred communities destroyed, and a million people displaced.[38] The massacres by the Guatemalan military government have been extensively documented, particularly by human-rights organizations such as Americas Watch and Amnesty International.

The counter-insurgency apparatus . . . was reactivated in 1978 by General Romeo Lucas Garcia in the face of the resurgence of armed opposition and continued during his four years in power. Once again the victims were students, workers, politicians, Indian peasants from the Guatemalan highlands, priests, nuns, doctors, lawyers and others. Since then the police, the army, and "death squads" acting with official sanction have been responsible for torture, "disappearance" and extrajudicial execution on a gross scale. People have been seized or gunned down in broad daylight by police and soldiers.

In 1982 many thousands of non-combatant civilians, most of them Indian peasants, were massacred in the Guatemalan countryside. They were the victims of the counter-insurgency strategy of a military government led by General Efraín Ríos Montt which seized power in March 1982; killed by the army in a drive to crush growing rural guerrilla opposition. The exact number of dead is not known, but all estimates put the toll in the tens of thousands. . . . [According to a defector from the Ministry of the Interior] the full plan envisaged a strategy based on the destruction of hamlets, burning of forests and the extermination of the civilian population in an attempt to stop the guerrillas. . . . Only occasionally had the people known of the guerrillas. But the army policy knew no nuances. The policy was to destroy, with the result that today there are large sections of the altiplano to the north of the Pan American highway that are virtual wastelands.[39]

One of the most remarkable and now widely publicized of these massacres was the extermination of virtually the whole population of the village of San Francisco, Nenton, in the department of Huehuetenango, in the course of an army sweep of the area. The list of those killed reconstructed from the few fugitives or survivors came to 302 names, 91 of which were children under the age of twelve.[40] Herod's "massacre of the innocents" pales by comparison.

In the ancient Roman empire Herod's role as client-king was to rule Palestine with an iron fist both as a bulwark of defense against any possible threat from the Parthian empire to the East and as a control over the peasant producers who sustained the ruling apparatus economically. In modern Central America the system of economic exploitation is different, and the rival empire is thought to be subverting the politicoeconomic order from within. The principal role of a client–military government such as that in Guatemala is to maintain an orderly and stable atmosphere for agribusiness and trade to flourish, in support of the indigenous oligarchy and the North American investment. In contrast to the ancient economy, in Guatemala the peasantry is dispensable as a productive force on the land. In fact, the more precarious the peasants' hold on their land, the greater the availability of a desperate mass of seasonal workers as a cheap labor supply. This dispensability of the peasantry to the dominant economic enterprises may make more understandable the extensive massacres that have occurred as the Guatemalan military government has pursued counterinsurgency with unprecedented vengeance.

CENTRAL AMERICAN PEOPLES

Peasants and Workers

As in ancient Palestine, so in Central America the vast majority of the people have been peasants. They were economically as well as politically subject to the rulers living in the cities, although they usually supported their rulers by their labor (as with some of the ancient shepherds) rather than by payment of a percentage of their agricultural produce in tithes or tribute. Central American peasants probably have a view of life very similar to the ancient Jewish (or many another) peasantry, namely, that it is rooted in the land, which is the God-given basis, not simply for the necessities of subsistence, but for their whole traditional way of life.[41]

Ancient rulers claimed their portion of the produce of the land by right of divinely sanctioned hereditary rule or by right of conquest. Because the peasantry was the labor force that went inseparably with the land, they took care to leave the producers at least a subsistence living on the land. The modern rulers of Central America, however, because they understand land in terms of private property (to much of which they themselves have the state-recognized and state-suported title) and because they depend on the cheap labor of the people, not their produce, are far less concerned with the minimal subsistence of the people on the land. Indeed, because the rulers themselves desire ever more land for commercial, export agriculture, peasants have been actively displaced from the land. Hence with the recent acceleration of investment and "development" and the corresponding obsession with security, the modern Central American peasants and workers have come directly or indirectly under attack from the politicoeconomic system to which they are subjected.

Many, probably the majority, of the native Central American people were killed by the Spanish guns or their diseases during the conquest. The population that emerged after the conquest was mixed but remained largely Indian in certain areas, particularly in Guatemala. Just as the feudal system was breaking up in Europe, the Spanish imposed it in Latin America. The state recognized communal village possession of land but set up requirements of centrally administered and mandatory labor levies for the peasants. The state thus guaranteed the availability of labor to the large landowners. After the achievement of independence from Spain, the Liberal parties were able to use these traditional arrangements and the power of the state to provide labor for the development of commercial agriculture for export. They also expropriated church and peasant communal lands. In El Salvador most traditional peasant communities had lost their lands to large landowners by the turn of the century, many people having become sharecroppers or otherwise dependent laborers. In Guatemala the process of expropriation was slower and less complete, but the requirement of labor services was effectively maintained by the state, only gradually passing over into wage-labor and massive seasonal migrations of landless or semilandless peasants.[42]

As long as communal village property was left intact and the economic pressures were not utterly impossible, the peasant communities could solve their own problems internally through traditional patterns of local interaction and land distribution. Moreover, particularly in Guatemala, "the community was the stronghold of indigenous culture, a refuge from national economic and political dominance, a reinforcing place where Indian identity was formed and maintained."[43]

Powerful economic forces, however, have disintegrated the village communities. As U.S.-sponsored "development" accelerated, principally the expansion of export agriculture, living conditions deteriorated for the majority of people, workers and peasants alike. Commercial agricultural ventures required more land, and peasants were already indebted and otherwise vulnerable. In El Salvador the number of completely landless rural families increased from just under 12 percent in 1961 to over 40 percent in 1974. In Guatemala between 1950 and 1970, the average size of family holding decreased from 8.1 to 5.6 hectares (from 20 to 14 acres), while the number of landless people increased to nearly one-quarter of the rural work force. In 1979, fully 88 percent of farms were too small to provide for the needs of a family. As peasants became landless or had too small a holding to make a living, they were increasingly dependent on laboring for the commercial estates. While 300,000 or more highland peasants migrate annually to coastal plantations for seasonal labor, an additional 100,000, displaced by hunger or repressive violence, have simply settled there. Meanwhile, the production of basic food needs of the population declined, so that Central American countries had increasingly to import them. But of course increasing landlessness and hunger guarantee a cheap supply of labor for the commercial agricultural enterprises.[44]

Given the overabundance of such cheap labor and, in contrast with the ancient world, the rulers' lack of interest in keeping a productive peasantry on the land, the increasingly impoverished peasants and workers are at the mercy of the system. This unhappy plight can be seen in the effects on the peasantry of the cotton boom in the 1960s and the dramatic expansion of beef production in the 1970s and 1980s. The rise of extensive cotton growing on the Pacific coastal plain was made possible by the financial support of the World Bank and government subsidies of cheap credit, new government-built roads, along with insecticides and chemical fertilizers. The abundant supply of cheap migratory labor, moreover, enabled the growers, bankers, and supporting agribusinesses to make substantial profits even when cotton prices dropped or other production costs rose. The effects on life for the common people were demeaning and distintegrating.[45] The easiest, hence the first, land to be planted to cotton was the land already being used by the peasants for their own corn production. Regardless of the particular form of peasant land tenure, they were evicted, sometimes by force. What had been the largest corn-producing areas of Nicaragua or El Salvador quickly became the largest cotton-producing areas. But cotton not only displaced corn, it displaced people. Denied land on which to raise their own food, the peasants were forced to move or migrate wherever the labor market offered seasonal work. Thus, for example, the traditional ways in which women had contributed to the family economy such as tending chickens or marketing vegetables had to be replaced by domestic labor in towns and cities. While the men roved the countryside looking for seasonal labor, the number of female-headed households in urban areas mushroomed.

The expansion of cattle production starting in the 1960s and escalating in the 1970s was a response to the demand for cheap beef, created partly by the fast-food industry in the United States.[46] Many peasants who had been pushed off their land by the cotton boom and other agricultural development for export had moved into the forest to start new farms on land considered too remote or too infertile for commercial ventures. But cattle ranching, not limited to the coastal lands and climate, pursued them, having learned from the cotton boom how to exploit them and then displace them. Where peasants had already opened up an area, either squatting on public lands or colonizing in an officially recognized project, the cattle ranchers could either obtain title to the land and legally evict the peasants or simply push them out with private and official strong-arm tactics. In other places, the land was rented to small farmers for a season or two, after which they were evicted and grass planted where the peasants had raised their corn. Whereas cotton production, like that of sugar and particularly coffee, had provided at least seasonal employment for the now landless peasants, cattle ranching offered few jobs for the displaced people (less than one-sixth as many). Far more than cotton had, beef now displaced people as well as the corn they had grown. In Guatemala, the northern provinces in which Indians and other peasants had been resettling (or officially resettled) became a prime area for potential development of cattle raising. Some of the very areas where AID or Catholic relief organizations or even the Guatemalan government had been promoting peasant cooperatives in resettlement ventures became prime zones of counterinsurgency operations by the military. In some cases the officers themselves were moving into the ranching business. "Barbed wire meant prosperity and prestige for ranchers, but for those who grew corn it came to symbolize a crown of thorns, the harbinger of crucifixion and death."[47]

Refugees

Although Roman conquest and reconquests and Herodian repression created thousands of refugees, the scale of displacement was nothing compared to what has occurred in the late twentieth century. Political repression and other violence during the 1980s have led to the dislocation of an estimated 2 million people in Central America. In Guatemala alone, a country of just over 7 million, roughly 1 million have been displaced, including 200,000 who have fled mainly to Mexico but also to other neighboring countries and the United States.[48] In their flight from harrassment and violence by army or death squads, ladinos and urbanites such as professionals and middle-class people have reacted as individuals or perhaps as whole families. Indian villages have often fled as whole communities. When the Guatemalan army launched one of its sweeps in a given area, Indians or other peasants might first try hiding out in nearby mountains or dense forests, hoping to return to their villages once the army had passed through. But the mounting scale of destruction and continuing military occupation led tens of thousands to seek safety across the border in Mexico. The total number of such refugees across the border in Mexico was still under 2,000 in 1981, as the United Nations, along with the Mexican authorities, began to take note of the escalating problem. As the counterinsurgency terror intensified dramatically in 1982, particularly after Ríos Montt seized power, the flow of refugees into Mexico escalated dramatically. By December 1982, there were 36,000 refugees in fifty-six camps; the next year, 46,000 in about ninety camps. In 1985, the director of the Mexican Refugee Commission estimated that the total of official (in camps) and unofficial refugees from Guatemala was closer to 200,000.[49]

Priests, Sisters, Catechists,
and Basic Christian Communities

However overwhelming the forces arranged against them, the people have organized themselves to protest, resist, and deal with their problems.[50] Central American peasants have protested and revolted periodically for centuries, usually in local actions uncoordinated with a broader alliance. Ordinary political participation, in the manner familiar to North Americans and Western Europeans, has been largely closed off by the ruling military regimes' sharp repression. Nevertheless, in recent decades concentrated efforts have been made to organize labor unions, teachers associations, and peasant cooperatives. Where these means of resistance and struggle for rights and a decent living were simply denied or seemed utterly impossible, some resorted to armed resistance as guerrillas based in remote areas. All such organization and resistance has been important and often effective. But at the risk of unbalanced and incomplete coverage, we will concentrate on the factor of the religiously motivated organizing and organizations because of its potential importance for our interpretation of biblical narratives.

There is no exact Central American equivalent to the ancient Jewish hereditary priesthood. The Roman Catholic church, in fact, was attacked and seriously weakened by the Liberal parties and the dictatorships they supported. As elsewhere in modern times, secular intellectuals have carried out many of the functions that priests performed in ancient societies. In recent decades, however, nuns, priests, and other religious workers who have "gone to the people," and indigenous catechists along with the emergence of numerous "basic Christian communities," have played religious and communications roles similar to those of the ordinary Jewish priestly families resident in the villages in ancient times. Religious workers in Central America, however, go beyond the role played by the ancient Jewish preists in two respects. As suggested in the excerpts from discussions in Solentiname above, members of basic Christian communities, like their clerical leaders, not only discern the parallels between their own situation in Central America and that portrayed in biblical narratives, but they are also motivated to seek liberation from that situation by those biblical narratives of liberation. Moreover, whereas the communications network formed by the ancient Jewish priests was confined to Jewish Palestine itself, the religious workers in Central America are part of an international network concerned for human rights and dignity.

Prior to the 1960s, the Roman Catholic church had been, if anything, in decline in Latin America. The Liberals had expropriated its lands and in some cases driven out its priests. So few were the latter that the people in some areas rarely saw a priest except on unusual ceremonial occasions. The clergy was divided into classes, as in ancient Judea, with the families of the oligarchy usually providing the bishops. But the priesthood did not provide a pervasive network of communications the way it had in ancient Palestine.

The orientation of the church changed dramatically beginning in the later 1960s. While the European and North American prelates who organized and dominated Vatican II concentrated on dealing with a world of human progress, the Latin American delegates, now led to look at the world, saw primarily poverty. The Latin Americans, however, refused to see the poverty of their people as indigenous backwardness. It did not take much critical analysis to realize that their poverty was the product of exploitation and dependency. Among ordinary religious workers there were already strong currents of motivation to work among the poor. The opening of the church toward the world in Vatican II, and particularly the Conference of Latin American Bishops at Medellin, Colombia, in 1968, gave powerful impetus and legitimation to those currents.

In "going to the people" with the primary aim of evangelization, the religious workers were now motivated to facilitate the people's own "consciousness raising" and to encourage the people, in their dignity as God's creatures, actively to shape their own lives. The traditional focal symbol of the passive resignation to the world as it is, the dead Christ hanging on the cross, was deemphasized. In its place came people learning how to read, often focusing on biblical narratives that were then openly discussed and related to their own life situation. What emerged were scores—even hundreds—of "basic Christian communities" in poor urban areas and villages throughout Latin America.

A frequent outgrowth of the interaction between religious workers and the people was that the latter would organize their own self-help measures. Numerous communities, besides continuing their prayer and Bible reading, developed other "bootstrap" operations such as schools, health care, and legal awareness, under the leadership of their own indigenous teachers, midwives, agronomists, and "delegates of the Word."[51] The Guatemalan Committee for Peasant Unity provides a case of sophisticated widespread organization. Catalyzed by activist Christian students working with pastoral agents and with church communities as the usual starting points, this large peasant organization operated with collective, decentralized leadership who did not appear in public, so that it was more difficult for the government or paramilitary groups to suppress their organizing. Led by this committee, eighty thousand plantation workers went on a strike that paralyzed the sugar-cane harvest in 1980 and won a 200 percent increase in the pitiful minimum daily wage.[52]

Central American military governments found the religiously motivated attempts to organize the people every bit as threatening as those of labor unions and peasant committees. Hundreds of modern-day martyrs from among the sisters, priests, and delegates of the word have joined the thousands of victims of repression. In the last years of the Somoza regime, the National Guard had begun to single out religious workers for persecution. The assassination of priests, nuns, and other religious workers in El Salvador in the late 1970s was more brutal and better known.[53] The escalation of general repression in Guatemala in 1980 included an apparent systematic attack on religious workers, an attack that became even more intense in 1981. In the department of Quiché, where Catholic pastoral agents had been most active during the 1970s, numerous priests and sisters and hundreds of catechists were killed. As the assassinations of his pastoral agents and threats against himself increased, the bishop in Quiché decided that he and the priests should simply leave, lest they all be killed. The remaining infrastructure of religious leadership, "the delegates of the Word," with deep local roots in the Indian villages, continued to be sought out systematically by the army or death squads.[54]

The religious workers in Central America, finally, constitute a communications network not only within a given country, as did the ancient Jewish (ordinary) priests, but between the subject countries and the dominant U.S. metropolis as well. For example, even when the bishop withdrew all the priests from the department of Quiché, the delegates of the Word still worked and moved among the villages. On occasion they would spend several days traveling to another area and often would bring in the already blessed Eucharist. In El Salvador, a conservative who was selected as archbishop, Oscar Romero, became steadily more aware of what was happening in the barrios and villages and visited the devastated churches and said funeral masses for his murdered priests.[55] Because most of the sisters and priests active in Central America were from abroad,[56] there were also numerous connections with their particular orders and the international church. Some of the best information about what was happening inside Central American countries has consistently been found in church publications rather than in the established North American news media. Most dramatically, when Archbishop Romero was assassinated on March 24, 1980, the general public internationally took note, and the rape and killing of four North American church women in December 1980 evoked sudden questioning as well as general outcry in the United States.

·8·

Liberating Narrative
and Liberating Understanding

A great deal of energy in biblical studies has been devoted to mitigating or avoiding the distancing effects of historical-critical analysis of biblical literature and history. Critical biblical scholarship, having become institutionalized in theological schools for the training of the clergy, had so distanced the Bible from the personal and ecclesial concerns of theologians, clergy, and laity that "what it meant" seemed virtually irrelevant for contemporary faith. Following upon legitimate objections to historical criticism's pretentions of "value-free" investigation and "objective" analysis in its concern to free biblical texts from traditional dogmatic biases of established Christianity, various ways were found to restore the Bible's relevance and revelatory power. Through all the emphasis on historical-critical study, its own practitioners had never come to grips with its implications for either the Bible or their own situation. Indeed, they, along with other theologians, had never really relinquished the older traditional understanding of the Bible as the "word of God." The whole discussion of what the Bible "meant" versus what it "means" is a manifestation of this schizophrenic dilemma of modern theologian-scholars torn between two ostensibly conflicting understandings of the Bible—as historical document or as the word of God.[1]

According to the latter view, the biblical text is not simply a means or medium of revelation but revelation itself; it not only communicates or mediates but is itself the word of God. But once biblical studies had successfully established an awareness of historical distance and difference in meaning, how could the "original" meaning of the text or the "historical" reconstruction of events still be "the word of God" for today? Some found relatively simple theological or ecclesial solutions. Certain neoorthodox theologians simply ignored the results of biblical studies and used the Bible as it stands in English or German as divine revelation, although not in a simplistic fundamentalist manner. Certain Catholic scholars still rigorously pursued their historical-critical methods for what the text "meant" but then deferred to the teaching authority of the Church for a definitive determination of what the text "means."[2] Theologically oriented biblical interpretation, of course, had simply never left off its practice of abstracting "proof texts" from literary or historical context to illustrate "early Christian," "New Testament," or "Matthean" christology or soteriology. In these ways the results of historical criticism— even though the infancy narratives might be dismissed as historically unreliable texts—would not affect the doctrines of the incarnation or of the virgin birth of Christ or of Jesus as "the Son of God."

More complex and sophisticated approaches to salvage the biblical text as the word of God for people today from the distancing effects of historical criticism are, like the simpler approaches just mentioned, either reversions to or contemporary versions of traditional ways of reading the Bible. All of these ways of reading, moreover, also either avoid or mitigate the historical reference of the biblical texts. Of great popularity recently is the reading of biblical texts simply as literature. Thus their intrinsic beauty or structure or their rhetorical power can be appreciated by the reader. On the analogy of modern drama, for example, an elaborate scheme of acts and scenes is discovered in the brief, twenty-three-verse narrative of Matthew 2.[3] Given the modern individualistic orientation, particularly in North America, it is not surprising that psychological interpretations are popular. Parts of the text or the whole are applied to the self; for example, in the birth of the Christ-child the self is being born (or the self is giving birth, or the child is being born in the heart).[4] Such psychological interpretations are, in effect, the modern equivalents of traditional allegorical interpretation, except that the system of spiritual understanding into which the text is being transposed is derived not from Plato but from Jung or Freud. How the fundamental motifs of the infancy narratives as a whole are transformed into a psychological pattern of meaning can be seen, of course, in Rank's Freudian treatment of "the myth of the birth of the hero" (see the Appendix).

The way most people have any contact at all with the Bible, of course, is in the context of a church service. There, when it is not simply utilized as a source for prooftexting and illustration, it is reduced to paragraph- or story-length "lessons" selected according to either the preacher's current agenda or an established liturgical lexicon. A historical understanding of the text may well inform the preacher's preparation of a sermon on such a text, but the people's reading is structured and oriented by the contemporary ecclesial (or personal piety) context. In such a case, of course, the infancy narratives are read in the context of the Advent season, which is part of an annual cycle of celebrations as well as part of the contemporary cultural Christmas atmosphere. With all of these approaches available and operative, the infancy narratives as "the word of God" would appear to have plenty of channels to the minds and hearts of the faithful with virtually no interference from the distancing effects of historical criticism.

HERMENEUTICS OF CONSENT

Others have attempted to find a way to let the text, the word of God, speak to the contemporary faithful, while still utilizing historical criticism. Anxious that historical criticism simply distances biblical text and history from the present, the "hermeneutics of consent" seeks an interpretation that listens as well as critically dissects, that allows the text to make a truth claim on the interpreter.[5] Bridging the gulf between historical criticism and word of God, or between past and present, is particularly important for theologians in the Lutheran tradition, for whom the very identity of the church depends upon its connection with Holy Scripture. For those anxious about this gulf, the historical criticism that once emancipated us from the constraints of tradition now appears even "absolutist." Consensual hermeneutics wants to utilize but to mitigate the effects of historical criticism by a new openness or consent to the textual spiritual tradition, which makes a claim on the interpreter.

This approach offers some concepts and concerns that might prove important for biblical interpretation if they could be implemented. First, in contrast with the Enlightenment and the "scientific" historical criticism that emerged from it, this hermeneutics attempts to take its prejudices or prejudgments (preunderstanding) into account rather than to escape or suppress them. The interpreter who seeks understanding of a text is unavoidably embedded in a particular situation, of which there is little possibility of any objective knowledge. In fact, the very presupposition of historical knowledge is that the interpreter is involved in a tradition, part of which is constituted by the effects that the text has had on her or his situation and preunderstanding. The power of those effects, moreover, does not depend on their being recognized.[6] Because "the self-awareness of the individual is only a flickering in the closed circuits of historical life," of course, one's prejudgments are far more determinative of understanding than one's judgments. "Thus the hermeneutically trained mind . . . will make conscious the prejudices governing our own understanding so that the text, another's meaning, can be isolated and valued on its own."[7]

Second, the concept of horizon has been used since Nietzsche with reference to how one's thoughts or views are determined by the situation. It includes potentially the whole range of vision, everything that could be seen from a particular vantage point. The implications are that one is not necessarily limited to seeing what is nearest but can see broad ranges of things with a certain perspective, even that one's horizon could be shifted and expanded. Historical understanding requires placing ourselves within the horizon out of which the tradition or text we are seeking to understand speaks. Simply to place ourselves in the situation or horizon of the text, however, would be like a one-way conversation in which we listen attentively to another person in order to understand another's views but without agreeing or letting it make a claim on us. If, on the other hand, we were to consent to the text's having something valuable or true for us, then we would have to engage in a genuine two-way conversation, allowing our own viewpoint or horizon to be further questioned and challenged. Genuine understanding would involve a "fusion of the horizons." Thus in seeking understanding of a text, we would not only place ourselves in another situation, within another horizon, but we would also resist a facile assimilation of the text or past to our own unexamined situation or horizon. Encounter with the texts from the tradition that has affected us is important to the testing of our prejudgments and the informing of our self-understanding.

There are a number of problems with this consensual hermeneutics, however, when it comes to the infancy narratives and other biblical materials. Some of the problems are simply inherent in the approach. Consensual hermeneutics appears still to assume that a religious dimension of life is separable from other dimensions, such as the political and economic. The Bible is understood, accordingly, as "the word of God," which evokes "faith" in the believer. Consensual hermeneutics does not appear to be any more open to nonreligious dimensions of life, past or present, than historical criticism is to transcendence (divine causation). Historical criticism, however, has made clear that most if not all biblical narratives and prophecies are concerned with life as a whole, and not simply a religious realm. As noted above, "he who was born king of the Jews" is not presented in Matthew 1–2 or Luke 1–2 as merely a spiritual savior. Consensual hermeneutics assumes an individualistic stance and focus. The infancy narratives, by contrast, manifest a sociopolitical stance and focus. Interconnected with the previous two points, consensual hermeneutics is concerned with self-understanding. The latter, moreover, is conceived in abstract, intellectual and spiritual terms of humankind in general. The infancy narratives, like the exodus narratives, however, are concerned with the concrete liberation of a whole people. Thus, insofar as this approach in effect confines itself to the claim of texts from its own religious tradition, it limits that claim to the impact that spiritual ideas from the past might have on its own self-understanding. The horizons involved are, in effect, the past and present spiritual and intellectual ones from the same religious tradition.

On the other hand, if this approach is seriously committed to pursuing historical criticism in a way that the concerns, foci, and horizons of past texts are allowed to challenge our own preunderstanding, then consent to and dialogue with biblical texts such as the infancy narratives should eventually have the effect of calling our limiting assumptions into question. Dialogic hermeneutics appears almost naive in its expectation that this openness will happen, virtually by sheer willpower, for there are severely limiting factors that it has apparently not taken into account. The placing of oneself in another horizon and the questioning of one's own prejudices supposedly takes place within a continuous religious or intellectual tradition, but no critical principle is supplied for the conversation other than the continuing circular dialogue between interpreter and text. We can predict how the conversation would work, for example, between North American interpreters and the infancy narratives. The history of effects of the biblical tradition is such that North Americans identify strongly with the biblical people of Israel and see themselves as those to whom the Christ-child was sent and to whom the "peace on earth" was proclaimed. No critical principle is provided that suggests that such an identification with the people of God in the tradition is invalid. Consensual hermeneutics relies on the willingness of Europeans and Americans (particularly those who are hermeneutically trained) to test their own prejudices. But biblical texts suggest that people in positions of relative power and privilege (kings, princes, priests, scribes, Pharisees) tend not to test their own prejudices and horizons but to use their power to impose them on others.

Perhaps consent to and confrontation with biblical texts are needed, but a far greater sense of suspicion is clearly in order with regard both to our own situation and prejudice (most of which we are unaware of) and to the ways in which the tradition has affected our situation and prejudices, the power of which goes unrecognized. We want to be near to the scriptural text once more, and an objectifying historical criticism is blamed for the alienation that has occurred. But perhaps, as the result of historical processes, we have in fact become distant from the biblical past in various respects (socially, politically, religiously), and historical criticism discerns the distance already there, however much it also tends to objectify. Thus historical criticism would appear to have a highly important role in two respects. Not only would critical historical reconstruction of the biblical texts and their circumstances discern the difference and distance of the biblical past from the situation and prejudices of the present. Historical criticism must also be applied to the ways in which the biblical texts or past has affected our situation and preunderstanding. Such critical distancing may provide one of the primary bases for suspicion and criticism of our own position.[8]

The distancing of historical criticism helps make possible the distancing necessary for difficult self-criticism. Schüssler Fiorenza delineates important ways in which historical criticism of the Bible can function in the interpretation and use of Scripture:

1. It asserts the meaning of the original witness over later dogmatic and social usurpations, for different purposes.

2. It makes the assimilation of the text to our own experience of parochial pietism and church interests more difficult.
3. It keeps alive the "irritation" of the original text by challenging our own assumptions, world views, and practice.
4. It limits the number of interpretations that can be given to a text. The "spiritual" meanings of a biblical text are limited by its historical meanings.[9]

Although consensual hermeneutics has critical intentions, its inherent problems are such that the very historical criticism whose effects it is attempting to mitigate must be pursued even more rigorously in order to accomplish its stated agenda of listening to the claims of biblical texts.

UNDERSTANDING THE BIBLE HISTORICALLY

The above discussion, however, assumes that the Bible is being understood as text, or more important, that what we are attempting to understand is text or "word." One of the results of historical criticism and of some recent hermeneutical discussions is that this is not the only way to view the Bible, particularly biblical narratives and prophetic material. The Bible was the product of communities of people.[10] The biblical text as we have it was preceded by oral and written traditions that were also produced and cultivated by historical communities, such as early Israel, disciples of the prophets, or followers of Jesus. The traditions and the texts they produced are expressions and reflections of their own experiences or events that were highly significant for them. The Book of Exodus provides accounts that express the significance of the people's deliverance from bondage in Egypt. The biblical text is a "word" about the event. It is the exodus event that Israel proclaims as its liberation, while the biblical "word" or account is a medium of communication about that liberating event (and becomes highly revered or "sacred Scripture" just for that reason). Similarly the infancy narratives are accounts of the significance of a liberating event. Because of our own recent objectifying and positivist historical orientation, we may be skittish or embarrassed with regard to the texts' imperviousness to discovery of "what really happened," but the infancy narratives originated and were cultivated and written as accounts of the significance of Jesus' birth. It is the latter event, not the "word" or text in itself, which is important—as is indicated by the subsequent formulation of the doctrine of the incarnation as one way to help protect it.

What may be only implicit in narratives such as the Exodus or the infancy stories is stated explicitly by Paul. Over against some of the Corinthians who were apparently reading the biblical text as a word of spiritual wisdom with salvific qualities, Paul insists that the Bible is about past historical events.

What had significance was not the word or the text itself but the events, which "were written down for our instruction" (or warning; see 1 Cor. 10:1–11). In fact, in his understanding of the Torah as an account of significant historical events, Paul has the audacity to insist that the function of the text or word was relative to its particular historical period in the overall sequence of events. That is, the Law as text or word served as the means of salvation from the time of its institution through Moses, but it had not so functioned in the prior events that it itself recounted and it was now historically superseded in its function by the events of Jesus' crucifixion and resurrection (Gal. 3). Thus, whether explicit in Paul or implicit in narratives such as the Exodus or the infancy narratives, much of the biblical text presents itself as an account about events of significance. The events, moreover, are not confined to a religious dimension but are events of politicoeconomic as well as (and inseparable from their) spiritual significance.

In a now-famous essay, the great literary critic Erich Auerbach delineated how leaders of the ancient church developed and medieval biblical interpretation elaborated the *figural* reading of the Bible as past history pertinent to subsequent history. A key step was the retention of the Jewish Scriptures as the Old Testament and the decision not to interpret it only abstractly and allegorically. Christianity thus maintained "its conception of a providential history, its intrinsic concreteness, and with these no doubt some of its immense persuasive power."[11] Not only are biblical narratives read as referring to concrete life and events, but they are also understood as pertaining to and elucidating later—including present—life and events, and not simply some spiritual dimension. This figural approach

> implies the interpretation of one worldly event through another; the first signifies the second, the second fulfills the first. Both remain historical events; yet both, looked at in this way, have something provisional and incomplete about them; they point to one another and both point to something in the future, something still to come, which will be the actual, real, and definitive event. This is true not only of Old Testament prefiguration, which points forward to the incarnation and the proclamation of the gospel, but also of these latter events, for they too are not the ultimate fulfillment, but themselves a promise of . . . the true kingdom of God.[12]

As recently as the American Revolution and formulation of the United States Constitution, many North Americans still understood the Bible as accounts of historical events, including politicoeconomic as well as religious affairs; and they understood that biblical life and events pointed forward and could illuminate subsequent history. In a sermon entitled "The Republic of the Israelites an Example to the American States," preached before the General Court (state legislature) of New Hampshire in June 1788, for example, Samuel Langdon declared that, "as to everything in their constitution of government . . . the Israelites may be considered as a pattern to the world in all ages; and from them we may learn what will exalt our character, and what will depress and bring us to ruin."[13] As noted in this discussion above (as well as in chap. 1), for understandable reasons established biblical interpretation retreated into a primarily religious reading of the Bible understood as a religious text. In recent times, however, black, women's, and third-world communties and liberation movements are showing the way toward rediscovery and critical appropriation of the Bible as history.

When the Bible is read as an account of experiences or events significant to the people of Israel or followers of Jesus, the focus is not on the text itself, removed from historical life to a separate sacred status, but on the people and their struggles. The Bible recounts the founding events of God's deliverance of the people, other paradigmatic events of liberation, and numerous experiences of conflict, failure, judgment, or renewal. When the account leaves off, however, the history of the people continues, being informed, inspired, and warned by biblical events and prophecies. For contemporary communities and movements that identify with or look seriously to biblical history, the reading and historical criticism of the Bible thus takes on some constructive roles or functions, while expanding the scope of its distancing and critical functions delineated in the preceding section. Several of these can be illustrated from the infancy narratives.

Any reconstruction of history is done for a group of people or for a certain position or purpose, whether it is consciously acknowledged or not.[14] But this fact accords well with the stance of biblical accounts such as the infancy narratives, in which God is, in no uncertain terms, effecting liberation for the subjected Israelite people, saving them from their enemies. Thus the infancy stories readily open toward a reconstruction of the historical relations involved in the birth of the Christ-child for purposes of liberation and movements among the oppressed. Liberative reconstructions, moreover, appear to be solidly supported by a reading of these narratives in the historical context of ancient Roman Palestine, judging from the materials explored in chapters 2–6 above. Biblical history, of course, can be reconstructed for purposes of domination as well as liberation. Herod consulted the biblical scholars of his day concerning messianic prophecies to determine where he should concentrate his military action to suppress any nascent resistance to his control. In today's more subtle reconstruction, the massacre of the innocents (or any indication of political conflict) is suppressed in order to produce a politically innocuous Christmas story for the holidays.

Bible reading and historical reconstruction are important for the cultivation of memory. Selective memory can be used in the service of domination. But unrestrained historical memory is usually threatening to oppressive or repressive order.[15] Memory of the infancy narratives would be "dangerous" in two respects especially. These stories and songs articulate the eager hopes and longings of ordinary people for deliverance from their domination by indigenous and alien rulers—indeed, their excitement over the birth of the one who is to lead their redemption. Elizabeth, Mary, Simeon, and Anna, as well as the shepherds (and the heavenly armies), were all ecstatic that here, finally, was "the consolation/redemption of the people." The stories also present a memory of suffering and struggle. The rulers were threatened and struck out violently; Joseph, Mary, and the child had to flee the country and, even when they returned, had to avoid recognition by the threatened and threatening rulers; and innocent children were slaughtered, and their mothers mourned. Memory of the longings and the sufferings of predecessors or forebears is subversive; it sustains the longings, mitigates the suffering, and nourishes the resolve to resist among those who remember.

In the interrelation between memory and the reconstruction of history (for particular purposes as well as of biblical events and relationship), biblical criticism can help determine what shall be remembered and how or in what connection it is remembered. Is the mention of Caesar and the census simply a literary device in Luke 2, as suggested in christologically oriented interpretations? Our awareness of the imperial situation of first-century Palestine indicates that the Roman demand of tribute evoked intense resistance among the Jewish peasants and teachers and was important in biblical memory (Acts 5:37). Is the memory of the liberative deeds of Jael or Judith to be evoked in the recitation of Elizabeth's greeting of Mary, "Blessed are you among women," or is it too threatening? The pre-Matthean traditions and pre-Lucan canticles along with Matthew and Luke make possible and encourage that Caesar's demand of tribute, Herod's cruel and violent repression, and Jael's and Judith's as well as Mary's acts of deliverance be remembered in connection with the birth of Jesus. Closely related to the issue of what is to be remembered, there may be more to the biblical history that can be remembered than initially meets the eye from reading the text. Historical criticism can discern, for example, that women were more important in the leadership of early Christianity than is portrayed in the androcentric New Testament texts. In the infancy narratives in particular, women play a more significant role than in other New Testament narratives, and the dialogue or songs by women in the stories allude to the tradition of women's prominence in historical deliverance as charismatic figures and prophets.

A particularly important function of both memory and historical criticism is the recovery of unfulfilled historical possibilities.[16] One of the dominant themes of biblical history is promise and fulfillment. The community of priests and scribes who wove revered traditions together and gave final form to the Torah included, in a prominent position, God's promise to Abraham and Sarah that their descendants would have land and would be a great people and that all peoples would receive blessings through them. But, writing in circumstances of exile or imperial rule over Judea, they end the historical narrative and covenantal exhortation prior even to Israel's entry into the land. History went on after the historical narrative of the Torah stopped, and the promises were partially fulfilled. Paul, in his excitement over the final fulfillment of the promises, proclaimed that the traditional social divisions between Jew and Greek, slave and free, and male and female were no longer valid (Gal. 3:28). But in his social practice he implemented only the first, and acquiesced in the perpetuation of the other inequalities and their attendant oppressions. Although the biblical account of people's struggles left off, the history of faithful communities continued. Finally in the nineteenth and twentieth centuries there was a serious return to the unfulfilled historical possibilities of liberation for slaves and women.

The narratives of the birth of Jesus occupy in the New Testament (or the new biblical history) the place that corresponds to the promises to the ancestors in the Hebrew Bible (and Israel's history). The savior and messiah is born, the good news of liberation is proclaimed, and the people rejoice as well as begin the difficult struggles involved. The infancy narratives set the theme and thrust of the gospel history as a whole: Israel is finally being redeemed, and then (at the end of Matthew and at the beginning of Acts) deliverance is opened to all peoples. After recounting Jesus' proclamation of the kingdom, his martyrdom and vindication, and the extension of the mission to the other peoples, the biblical story leaves off before the anticipated final fulfillment in the *parousia*. (Of course, by the end of Acts the gospel has at least finally reached the imperial capital.) But the history of peoples' yearning and struggle continues. The memory of Christmas in the infancy narratives, however, keeps alive the hopes for and the commitment to the unfulfilled historical possibilities that the birth of the child inaugurated. There is nothing in the infancy narratives themselves or in the rest of Matthew or Luke to suggest that the possibilities of "deliverance from our enemies" is deferred as only eschatological, that is, possible only at the end of historical conditions. That view is a carryover from the older tendency to read the biblical text literalistically. In fact, the eschatological reading only serves to discourage the yearning and struggle toward realization of the unfulfilled historical possibilities as illegitimate (according to the authoritative scholarly reading of the "word of God") and to dissipate the subversive memory that Christmas would keep alive.

Like history that is reconstructed for some purpose or community, memory is not necessarily oriented toward the past. Considering the prominence of promise and fulfillment and the memory of unfulfilled historical possibilites that are juxtaposed with concrete, formative experiences of deliverance in the Bible, biblical memory and biblical history are if anything oriented toward the future (or as Paul says, biblical history was written down "for us"). Thus yet another function of biblical history and memory is "to provide paradigms in which the life of a later time, i.e., the future from the viewpoint of the texts themselves, may be illuminated."[17] Not only prophecies but many narrative passages, which ostensibly refer to the past, become paradigmatic for present experiences.[18] Stories of Abraham and Sarah were told or written not to provide information about the past but to offer patterns of hope and trust, or the lack thereof, in the fulfillment of God's promises. Such stories still function paradigmatically in the present. The same illumination of present historical experience by the biblical past happened for black slaves in North America and is happening today for Central Americans on the basis of biblical memories of the exodus and the birth of Jesus, respectively.

Historical criticism has an important role in relation to this future orientation and pertinence of biblical history, but its function is more enabling than definitive.

> The future direction of scripture can be rightly realized and exploited only in conjunction with its past references, for it is the past references that, though historically imprecise, provide the historically given definitions of its terms. And here again we have a reason why the Bible has to be understood with a fully historical understanding, aligned with disciplines lying outside the biblical and theological fields: only that can guard us from systematic misunderstanding of the range of possible meanings of biblical terms in their reference of present and future.[19]

The role of historical criticism and reconstruction here, however, is only that of assistance to communities or movements. The illumination of present experience and events from the biblical past is a matter of discernment, although without historical criticism there would be less to discern.[20]

In a number of respects these functions of memory and criticism of biblical history, such as the attention to unfulfilled historical possibilities and the discernment of how biblical paradigms illumine present affairs, represent a rediscovery of the figural interpretation prominent prior to the Reformation and rise of rationalism. Yet, they differ in important respects as well. That is, they are no longer tied to the Platonic cultural heritage of late antiquity, with the historical *figurae* as a tentative form of something eternal and timeless as well as concrete in themselves. And with less standardized patterns fixed in the minds of contemporary historical actors, they allow current events their own full concrete integrity and flow without conforming them to biblical prototypes.

A LIBERATING CHRISTMAS STORY

The infancy narratives are about liberation. The birth of the Christ-child means that God has inaugurated the long-awaited deliverance of the people of Israel from their enemies. More precisely, God has begun to free the people from domination and exploitation by the imperial ruler and from their own rulers, particularly the tyrannical king. The people's liberation evokes brutal repression and involves suffering, but the dominant tone is one of relief and excitement as the people respond readily to God's initiative.

Memory of the stories of Jesus' birth have been among the most cultivated of all biblical narratives, partly because of the widespread celebration of Christmas. Correspondingly, however, with regard to the history of its influence on cultural tradition, there has been all the more opportunity for that memory to have become selective and for the stories to have become used with other than liberative effects. Nevertheless, these biblical narratives are among the most laden with unfulfilled historical possibilities because they tell of and rejoice in liberation initiated but remaining potential rather than actualized. Like the stories of the promises to Abraham and Sarah and those of the temporary heavenly enthronement of Jesus, they are strongly oriented toward future historical realization.

Those in the present likely to find themselves particularly addressed by these stories are people of similar life circumstances. People dominated and exploited by local or foreign rulers are the ones likely to discern that these biblical stories illuminate their own situation and experiences. The campesinos of Solentiname under the rule of Somoza provide a vivid illustration, as sketched briefly at the opening of chapter 7. By contrast, North American society generally has moved away from its earlier identification with and celebration of the birth of the Christ-child, or strikingly domesticated adaptable parts of the Christmas story, into a festival of gift-giving consumption legitimated and motivated primarily by the symbol of Santa Claus. Vast numbers of North Americans, living in a culture no longer familiar with the Bible as people's history, have little sense of how the stories behind "Christmas" could be about the deliverance of an oppressed people. Thus it may be useful to explore the liberative function of the infancy narratives as memory or history for basic Christian communities, focusing particularly on the process of "conscientization" (consciousness raising) that takes place in many of these small Latin American communities of the poor.[21] In the process some interesting points of difference will emerge between the attitudes and approaches of established European and North American biblical studies and those of the basic Christian communities.

For many if not most peoples in oppressive situations, the world appears as fated. Given their own utter powerlessness, combined with the traditional religious and other cultural forms utilized by their rulers to legitimate their own rule and control their subjects, it is not surprising that the people's stance toward reality is often fatalistic. It is not difficult to appreciate how the infancy narratives, like much other biblical material, provide a direct challenge or alternative to such fatalism. A benign god not only is in full control of the situation but is acting to liberate the people. The old myths and mystification are exposed by the birth narratives, and alternative explanations are suggested. The emperor or other ruler is not divine; tribute and taxes are not the legitimate claim of rulers and conquerors. And true peace is not tranquility and prosperity for the privileged on the basis of the people's subjection. Moreover, the infancy narratives portray the people's difficult circumstances of life, which they would otherwise have accepted as simply "the way things are," as caused by human agents to whom God's action is sharply opposed. It is a powerful but mortal Caesar who decrees taxation, not God. Those who dominate and exploit the people are viewed as enemies whom God is about to overthrow. Rulers can be seen to exercise such violence against the people because they sense the illegitimacy and insecurity of their own domination.

In contrast to oppressed peoples' internalized sense of subjection to and dependency on their masters, the infancy narratives present a striking case of God's dealing directly with the ordinary people. The divine will and action, moreover, is for their own liberation, not their further oppression. If ordinary people are valued by God, then perhaps they can value themselves. The ordinary people in the infancy narratives, moreover, display no deference to their rulers and have no apparent anxieties or hesitation about their own imminent liberation. The people in the birth narratives thus become paradigms or prototypes for later readers or hearers: seeing that God helped earlier people, who ventured to assert their freedom, they come to believe that God will help them as well and are able to take action in shaping their own lives.

As has been noted by reflective participants in the discussions of communities of the poor, and as can be readily observed in Cardenal's transcripts from Solentiname, the people readily relate or even mix biblical stories, events, or figures with their own lives and circumstances, and vice versa. *They* are Mary or the Christ-child or the shepherds. Herod's killing of the children is Somoza's National Guard turned loose on fellow Nicaraguans. Or *they* are in bondage in Egypt. Biblical stories are history for the people but are also reflections or portrayals of their own lives and situations. Hearing and discussing the biblical stories is a way of beginning to understand their own situation and of reflecting what might be done about it. They are not focused on trying to interpret the Bible as an activity in itself (and separate from other activities). In effect, they are interpreting their own lives and circumstances with the help of or by means of the biblical stories. The word of God is not in the Bible but somehow emerges from the community's discussion of their life situation in relation to biblical figures and events. In contrast with the traditional European and North American Protestant emphasis that the reading and exposition of Scripture evokes faith, but in a separate religious dimension, the basic communities' reading and discussion of biblical stories do not differentiate life and faith, do not separate politicoeconomic concerns from religious activities.[22]

It might legitimately be charged that such communities are giving the Bible only a relative position or even second place. But that position is in integral relation with life as a whole, whereas when North Atlantic Christians, particularly Protestants who emphasize the *sola scriptura* principle, give the Bible first place, it is only within a separate sphere of faith or religion. Finally we should note the basic communities' stengthening conviction that God is with them in their struggles, and not simply active in past struggles. Directly or indirectly, this conviction leads to taking action in regard to their own lives on matters such as education, labor organization, access to land, or health care, as well as the Eucharist and prayer. But such actions should not be surprising, since biblical stories have provided some suggestive prototypes of organization for taking control of one's own life and having land as well as a positive self-image and a spirit of group solidarity.

How might North Americans learn to read the liberating story of Christ's birth and begin to discern how it might illumine our situation? Because we have become so distant historically (i.e., socially, economically, politically, and religiously) from the birth narratives, historical criticism may indeed have an important role in preparation for discernment. One of the ways that has been developed to deal with the historical distance is the principle of "dynamic analogy." In interpreting biblical statements such as prophecies or the teachings of Jesus (i.e., the Bible as word), for example, one would apply the message to "those dynamically equivalent to those challenged in the text."[23] If this principal of dynamic analogy can be expanded in scope and complexity to deal with the Bible not only as word but as history as well, then it might well provide a device by which some discernment could be induced.

As noted above, in early generations analogies (often elaborate) were made between biblical history and United States history. More recently, with the scope of history narrowed to that of religious institutions, analogies have frequently been drawn between facets of the biblical people of God and their modern equivalents. Not only do theologians often see themselves in Paul's image, but (more self-critically) they even acknowledge that the established clergy correspond to the Pharisees in ancient "Judaism." Were we to draw a dynamic analogy between United States society and ancient Jewish society as a whole as portrayed in the infancy narratives, then the wealthy and powerful generally would correspond to Herod and the high priests, and educated professionals generally would correspond to the scribes, and so forth.

However, to press such an analogy between a tiny ancient society and one of the great modern world powers strains historical credibility. The analogy discerned by the peasants in Solentiname is far more credible. What corresponds to Jewish society under Roman rule in New Testament times is a third-world country such as their own Nicaragua, while the United States, with a number of small countries under its domination, corresponds to Rome. Such an analogical interpretation simply extends a prophetic principle used in biblical history itself both in Amos and by John the Baptist. A people that confidently understood its continuity with those specially favored by God in the past as a guarantee of continued divine blessing (whether because of the promise to Abraham or because of the redemption from Egyptian bondage) is disabused of its presumptuous illusion: God can raise up children to Abraham out of stones; and perhaps God is concerned as much about the Philistines and Syria as about Israel (Luke 3:7–9; Amos 9:7–8). The extension here, in broad analogy to the infancy narratives, is from the recognition that the United States can no longer pretend to be "God's New Israel" to the realization that it has apparently become the new Rome.

Once we recognize the imperial position of the U.S. in the dynamic historical analogy, it may be possible to discern important facets of the present-day "Caesar's" rule through a fresh reading of the infancy narratives, informed additionally from our historical-critical reconstruction of their broader context. Thus we can discern that the equivalent of Caesar's decree that all the world should be laid under tribute is North American economic exploitation of smaller countries. And just as Caesar sent in the legions to enforce Rome's extraction of tribute, so U.S. military power is used to protect investments, profits, and trade. One of the purposes of Rome's economic exploitation of subject peoples was to provide the "bread and circus" necessary to keep the Roman mobs under control. Moreover, just as Rome dominated through client-rulers such as Herod, so the U.S. maintains its interests and influence through governments, often military, that it designates and supports. Pressing the analogy to greater complexity, we can see our own equivalent to the ancient Roman religious ideology of "peace" established by the imperial "savior." "Democracy" and "development" or "progress" are the blessings of the "free world" established and dominated by U.S. military power.

The foregoing aspects of a dynamic analogy were all drawn from ancient Roman history, as represented in the infancy narratives (Caesar, tribute, peace, Herod) and applied to contemporary United States practices. The analogy could be drawn or discerned in the other direction as well. Thus, for example, the hundreds of thousands of Central American refugees in the United States might have an analogue in the flight of the Christ-child and parents to Egypt, especially considering the similar causes of their flight (repression by client-regimes threatened by nascent liberation movements).

Having determined the corresponding cast of characters and some of their practices by means of the expanded dynamic analogy with the infancy narratives, we can probe the thrust of the stories as well, particularly the implications for "Caesar" and other "Romans." In the stories and songs about the birth of Jesus, God, in acting for the people, is acting against Caesar and Herod. The emphasis, particularly in Luke 1–2, is that the birth of Jesus means salvation of the people from their enemies. But it is abundantly clear, both from the fundamental relationships portrayed in the narratives and from the Magnificat in particular, that raising up the lowly and feeding the hungry also entails pulling down the mighty from their thrones and sending the rich away empty. The unmistakable implication in the birth stories that God is rejecting the rulers, moreover, is part of a consistent pattern of God's historical action. In liberating the Israelites from bondage in Egypt, for example, God took action against Pharaoh and his armies (Exod. 15); in reasserting the independence of the covenant people in their land, God fought against Canaanite kings (e.g., Judg. 5); in delivering Israel from the harsh rule of Ahab and Jezebel, God inspired a revolt through the prophets Elijah and Elisha (1 Kings 19 and 2 Kings 9); to preserve the traditional covenant with the people, God inspired resistance and revolt against the imperial rule of Antiochus Epiphanes (e.g., Dan. 11; 1–2 Maccabees). Thus if the infancy narratives are to be read analogically, the present-day Caesars and their client-rulers are implicated. If, analogous to God's action recounted in the infancy narratives, and in pursuit of the unfulfilled historical possibilities that opened in the birth of Jesus, God is still today acting for the liberation of poor and subjected people, it would seem clear that such action entails opposition to their domination and exploitation by North American political and economic practices.

The infancy narratives and the Gospels that they introduce, however, are neither deterministic nor vindictive. The Magnificat and the Beatitudes are not announcements of "eschatological reversal," whereby the downtrodden will finally lord it over their oppressors in some end time. And there are no lurid descriptions of how cruel and arrogant rulers are to suffer horrendous torments. Although under the influence of powerful social and cultural forces, the wealthy and powerful are not thought to be inevitably and hopelessly condemned. Later in the gospel story, Jesus does not simply turn away the "rich young ruler" (Luke 18:18–25). What the Gospels, like the prophets, appear to be calling for is a change of practice, and not simply an expansion or adjustment of one's "horizon." In this connection the actions of certain groups—some of them church or church-related organizations—rather than hermeneutical discussions, are providing indicators of how the citizens of today's "Rome" might respond to the implications of the infancy narratives.

Some churches or church groups have taken advantage of the supposed "separation of church and state" to offer a biblically based sanctuary to refugees. A number of independent organizations help channel private donations for medical aid and other forms of relief from the effects of U.S.-sponsored destruction of life, limb, and livelihood. The complex politicoeconomic system centered in the United States, however, calls for a more systematic approach, including use of contemporary social criticism along with historical criticism, by biblically informed citizens of the modern analogue to Rome. Although the economic system has become highly intricate, for example, with union and professional retirement funds being invested in multinational corporations that exercise extraordinary power in "underdeveloped" countries, there is still a degree of structural differentiation among political and economic institutions, and some degree of pluralism, hence of personal and group independence of any particular institution. Hence it is possible for North American individuals and groups to quit (at least partially) living from the "bread and circus" provided, for a profit, by the huge agribusinesses that are exploiting dependent laborers in Central America. North Americans, who still enjoy political rights, can demand that their own government cease enforcing the "tribute" taken by U.S.-based corporations and cease placing and supporting in power client-regimes that expropriate and brutalize their subjects. Some groups, with substantial church participation, have already pledged resistance by civil disobedience to any further direct military intervention in Central America by the United States government. Although perhaps to a diminishing degree, the present-day "Caesar" is still dependent on the consent of the citizenry, which was not the case in ancient Rome.

In the heyday of rational criticism, biblical expressions of future hope were dismissed as utterly unrealistic, as fanciful myths. Besides being viewed as "mythical" (hence to be rejected as accounts of anything that might really have occurred), the stories surrounding Jesus' birth were dismissed as fantasies with regard to their hopes of salvation. Like Jesus' promise of the kingdom of God (read, of course, in Matthew's wording of "the kingdom of heaven"), the Christmas story's proclamation of peace on earth and salvation of people from their enemies appeared to rational modern men as expressions of pious fantasies that merely provided spiritual compensation for unenlightened people's suffering. Memory that the birth of Jesus included the promise of peace on earth and excited responses to God's nascent deliverance by ordinary people such as Mary, Elizabeth, Simeon, Anna, and the shepherds was cultivated in the traditional celebration of Christmas. But that event too was understood as a special, mythical, magical time.

The increasing abandonment or subordination of the biblical Christmas story in contemporary North American celebration of "the holidays" invites us to read the former over against the latter. The current celebration of "Christmas" now appears to take place in a fantasyland, a magical, fairy-tale world—which no one takes too seriously, of course. Whereas Enlightenment reason was driven to criticize the stories of Christ's birth and other biblical "myths" as parts of the traditional forms of authoritarian domination, few today are bothered by the new forms of myth and magic. The latter are forms of domination no less than were the biblical revelation and the Christian theological doctrines attacked by Enlightenment rationalists. If they were not effective in inducing massive retail spending from Thanksgiving to Christmas, then manufacturers and retailers would hardly utilize them so extensively in costly advertising in the communications media. Perhaps the fact that these new forms of myth and magic help keep the economy humming tends to mitigate any discomfort over the manipulation and domination involved.

The infancy narratives of Jesus, on the other hand, once freed both from the domesticating cultural context of "the holidays" and from rationalist dismissal as "myth," can be read again as stories of people's liberation from exploitation and domination. The people who may respond most immediately are probably those whose situation is similar to that portrayed in the stories. But for the modern-day citizens of "Rome," uncomfortable about their intricate involvement in the web of the new forms of domination, they also offer a challenge and inspiration to regain control of their own lives in response to God's liberating initiative in the birth of Jesus.

APPENDIX

Legends of the Birth of the Hero: A Critical Appraisal

Psychologists and mythophiles were attracted to the infancy stories of Jesus for the same reason that critical biblical scholars were neglecting them: their "mythical" qualities. As noted in chapter 1, both Freudians and Jungians were fascinated with the stories of the births of heroes for the light they believed such accounts shed on the development of personality. The earliest, most focused treatment of such material was the collection of stories with analytical commentary by Otto Rank, *The Myth of the Birth of the Hero,* published in 1909. With the recent interdisciplinary opening of New Testament studies in the 1970s, distinguished folklorists were asked to apply the patterns they had discerned in cross-cultural materials to the Gospels.[1] Practitioners of biblical interpretation can surely benefit from the comparative perspective of folklorists and others.[2] Such benefits can be appropriated, however, with the full retention of the critical literary and historical analysis already developed in biblical studies. In the following discussion it is important to remember that, in accordance with recently converging interdisciplinary definitions, the appropriate narrative category for the hero stories is *legend,* and not *myth,* the term used particularly by psychologists and mythophiles.

RAGLAN'S QUESTIONABLE HEROES AND JESUS

Unaware of previous work by Rank and von Hahn,[3] in 1934 Lord Raglan laid out a scheme of what he called "The Hero of Tradition" in twenty-two incidents, based on what he thought were the absolutely nonhistorical and ritual-based accounts of twenty-one "heroes."[4] According to the distinguished folklorist Alan Dundes, Raglan avoided mentioning Jesus in order not to upset anyone. Apparently less concerned about the upset a generation later, Dundes himself has adapted Raglan's "hero of tradition" and applied the so-called hero-pattern to Jesus.[5] He did so somewhat loosely, however, missing some obvious points and stretching others. He was criticized by biblical scholars concerned with the official canon of Scripture. Perhaps two semi-separate analyses would be appropriate, given the dispute about the relevant or legitimate materials to be used. Since Raglan and Dundes were dealing with heroes as portrayed in popular tradition, the first should include such data as the apocryphal gospels, painting, and popular iconography. It would then be useful for critical comparison to do a second analysis solely on the basis of the four canonical Gospels.

On the basis of the canonical Gospels *and* popular traditions, Jesus fits Raglan's sketch of the "hero of tradition" more completely than most of the figures Raglan used. (In the following survey, Raglan's twenty-two incidents are placed in italics.) (1) His *mother* was *a virgin,* but her *royalty* may derive from her husband, through whom the genealogy is traced in both Matthew and Luke. (2) His *father* was thus ostensibly descended from the Davidic *royal* line. But, contrary to no. 3, there is no indication that *his father* may have been *related to his mother.* (4) The circumstances of *his conception* were *unusual;* and (5) he was portrayed as *the son of god.* (6) At his birth an *attempt was made to kill him,* but (7) *he was spirited away* and (8), at least for a short time, *reared in a far country* (even if by his own mother; one might consider Joseph his foster father, but that would then skew no. 2). Traditions about Jesus in both Luke 2 and apocryphal gospels *do* tell about his childhood; hence, no. 9 does not fit. (10) He went or *returned to his future kingdom,* either as a child returning from Egypt or in the "triumphal entry" into Jerusalem. (11) He fought and was *victorious over a "dragon,"* in the temptations by Satan (the prince of demons) in the wilderness. But, unless one considers that, as Christ the king, Jesus takes the church as his "bride," he did not *marry a princess;* hence no. 12 does not fit. (13) He *became a king,* at least as declared by Peter and acclaimed in the "triumphal entry" and as mocked at his crucifixion. He even (14) *reigned uneventfully* for a time in Galilee, and for at least a few days in Jerusalem, while (15) *prescribing laws.* Then, (16) *losing favor with the people* (Christian tradition accused the Jews generally of turning on Jesus), (17) he was *driven from the throne,* at least figuratively. There was nothing *mysterious* about his *death;* hence, no. 18 is inapplicable. (19) He was *killed at the top of a hill.* (20) He was *not succeeded by his children,* since he had none. His *body was buried* only temporarily; hence, no. 21 applies only in a sense. And (22) he *has holy sepulchres.* Jesus' "score" would thus appear to be 17+, rivaling the most heroic of Raglan's heroes.

If we confine ourselves to the texts of the four canonical Gospels, of course, the score would be considerably lower. Jesus explicitly refuses to become a king (at least during his earthly ministry), hence does not really reign at all, hence cannot have earlier "returned to his kingdom" and is not then "driven from the throne." He loses favor only with the rulers and their retainers (scribes and Pharisees), but not with the people generally or with God. The canonical Gospels do not say that he was crucified on a hill, and they are very explicit that he was buried, although the tomb is surrounded with no special holiness. Hence numbers 10, 13–14, 16–17, 19, 21–22 become inapplicable along with 9, 12, and 18. One might also question whether Satan in the temptation narrative is really portrayed as a dragon or a king as well. Thus, once we are past the birth and infancy narratives, all we have left of the hero pattern is number 15, "prescribes laws," and the innocuous number 20 about the nonchildren's nonsuccession. In fact, Jesus as portrayed in the Gospels is not only nonheroic but is virtually an antihero as measured by Raglan's (and Dundes') criteria. On the other hand, with the exception of number 3, and if we allow for Mary's not being a *royal* virgin and Joseph's not actually being a king but nevertheless in the royal lineage, the portrayal of Jesus in Matthew 1–2 and Luke 1–2 matches the motifs of the hero pattern point for point (nos. 1–2, 4–8) as regards birth and infancy—to which we return below.

Dundes follows the important folklorists' elementary distinctions among types of narratives, namely, between fairy tales, myths, and legends. Since most hero narratives were told as true stories, they are therefore classed as legends and not fairy tales, in apparent contrast to some earlier discussions that had called some of the component motifs *Märchen*. However, Dundes fails to draw the obvious critical conclusions from some of his own observations about the arbitrariness of Raglan's and others' selection of heroic traits. He assures us that

> the overall advantage of the fact that von Hahn, Rank, and Raglan made independent investigations of essentially the same textual material is the support it provides for the reliability of their hypothesized accounts of the hero pattern. In other words, since all three were able to inductively extrapolate hero biographical incident sequences which reveal a fairly high degree of uniformity, it is more reasonable to defend the proposition that an empirically demonstrable hero biography pattern for (Indo-)European (and Semitic) heroes exists.[6]

A review of the chart he provides on the next pages, however, reveals nothing of the kind. Next to Raglan's twenty-two motifs or incidents, von Hahn has only sixteen, and Rank only twelve. Moreover, once we pass the first eight, von Hahn has motifs that correspond only to numbers 10–11 and 18 in Raglan's sequence. Indeed, unless one is convinced simply on the basis of Raglan's first five (Greco-Roman) heroes (Oedipus, Theseus, Romulus, Heracles, and Perseus) plus Dionysus and Moses (and perhaps Arthur) that such a "hero biography pattern" exists, there is little or nothing in the other studies to make it "empirically demonstrable." On the other hand, what is at least impressive, on the basis of Dundes's comparison of von Hahn, Rank, and Raglan, is the close correspondence of the first eight motifs in their respective schemes and the degree to which their respective case studies exemplify all or most of those motifs. What appears to exist is not an overall biographical hero pattern but something closer to what Rank called "the myth of the birth of the hero."

It would surely not be methodologically too strict to insist that lists of motifs do not constitute a pattern or elucidate meaning. The hero pattern posited by Raglan (or those by von Hahn or Rank or the composite by Dundes) is simply a list of incidents, details, or motifs and does not correspond to any form or genre of literature, oral or written. In Dundes' presentation of the supposed pattern, the interpreter is apparently free to combine hero traits and incidents indiscriminately from different lists and to stretch or interpret the motifs in order to maximize a particular hero's correspondence to the pattern.[7] However, whereas Vladimir Propp's morphology of folk tales was based on numerous actual fairy tales, the hero pattern as presented by Raglan and Dundes includes traits and incidents from a variety of sources and types of literature. They apparently assume that their subject and materials are traditional popular legends of folk heroes. Yet, most of their sources for most of the heroes included consist of formal literature, such as Greek drama, history, mythography, and so forth. Even if we could isolate the features of popular legend behind the literary in some cases, nevertheless, as Dundes himself point out, "as a genre, legend rarely exists in any one single version in any community in the world. Rather a cluster of legends surrounds an important political or religious figure. . . . For this reason, a folklorist normally collects as many versions of a legend as possible before trying to reconstruct a composite notion of a legendary figure's life story."[8]

Lord speaks similarly of oral traditional narratives: "Most commonly, the separate elements or incidents in the life of the hero form individual poems or sagas."[9] In the case of the supposed hero pattern, however, we are offered a somewhat arbitrary list of incidents or motifs collected from often limited and fragmentary sources and from a wide variety of times and societies. Indeed, insofar as the legends surrounding heroes tend to focus on particular incidents or motifs, it may not be possible to posit any overall biographical hero pattern.

Previous discussions of the hero pattern also have not clarified the relation between structure (the posited pattern or scheme) and meaning. Lord's work with oral traditional literature would appear to be pertinent. By "mythic pattern" he appears to be referring to how elements of stories are "repeatedly structured into larger wholes in a similar way" across different cultures and considerable spans of time. With this persistence, the mythic pattern itself would appear to be the bearer of meaning, whereas in any particular story the specific details, or "local color," make the meaning of the pattern concrete. The pattern attracts particulars of time and place, but "traditional narrators tend to tell what happened in terms of already existent patterns of story."[10] The mythic patterns that Lord describes and applies to the Gospels as oral traditional literature ("cosmic dragon-slaying," "the dying and resurrected god," and narratives clustering around the "transitional points in the man's life" such as birth, initiation, marriage, and death) are even more diffuse and less convincing than Raglan's as adapted by Dundes. Lord's implicit definition of the kind of legendary pattern we might find in traditional hero stories, however, is much clearer than that of Raglan and Dundes. Given the greater coherence and frequency of motifs that revolve around the birth and infancy of heroes noted above in von Hahn's and Rank's as well as Raglan's analyses, Rank's "myth of the *birth* of the hero" may be worth further critical exploration.

RANK'S "MYTH OF THE BIRTH OF THE HERO" AND JESUS

Rank included the stories of Jesus' birth and infancy as one of the principal illustrations of his hypothesized "myth of the birth of the hero." He suggested that "a standard saga" could be reconstructed from "a series of uniformly common features" found in stories about such figures as Moses, Cyrus, Oedipus, Paris, Perseus, Romulus, and Hercules.

> (1) The hero is the child of most distinguished parents; usually the son of a king. (2) His origin is preceded by difficulties, such as continence, or prolonged barrenness, or secret intercourse of the parents, due to external prohibition of obstacles. (3) During the pregnancy, or antedating the same, there is a prophecy, in form of a dream or oracle, cautioning against his birth, and usually threatening danger to the father, or his representative. (4) As a rule, he is surrendered to the water, in a box. (5) He is then saved by animals, or by lowly people (shepherds) and is suckled by a female animal or by a humble woman. After he has grown up, he finds his distinguished parents, in highly versatile fashion; takes his revenge on his father, on the one hand, is acknowledged on the other, and finally achieves rank and honors.[11]

Most of these features can be found in most of the summaries of stories about the heroes cited by Rank. The series of features is most evidently manifested by Cyrus, Perseus, and Romulus. At first glance, however, the Gospel stories about Jesus would not appear to fit very well into Rank's series of features. Although Matthew's and Luke's genealogies place Joseph in the lineage of King David, Joseph and Mary are themselves not distinguished. In contrast to many other biblical "heroes" such as Isaac or Samuel or John the Baptist, Jesus' birth is not preceded by difficulties (typically prolonged barrenness) at all; Mary is suddenly pregnant, not having "known a man." There are indeed prophecies that the child about to be born will become king or savior of his people, but those prophecies are not threatening to the father or his representative. In contrast to Moses in the Exodus story, Jesus is not surrendered to water in a box. Nor is he rescued or suckled by animals; and the "lowly people" who care for Jesus are his own parents. After he has grown up, rather than finding his parents, he leaves them but does not take revenge on his father; and although he is temporarily acknowledged in the "triumphal entry," he is then ignominiously executed, with ironically mocking "honors." Only after death does he receive "rank and honor," but then it is from God and not from his own people. Of Rank's six motifs, only parts of the first, third, and sixth apply to stories about Jesus. In many other respects he would appear almost to be an antihero.

A second look may be necessary, however, because Rank did not very carefully describe the features of his own "hero myths." The difficulties are both descriptive and theoretical.[12] Apparently he did not attend to the details of the very stories he cites or summarizes. This oversight was surely partly due to his already having a sense of what particular symbols mean. For example, the motif of surrendering the baby hero to the water in a box occurs in barely half of his "myths," but from his study of dream symbolism he already has in mind that "the exposure in the water signifies no more and no less than the *symbolic expression of birth,*" with the box being the womb.[13] Indeed, Rank appears to have in mind a scheme for what any of the myths as a whole means: "This complicated myth with its promiscuous array of personages is thus simplified and reduced to three actors, namely the hero and his parents."[14] Not surprisingly, Rank has found that the prophecy of the hero's birth is threatening to the "father," with Herod being simply another father figure for the nascent hero Jesus. Thus, besides foreclosing the discovery of more complex meaning from the more complex details in the hero stories in his reduction of the myth to three actors, Rank's Freudian scheme is objectionable as a psychoanalytical and psychosocial interpretation of symbol and myth. It personalizes or individualizes what should be understood at a transpersonal cultural level, where a more complex set of relations may be involved.

If we attend more closely to the very "myths" cited by Rank, some significant revision of his descriptions of features becomes necessary. Thus (1) it is not always the immediate parents who are "distinguished" (esp. royal) but often the paternal or maternal grandfather or other ancestor; and the hero is often the son of a god as well, with his mother often being a virgin. (2) The difficulties preceding (or surrounding) the hero's birth seldom include prolonged barrenness, but they do often include obstacles placed in the way by the present ruler. That factor, moreover, is often closely related to (3): the birth prophecy is usually threatening not to the hero's own father but, as just noticed, to the present ruler, who may or may not be related. (4) The infant hero may indeed not always or even ordinarily be "surrendered to the water in a box," but he is usually exposed or threatened with death in some way. (5) The infant hero is often saved (and suckled) by animals or lowly people, but while many are then also raised by lowly foster parents, some are raised by "distinguished" or royal foster parents.

This correction of Rank's descriptions better to fit the other hero myths he cites was done without taking the Jesus stories into account. Thus it is all the more striking that the stories about Jesus' infancy display parallels to nearly all of the features integral to stories about the other heroes. (1) Besides his distinguished royal ancestry, Jesus is born of a virgin and is the son of God as well. (2) While the Jesus stories do not contain the motif of the mother's prolonged barrenness, which is infrequent in the hero myths anyhow, they do involve the more frequent motif of obstacles thrown in the way by rulers: the journey made necessary by Caesar's census decree. (3) Closely connected, the prophecy of the child's eventual heroism implicit in the Magi's star is taken by King Herod as a direct threat to his own rule. (4) Herod's hostile reaction threatens death for the newly born hero Jesus, who is "spirited away" (as in many of Raglan's traditions as well as Rank's). (5) Especially if the "son of God" (distinguished parent) motif is emphasized in (1), then it is clearly the "lowly people" Joseph (foster father or stepfather) and Mary who rescue and raise the hero Jesus. The series of parallels between the Jesus stories and the myths cited by Rank is impressive, especially considering that they constitute many of the central motives and relationships of the Gospel infancy narratives. More particularly, in terms of typical scholarly biblical studies, nearly all of these features and relations occur in the fundamental (often pre-Matthean and pre-Lucan) traditions to which the distinctive Matthean and Lucan interpretative touches have been added.

Once we begin to scrutinize Rank's myths more closely, however, it is tempting to analyze their motifs and relations even more precisely. With regard to the ancestry, consider, for example, the distinguished "father" (the figure threatened by the prophecy or oracle). It is relatively rare among Rank's stories that the hero's own father is the focal figure, as in the Oedipus myth. The grandfather (or great-uncle), particularly the maternal grandfather, is far more frequently the focal (threatened) figure. In some of those same myths, moreover, the actual father is a god. Furthermore, the mother, besides being distinguished and usually royal, is often a virgin. Thus whereas nearly all of the heroes have distinguished parents, heroes such as Heracles, Perseus, and Romulus all have divine fathers along with virginal royal mothers; and with

Cyrus they share a threatened and hostile grandfather or great-uncle as the focal father figure in the story.

With regard to Rank's features (2), (3), and (4), as the one to whom or against whom the prophecy is given, the focal grandfather is often the agent of the difficulties surrounding or preceding the hero's conception (by his own daughter), and he is the one who threatens the infant hero's life, either by direct action or more often by ordering the child exposed. Only rarely does the actual father attack the child or order it exposed, as in the Oedipus story again. In the case of Heracles the threatened hostile figure is the goddess Hera, and the agent of exposure is his own mother. The exposure itself, while often on water in a box, basket, or tub, can also be in a field or on a mountain. The rescue and raising of the hero, finally, can be divided or shared between animals and lowly parents, although the raising is often done by distinguished foster parents, as again with Oedipus.

Greater specificity is also pertinent with regard to the overall career or content of the hero's heroism, left rather vague and fluid in Rank's treatment. Some of his heroes happen to have died in their pursuit of heroism, and some were simply an embarrassment (e.g., Paris). But most of the heroes cited by Rank were kings, and many of them were founders of cities or a royal dynasty, perhaps by replacing the previous ruler. Even more striking with regard to some of the basic motives in the Jesus stories, it has to be significant that Cyrus, the founder of the Persian empire (and the "messiah" who liberated the exiled Jews from Babylon), Perseus, the king of Argos and founder-builder of Mycene, and Romulus, the founder of Rome, all share most of the same particular features delineated just above.[15] The grandfather, who is the existing ruler, is the focal "father" who is threatened by the prophecy of the hero's birth and the agent of both the difficulties in conception and the attempt on the hero's life or the exposure in all of these cases. Moreover, although the means of exposure varies somewhat, the rescue and raising is accomplished either by animals or by lowly people or both. In all of these cases, of course, the hero eventually succeeds in founding a city or an empire.

The stories of all these founding figures were current in the Hellenistic culture in which the Jesus stories were shaped. Hence it is significant that the stories about Jesus' infancy share some of the particular features and relationships present in the myths of these founders. Most striking are the parallels in the divine fatherhood and the virgin mother that Jesus shares with Perseus and Romulus (and perhaps Heracles), the prophecy of the hero's threat to the existing ruler, shared with Cyrus and Perseus (and Aelian's Gilgamesh), and the threat to the child hero's life by the threatened existing ruler in all of these cases. The most complete and striking cases of "the myth of the birth of the hero" revolve around the person, relationships, and potential for heroism of the founder of a new sociopolitical order. It has been argued that readers or hearers of the infancy stories of Jesus would have been familiar with features such as dreams, portents, and childhood prodigies from contemporary accounts of important figures, such as the biographies of the Caesars by Suetonius.[16] Judging from stories of figures such as Perseus, Theseus, Cyrus, or Romulus, people in the Hellenistic-Roman world would have been familiar with an even more deeply rooted pattern, implicit in the infancy narratives of Jesus, of birth of the founder of a new sociopolitical order.

Rank, the Jungians, and their avid recent readers were searching for the psychological or spiritual significance of the hero (birth) myth, with little thought for the sociopolitical circumstances or implications of myths that they viewed as analogous to (collective) dreams. But there is no reason to separate the psychospiritual dimension from the sociopolitical, much less to argue the validity of the one as opposed to the other. In fact, we should work at countering our modern individualistic presuppositions and biases. The Jungians insisted on the "transpersonal" meaning of hero legends over against Rank's Freudian reduction in terms of the relations of child and parents. We, in turn, can insist on inclusion of the social and historical dimensions over against the Jungian psychospiritual reduction, particularly in terms of "archetypes" conceived in terms of patriarchal familial relations. In fact, many of the Jungian interpretations of "the hero myth" make far more sense if understood in social as well as psychological terms. Since few of us would claim that the self develops apart from social relationships in a historical context, it makes no sense to interpret myths as if the real subject were the self that projects inner development onto the outside world. Myths or legends, rather, are rooted in social relationships, which is the persupposition of their serving as paradigms or models of personal or transpersonal development.

It is not difficult to reformulate in more adequate sociopolitical (along with psychological) terms some typical Jungian interpretations of "the hero myth."[17] The grandfathers or sometimes the fathers (who are significantly mentioned explicitly as the existing rulers, hence are not merely symbolic) represent the old order, the established sociopolitical relationships as well as the legitimating cultural canons that would normally simply be handed down from one generation to the next. The hero, however, is about to challenge the old order, the ruling system, and the old cultural values. The divine parentage represents the higher order, power, and new values that transcend the old order. That the hero is descended from the reigning king, his grandfather, provides a link with and a legitimate claim to his rule or the rule of the new order. The dominant theme of the whole story or set of stories is the struggle for rule. The king-grandfather has a premonition or receives a prophecy that his rule (the old system) is threatened and understandably takes steps to secure it—in particular, by eliminating the threat in its "infancy." But the inner drive and the higher source, calling, or loyalty of the hero is so powerful that it can overcome exposure in the wilderness or chaotic waters and other obstacles thrown in the path in realizing the new order. "The hero serves as a model. . . . The formation of the personality is symbolically portrayed in his life—he is the first 'personality', and his example is followed by all who become personalities."[18] But that development is dependent on what happened in the sociohistorical context represented in the legends. As the folklorists and anthropologists point out in their very definitions, the legends are taken seriously, are regarded as true in the society in which they function.

An important conclusion to be drawn from the preceding analysis is that, even when the infancy narratives of Jesus are understood as legends of the birth of the hero, the meaning cannot be reduced to a psychospiritual one, but has a sociopolitical dimension as well. Jesus is the hero of a new order, which becomes internalized in those persons who look to him as the model of the new humanity. But that new order, both social and personal, is not merely "religious" or "spiritual." Like the birth legends of Romulus, the founder of Rome, the birth legends of Jesus have sociopolitical implications.

It was argued in Chapter 1 above, of course, that the infancy stories of Jesus differ from or transcend the usual legends of the birth of the hero in a number of significant respects. When we focus on the particular details in the narratives rather than on the motifs similar to hero legends, then Jesus begins to look almost like an antihero. The whole pattern of relationships portrayed in the stories of Jesus' birth, moreover, is much more complex and significantly different from that we have discerned in the legends of the heroes cited. Both the narrative detail and the typically biblical literary patterns in the infancy stories of Jesus indicate that they originated in and reflect a distinctive Palestinian Jewish ethos, not the Hellenistic milieu presupposed and expressed in the hero legends. Thus the stories of Jesus' birth, like those of Moses' birth, appear to be narratives about the liberation of subjected people rather than typical hero legends.

Nevertheless, it is clear that, when the focus lies on the motifs similar to those in legends of the birth of the hero, the stories of Jesus' birth are easily understandable in terms of the typical hero pattern, which, we have now seen, has a clear sociopolitical dimension. In fact, the stories of Christ's birth were very likely understood in such terms, particularly considering that the hero pattern was already prominent, with numerous representative heroes such as Hercules and Romulus, in the Hellenistic-Roman culture in which Christianity became established. If the above sketch of the meaning of the basic pattern implicit in legends of the birth of Jesus and other heroes is even close to adequate (i.e., that the [grand]father/old order is confronted by the new order in the person of the infant hero, who has transcendent divine parentage and the divinely given power to overcome obstacles placed by the old rule[r]), then by late antiquity it was evident that Christ was the hero who established the new order in opposition to the old order, whether that of Judaism, represented by Herod and Jerusalem, or that of Rome, represented by Caesar Augustus.

In any case, the humble origins of the infancy narratives would have been understood as the appropriate (typical) origin that led to the imperial outcome of Christ as the ruler of the world. One might even argue that the pattern expressed in the hero legends is still operative in in certain theologically determined biblical interpretation. That is, the old rule/old order was Judaism, with the law and salvation by merit, which is confronted by the hero Jesus Christ, who breaks the law and is rejected and attacked by the representatives of Judaism/the law but who finally, vindicated by God, ends the reign of the law and brings the new rule of grace and love. That interpretation of "the myth of the birth of the hero" is not simply implicit in certain Christian theological interpretation, for example, of Paul and the law in Galatians or Romans, but its components are displayed explicitly in commentaries on Matthew 1–2 and Luke 1–2, representative items of which were cited in chapter 1.

This examination of the hero legends and the hero pattern thus leads finally to the same critical point already articulated in chapter 1. That is, when the emphasis is on the general pattern typical of the hero legends across several cultures, the meaning of the infancy stories of Jesus may be assimilated or reduced to dominant cultural or theological concerns. Attention to the concrete particulars in the birth narratives of Jesus is important precisely to provide some minimal control on any proclivity to our own dominant, and perhaps unconscious, views and concerns.

Notes

Abbreviations

ANRW	*Aufstieg und Niedergang der Römischen Welt*
BJRL	*Bulletin of the John Rylands Library*
CBQ	*Catholic Biblical Quarterly*
HJP	E. Schürer, *The History of the Jewish People in the Age of Jesus Christ: A New English Version*. Revised and edited by G. Vermes and F. Millar. 3 vols. Edinburgh: T. & T. Clark, 1973–86.
HTR	*Harvard Theological Review*
ICC	International Critical Commentary
IDB	*The Interpreter's Dictionary of the Bible*
IDB Sup.	*IDB* Supplementary Volume
IG	*Inscriptiones Graecae*
JBL	*Journal of Biblical Literature*
JJS	*Journal of Jewish Studies*
JPFC	*The Jewish People in the First Century*. Edited by S. Safrai and M. Stern. 2 vols. Assen: Van Gorcum, 1974–76.
JR	*Journal of Religion*
JTS	*Journal of Theological Studies*
NTS	*New Testament Studies*
OGIS	*Orientis Graeci Inscriptiones Selectae*
RB	*Revue Biblique*
RQ	*Revue de Qumrân*
RSV	Revised Standard Version
SBLDS	Society of Biblical Literature Dissertation Series
TDNT	*Theological Dictionary of the New Testament*
WHJP	*The World History of the Jewish People*. First Series: Ancient Times. Edited by A. Schalit. Vol. 6: *The Hellenistic Age*. Edited by A. Schalit. Vol. 7: *The Herodian Period*. Edited by M. Avi Yonah. New Brunswick, N.J.: Rutgers University Press, 1972–75.
ZNW	*Zeitschrift für die neutestamentliche Wissenschaft*

Introduction

1. R. E. Brown, *The Virginal Conception and Bodily Resurrection of Jesus* (New York: Paulist, 1973); and "Appendix 4: Virginal Conception," in his *Birth of the Messiah: A Commentary on the Infancy Narratives in Matthew and Luke* (Garden City, N.Y.: Doubleday, 1977), 517–33 (hereafter cited as *BM*).

Chapter 1/The Christmas Story

1. Johann Philipp Gabler, a student of Eichhorn, writing in 1800, as quoted in W. G. Kümmel, *The New Testament: The History of the Investigation of Its Problems* (London: SCM, 1970), 103.

2. D. F. Strauss, *The Life of Jesus Critically Examined* (trans. George Eliot; Philadelphia: Fortress, 1972; German original, 1835), 757.

3. A. Harnack, *What Is Christianity?* (New York: Harper & Row, 1957; German original, 1900), 51.

4. R. Bultmann, *Jesus and the Word* (New York: Scribners, 1958; German original, 1926); G. Bornkamm, *Jesus of Nazareth* (New York: Harper & Brothers, 1960).

5. Brown (*BM*) has summarized and critically discussed virtually all such material for both Matt. 1–2 and Luke 1–2; J. Fitzmyer, *Gospel according to Luke* (Anchor; 2 vols.; Garden City, N.Y.: Doubleday, 1981–85), has supplied most of it for Luke 1–2.

6. A. Plummer, *The Gospel according to Saint Luke* (ICC; Edinburgh: T. & T. Clark, 1896), 6. Indeed, the origin of the story of the Magi cannot be explained unless it is true, says Plummer, *An Exegetical Commentary on the Gospel according to Saint Matthew* (London: Scott, 1909), 11–12. H. Balmforth, *The Gospel according to Saint Luke* (Clarendon Bible; Oxford: Clarendon, 1930), 121; and G. B. Caird, *Saint Luke* (Westminister; Philadelphia: Westminister, 1963), also find a substratum of historical facts behind the legendary or mythical narratives.

7. Balmforth, *Luke*, 121.

8. W. Manson, *The Gospel of Luke* (Moffatt; London: Hodder & Stoughton, 1930), 4.

9. F. V. Filson, *The Gospel according to St. Matthew* (Harpers; New York: Harper & Brothers, 1960), 56; Caird, *Saint Luke*.

10. Plummer, *Matthew*, 13, 16; Balmforth, *Luke*, 124; B. S. Easton, *The Gospel according to Saint Luke* (New York: Scribners, 1926), 15.

11. Manson, *Luke*, 12.

12. Caird, *Saint Luke*, 58.

13. F. W. Green, *The Gospel according to Saint Matthew* (Clarendon Bible; Oxford: Clarendon, 1936), 106.

14. E. E. Ellis, *The Gospel of Luke* (New Century; London: Nelson, 1966), 81–82.

15. Plummer, *Matthew*, 14; Filson, *Matthew*, 57–58; J. C. Fenton, *Saint Matthew* (Westminster; Philadelphia: Westminister, 1963), 44; E. Schweizer, *The Good News according to Matthew* (Atlanta: John Knox, 1975), 37; prominent also in Brown, *BM*.

16. E.g., Balmforth, *Luke*, 123–24.

17. E.g., Plummer, *Luke*, 65; Balmforth, *Luke*, 119, 129; Caird, *Saint Luke*, 48; Brown, *BM*, 450; Fitzmyer, *Luke* 1.426.

18. Ellis, *Luke*, 75; Caird, *Saint Luke*, 55.

19. Caird, *Saint Luke*, 48.

20. H. Conzelmann, *The Theology of St. Luke* (New York: Harper & Row, 1960; German original, 1954).

21. K. Stendahl, "Quis et Unde? An Analysis of Mt 1–2," in *Judentum, Urchristentum, Kirche* (Festschrift J. Jeremias; ed. W. Eltester; Berlin: Töpelmann, 1964; reprinted in *Interpretation of Matthew* [ed. G. N. Stanton; Philadelphia: Fortress Press, 1983], 56–66), 97. Stendahl's article is important and influential and is followed with further refinement by Brown (*BM*, chaps. 1 and 5).

22. Stendahl, "Quis et Unde?" 98; Brown, *BM*, 179–80.

23. As Stendahl himself points out, the text mentions "Herod's name 9 times, and at all points of progress in the account" ("Quis et Unde?" 99).

24. Cf. Brown, *BM*, 180; but Brown himself points out in Appendix 3 that expectation of the messiah's birth at Bethlehem is not attested "until considerably later in Jewish writings."

25. For a sketch of these popular Jewish kings and their movements, see R. A. Horsley and J. S. Hanson, *Bandits, Prophets, and Messiahs* (Minneapolis: Winston-Seabury, 1985), chap. 3.

26. Brown, *BM*, 183; see further pp. 180–83.

27. Ibid., 183.

28. J. D. Kingsbury, *Matthew: Structure, Christology, Kingdom* (Philadelphia: Fortress, 1975), 46.

29. Contra ibid., 36, etc.

30. H. H. Oliver, "The Lucan Birth Stories and the Purpose of Luke-Acts," *NTS* 10 (1964) 203–26.

31. Respectively, Fitzmyer, *Luke* 1.10 (Acts 24:5, 14; 28:22 are hardly Luke's own view of "the way" but are his depiction of other Jews' characterization of it as a *hairesis*, or "party/sect"); and Brown, *BM*, 242–43, etc.

32. C. H. Talbert, *Reading Luke* (New York: Crossroad, 1982), 22–24. Similarly, the "miraculous conception" was necessary theologically in order to prevent claim to salvation by human merit, such as Paul encountered in Galatia, according to highly influential mid-nineteenth-century German Lutheran scholarship (p. 21). It is highly questionable that "the Lucan view" is accurately reflected by a late-twentieth-century advocate of "the nonresistant church" (p. 25).

33. E.g., C. Clemen, *Religionsgeschichtliche Erklärung des Neuen Testaments* (Giessen: Töpelmann, 1909); H. Usener, "Geburt und Kindheit Christi," *ZNW* 4 (1903) 1–21; H. Gressmann, *Das Weihnachts-Evangelium* (Göttingen: Vandenhoeck & Ruprecht, 1914); E. Norden, *Die Geburt des Kindes: Geschichte einer religiösen Idee* (Leipzig: Teubner, 1924).

34. Otto Rank, *Myth of the Birth of the Hero* (New York: Vintage, 1959; German original, 1909).

35. See especially E. Neumann, *The Origins and History of Consciousness* (New York: Bollingen Foundation, 1954; numerous reprintings, including Princeton: Princeton University Press, 1970; German original, 1949).

36. Joseph Campbell, *The Hero with a Thousand Faces* (New York: Bollingen Foundation, 1949; numerous reprintings, including Princeton: Princeton University Press, 1968).

37. It may be a significant indicator of the intensity of interest in Jungian thought that, in many university and seminary libraries, *all* volumes by Jung were listed as "missing" in the early 1970s.

38. A. Dundes, *The Hero Pattern and the Life of Jesus,* published with numerous responses (ed. W. Wuellner; Berkeley, Calif.: Center for Hermeneutical Studies, 1977). The most incisive response is by the Slavicist M. P. Coote, pp. 42–43. The lecture

itself is reprinted in A. Dundes, *Interpreting Folklore* (Bloomington: Indiana University Press, 1980). A. B. Lord, "The Gospels as Oral Traditional Literature," in *The Relationships among the Gospels* (ed. W. O. Walker; San Antonio: Trinity University Press, 1978).

39. W. Bascom, "The Forms of Folklore: Prose Narratives," *Journal of American Folklore* 78 (1965) 4. Cf. the similar definition by the anthropologist P. S. Cohen, "Theories of Myth," *Man*, n.s., 4 (1969) 337. For Cohen, myth is a sacred narrative in symbolic form referring to origins, some of the objects and events in which do not exist or occur in the world outside of itself. There is general agreement that the term *myth* be used for sacred traditional narratives about supernatural or superhuman (or nonhuman) beings such as spirits or gods (or animals); see J. Fontenrose, *The Ritual Theory of Myth* (Berkeley: University of California Press, 1966), 54–55.

40. Cf. further Cohen, "Theories of Myth," 337: "The sacred quality and the reference to origins and transformations distinguish myth from legend and other types of folktale. The narration of events and reference to objects unknown outside the world of myth differentiates myth from history or pseudohistory." See also G. S. Kirk, *Myth: Its Meaning and Functions in Ancient and Other Cultures* (Berkeley: University of California Press, 1971), 31–41. Saying that folktales are not taken seriously does not imply that they do not have a serious social function or effect.

41. R. A. Oden (*The Bible without Theology* [San Francisco: Harper & Row, 1987], 58) quickly broadens the definition when he moves from biblical materials to a traditional narrative, "at least one of whose characters" is superhuman. His discussion of myths (pp. 59–90) is based in substance and procedure largely on Cohen, "Theories of Myth."

42. Oden's reflections in *Bible without Theology*, chap. 2, appear to accept rather than to challenge those alternatives.

43. Rank's "myth of the birth of the hero," along with related work of Lord Raglan and A. Dundes, is critically examined in the Appendix below.

44. In a seeming reversal of the typical hero pattern, Moses is rescued and raised by exalted royal foster parents at the court of Pharaoh.

45. "In fact, these chapters are so thoroughly permeated with the words of the ancient prophecies that they suggest a close community setting where a kind of archaic scriptural rhetoric is the living language of faith" (D. L. Tiede, *Prophecy and History in Luke-Acts* [Philadelphia: Fortress, 1980], 25).

46. Brown lays out the form in graphic detail in *BM*, Table 8, p. 156. He discusses the use of the pattern in Luke 1 on pp. 292–98.

47. E.g., M. M. Bourke, "The Literary Genus of Matthew 1–2," *CBQ* 22 (1960) 160–75; cf. the judicious discussion in Brown, *BM*, Appendix 8, pp. 557–63.

48. Brown, *BM*, 155–59.

49. Ibid., 108–9, Tables 6 and 7, both demonstrates the pattern and reconstructs the hypothesized "source."

50. Brown, *BM*, 117, 192. Cf. the delineation of pre-Matthean sources by C. T. Davis, "Tradition and Redaction in Matthew 1:18–2:23," *JBL* 90 (1971) 404–21; and G. M. Soares Prabhu, *The Formula Quotations in the Infancy Narratives of Matthew* (Rome: Biblical Institute Press, 1976), 294–99 and charts.

51. See Brown's list of ostensible parallels between Jesus and Moses, in *BM*, 113.

52. See ibid., 114–15.

53. See further the Appendix below.

54. For a recent literary and historical analysis that indicates how intertwined the legendary reports of Herodotus are with apparently historical figures, relationships,

and events, see I. M. Diakonoff, "Medea," in *The Cambridge Ancient History of Iran* (Cambridge: Cambridge University Press, 1985), 142–48.

55. In these cases, historical figures would appear to have attracted motifs from the legendary pattern rather than particular legends focused on heroic motifs having attracted particular details from historical figures, as is illustrated also in the analysis above of Josephus's report of Moses' birth.

56. E.g., Talbert, *Reading Luke*. By contrast, Tiede *(Prophecy and History in Luke-Acts)* places analysis and understanding of the narrative squarely and critically in the broadest concrete historical context.

Chapter 2/Caesar and Census

1. Fitzmyer, *Luke* 1.393.
2. Brown, *BM*, 414–15.
3. Fitzmyer, *Luke* 1.393–94.
4. Brown, *BM*, 415.
5. Fitzmyer obscures the issue by framing his interpretation in dogmatic terms of the different phases of Jesus' existence (*Luke* 1.204).
6. *British Museum Inscriptions*, 894; see this and the other inscriptions translated in F. C. Grant, *Ancient Roman Religion* (New York: Liberal Arts, 1957), 174–76.
7. W. Dittenberger, *Sylloge Inscriptionem Graecarum* (4 vols; 3d ed.; Leipzig: Teubner, 1915–24), 2.364; 3.797.
8. Translation of E. R. Goodenough, *Yale Classical Studies* 1 (1928) 67–68.
9. E. Barker, "The Concept of Empire," in *The Legacy of Rome* (ed. C. Bailey; Oxford: Clarendon, 1923), 65.
10. C. H. V. Sutherland, *Roman Imperial Coinage* (London, n.d.), 120, nos. 210–11; cf. 119, no. 209; 181, no. 335.
11. Aelius Aristides, *To Rome* (trans. S. Levin; Glencoe, Ill., 1950), 30, 60.
12. Brown, *BM*, 394–95, and Appendix 7, 547–55; Fitzmyer, *Luke* 1.400–405.
13. Brown, *BM*, 412, 414.
14. Fitzmyer, *Luke* 1.393.
15. R. A. Horsley, *Jesus and the Spiral of Violence* (San Francisco: Harper & Row, 1987), 162–63.
16. See further below; and see ibid., 306–17.

Chapter 3/Herod, Jerusalem, and the Magi

1. K. Stendahl, "Quis et Unde?"
2. So Brown, *BM*, 181–82.
3. Following Brown or the Jerusalem Bible, instead of the RSV's "troubled."
4. Schalit (*WHJP*, 60) suggests that "the whole country" as well as Jerusalem had risen in revolt against Herod and Phasael.
5. M. Stern, "The Reign of Herod," *WHJP*, 79.
6. *OGIS 2*, no. 414; *IG* 2, nos. 3440–41.
7. Josephus's comments on the Jews Herod settled in Batanea, initially free of either taxes or tribute, show how the imposition of only one of these layers of taxes could crush people economically (*Ant.* 14.23–28).
8. See Horsley, *Jesus and Violence*, 99–105.
9. A. Schalit, *König Herodes: Der Mann und sein Werke* (Berlin: de Gruyter, 1969), 473–79.

10. As attested in an inscription (*OGIS 2*, no. 415).

11. See further Horsley, *Jesus and Violence*, 71–77.

12. Macrobius, *Saturnalia* 2.4.2. That the non-Christian writer Macrobius, about A.D. 400, who shows no other sign of Christian influence, has this quip linked with Herod's massacre of the children from Matt. 2 indicates that the two separate incidents had already come together in popular or literary tradition.

13. Similarly, to focus on the seemingly continuous intrigues and suspicions at Herod's court and on his periodic execution of political rivals, wives, and other sons, while it further dramatizes his brutality, would divert attention from the whole system of exploitation, repression, and fear that Herod instituted and symbolized.

14. Y. Yadin, *Masada* (New York: Random House, 1966) is the most accessible book (with pictures) on Masada, although his assertions about the Zealots on Masada lack historical evidence.

15. Josephus suggests that Herod's gifts to Hellenistic cities and other rulers were also made with an eye toward his security: "He also surrounded himself with security on the outside, as though making this a reinforcement for himself against his subjects" (*Ant.* 15.326).

16. "To keep them from starting any trouble without his learning of it [he had] men stationed near them at all times and thus could discover and prevent it" (ibid., 295).

17. See further Schürer-Vermes, *HJP* 1.505 n. 20.

18. See further Horsley and Hanson, *Bandits, Prophets, and Messiahs*, chap. 3.

19. Brown, *BM*, 183, etc.

20. On the concentration of the Temple revenues under the control of the high priests, see the section entitled "Priests" in chap. 5.

21. There is no evidence, for example, that the revolt took the form of a messianic movement, as happened in 4 B.C.E. or 68–70 C.E.

22. Because of his disfigurement, Hyrcanus no longer qualified to serve as pontiff.

23. See Josephus, *Ant.* 15.18–22, 40–41, 51–56, 319–22; 17.78, 161–67.

24. Ibid. 20.180–81, 206–7, 213–14; see further in the section entitled "Priests" in chap. 5.

25. There is no concern with complexities such as the scribal and scholarly resistance to Herod noted above. The experience of most Palestinian Jews was surely similar to that portrayed in the gospel tradition, that the Pharisees and scribes generally represented the established order.

26. See further chap. 5.

27. M. Hengel and H. Merkel, "Die Magier aus dem Osten und die Flucht nach Ägypten (Mt 2) . . . ," in *Orientierung an Jesus* (Festschrift Joseph Schmid; ed. P. Hoffmann; Freiburg: Herder, 1973), 152; and F. W. Beare, *The Gospel according to Matthew* (Oxford: Blackwell, 1981), 72.

28. Brown, *BM*, 178, 182–83, 196, 199.

29. J. C. Marsh-Edwards, "The Magi in Tradition and Art," *Irish Ecclesiastical Record* 85 (1956) 3.

30. Herodotus 1.107–8, 120, 128, 204. See Further Cicero, *Div.* 1.23.46; Ammianus Marcellinus 33.6.32–35.

31. Herodotus 1.132, 140; 7.191, 133–34; Strabo 15.3.13–14 (732); 15.3.18 (733); Xenophon, *Cyropaedia* 7.5.35, 57; 8.1.23–24.

32. S. K. Eddy, *The King Is Dead* (Lincoln: University of Nebraska Press, 1961), 67, with references, n. 7.

33. Ibid., 65–67.

34. Brown seems to assume that the Magi as kings is a product of Christian interpretation (*BM,* 197–98).
35. See, e.g., J. H. Charlesworth, "Jewish Astrology in the Talmud, Pseudepi-
grapha, the Dead Sea Scrolls, and Early Palestinian Synagogues," *HTR* 70 (1977)
183–200.
36. Herodotus 7.136; Justin 6.2; Plutarch, *Arat.* 22.4; Aelian, *Var. Hist.* 1.21;
cf. the throne-hall reliefs in E. F. Schmid, *Persepolis* (Chicago: University of Chicago
Press, 1953), vol. 1, plates 98–99.
37. Strabo, 15.3.14–15 (732–33); Pliny, *Nat. Hist.* 25.13—or is Pliny using *magi*
as a generic term, i.e., as "the sacred philosophers" or "the magicians" of Persia, Arabia,
Ethiopia, and Egypt?
38. Thucydides 8.109; Cicero, *Div.* 1.23.47; Plutarch, *Alex.* 3.4.
39. Eddy, *King Is Dead,* chap. 3.
40. J. W. Swain, "The Theory of the Four Monarchies: Opposition History under
the Roman Empire," *Classical Philology* 35 (1940) 1–21.
41. Eddy, *King Is Dead,* 23–36.
42. Ibid., chaps. 1–3.
43. Recounted in Dio Cassius, *Roman History* 63.1–7; Suetonius, *Nero,* 13; Pliny,
Nat. Hist. 30.6.16–17.
44. The laurel wreath was laid only when a *triumph* was celebrated, and the doors
of the temple of Janus were closed only very rarely, as when Augustus had brought
"peace" to the whole world (on which see above). Cf. the more elaborate description
in Dio Cassius, *Roman History* 67.1–7, where he notes briefly, apropos of Matt. 2:12,
that Tiridates "did not return by the route he had followed in coming."
45. Beare, *Matthew,* 74–75.
46. R. D. Aus, "The Magi at the Birth of Cyrus and the Magi at Jesus' Birth in
Matt 2:1–12," in *Religion, Literature, and Society in Ancient Israel: Formative Christianity
and Judaism* (Festschrift H. C. Kee; 2 vols.; ed. J. Neusner, P. Borgen, E. S. Frerichs,
and R. A. Horsley; New York: University Press of America, 1987), 99–114.
47. Brown, *BM,* 109–16 and 190–92. Brown then finds the background of the
Magi story in the Balaam narrative in Num. 22–24; but what he reconstructs as the
pre-Matthean story of the Magi shows little similarity to the Balaam material.
48. See further *BM,* 191–92, for Brown's own explanatory notes and discussion.
49. See H. Greeven, *"Proskyneō," TDNT* 6.763–64.

Chapter 4/"To All the People"

1. On this point and the following, see the recent survey of scholarship by N.
Lohfink, "Von der 'Anawim-Partei' zur Kirche der Armen: Die bibelwissenschaftliche
Ahnentafel eines Hauptbegriffs der 'Theologie der Befreiung,' " *Biblica* 67 (1986)
153–76.
2. See particularly A. Gelin, *The Poor of Yahweh* (Collegeville, Minn.: Liturgical
Press, 1964; French original, 1953), to which Brown directs us.
3. Besides Lohfink, "Von der 'Anawim-Partei,' " see, e.g., D. P. Seccombe, *Possessions and the Poor in Luke-Acts* (Linz: Studien zum Neuen Testament und seiner
Umwelt, 1982), 24–28.
4. P. Davies, "Hasidim in the Maccabean Period," *JJS* 28 (1977) 127–38.
5. Brown, *BM,* 267–68 n. 13; 351.
6. The scholarly basis cited by Brown (*BM,* 267) is a three-paragraph article, R.
Schnackenburg, "Tempelfrömmigkeit," in *Lexikon für Theologie und Kirche* (2d ed.,

vol. 9, cols. 1358–59), the relevant paragraph of which is a highly synthetic reference to various facets of the significance of and attitudes toward the Temple, particularly in the Psalms and postexilic prophetic books.

7. The RSV translation "attending the temple," in Acts 2:46, is misleading insofar as we think of "attending church" or "attending mass."

8. Brown, *BM,* 353.

9. Brown writes also of "the Temple cult," "the holy place of Israel," and of Simeon's "standing before the sanctuary" (ibid., 453). However important these motifs are for a christology that sees Jesus' embodying "much of what was associated with the Temple," none of them is present in the story.

10. According to Brown (ibid., 452–53, 466–67).

11. As Brown himself suggests (ibid., 467).

12. So also ibid., 468.

13. Simple class conflict within Judah (or within the priesthood) and the special piety of the spiritually "poor" are clearly not only false alternatives for these psalms (and other biblical materials) but categories into which they do not fit.

14. Eric Wolf, *Peasants* (Englewood Cliffs, N.J.: Prentice-Hall, 1966), 3–4; see also pp. 12–17 on the following discussion.

15. We need more evidence and analysis of the economic situation of the Jewish peasantry in Roman Palestine. Perhaps the most informative presentations available currently are those of S. Applebaum, "Economic Life in Palestine," *JPFC* 2.631–700; and "Judaea as a Roman Province; the Countryside as a Political and Economic Factor," *ANRW* 2.8.355–96.

16. On the economics of debt and social conflict, see M. Goodman, "The First Revolt: Social Conflict and the Problem of Debt," *JJS* 33 (1982) 417–27.

17. For the early tradition of the Lord's Prayer, see J. Jeremias, *The Lord's Prayer* (Philadelphia: Fortress, 1973).

18. Brown, *BM,* 549; Fitzmyer, *Luke* 1.405.

19. P. Oxy., 2669; P. Ryl., 595; N. Lewis, *life in Egypt under Roman Rule* (Oxford: Clarendon, 1983), 161–65.

20. See further Horsley and Hanson, *Bandits, Prophets, and Messiahs,* chap. 2; and on Egypt, cf. Lewis, *Life in Egypt,* 203–4.

21. On this Jewish peasant strike, see further Horsley, *Jesus and Violence,* 110–16.

22. See, e.g., E. N. Luttwak, *The Grand Strategy of the Roman Empire* (Baltimore: Johns Hopkins University Press, 1976), 25–33, 41–47.

23. E.g., Mishnah, Nedarim 2.4: "The men of Galilee know naught of the terumah of the Temple chamber." Some of this evidence has been brought together in S. Freyne, *Galilee, from Alexander the Great to Hadrian* (Wilmington: Glazier, 1980), 277–87; curiously, Freyne draws a conclusion opposite of that indicated in his evidence, partly because he is attempting to refute the older stereotype that Galilee was a special hotbed of revolution.

24. See further W. Horbury, "The Temple Tax," in *Jesus and the Politics of His Day* (ed. E. Bammel and C. F. D. Moule; Cambridge: Cambridge University Press, 1986), 266–73; and Horsley, *Jesus and Violence,* 279–83.

25. See further F. M. Cross, *Canaanite Myth and Hebrew Epic* (Cambridge: Harvard University Press, 1973), 219–29; R. A. Horsley, "Popular Messianic Movements around the Time of Jesus," *CBQ* 46 (1984) 471–95.

26. E.g., Brown, *BM,* 442–43.

27. With Fitzmyer, *Luke* 1.432, but against his note on p. 427.

28. In *Discoveries in the Judean Desert* (ed. P. Benoit, J. T. Milik, R. de Vaux; Oxford: Clarendon, 1957), 2.124–32, 135; cf. coins from the revolt, in L. Cadman, *Coins from the Roman-Jewish War of 66–73* (Tel Aviv: Schocken, 1960).

29. J. Fitzmyer, review of J. P. Meier, *Law and History in Matthew's Gospel* (Rome: Pontifical Biblical Institute, 1976), *CBQ* 39 (1977) 438.

30. P. D. Miller, *The Divine Warrior in Early Israel* (Cambridge: Harvard University Press, 1973), 308 n. 11.

31. See further Horsley and Hanson, *Bandits, Prophets, and Messiahs*, 161–72.

32. See further ibid., 119–25.

Chapter 5/"A People Prepared"

1. E. Schüssler Fiorenza, *In Memory of Her* (New York: Crossroad, 1983), 29.

2. See, e.g., S. R. Johansson, " 'Herstory' as History: A New Field or Another Fad?" in *Liberating Women's History* (ed. B. A. Carroll; Urbana: University of Illinois Press, 1976), 415.

3. Schüssler Fiorenza, *In Memory of Her*, esp. pp. 138–40; idem, "Word, Spirit, and Power: Woman in Early Christian Communities," in *Woman of Spirit* (ed. R. Ruether and E. McLaughlin; New York: Simon & Schuster, 1979), 29–70; and L. Schottroff, "Women as Followers of Jesus in New Testament Times: An Exercise in Social-Historical Exegesis of the Bible," in *The Bible and Liberation* (ed. N. K. Gottwald; Maryknoll, N.Y.: Orbis, 1983), 418–27.

4. See further J. C. Exum, "You Shall Let Every Daughter Live," *Semeia* 28 (1983) 63–82.

5. See further F. Gottlieb, "Three Mothers," *Judaism* 30 (1981) 194–203.

6. See the incisive treatment of these four women in J. Schaberg, *The Illegitimacy of Jesus* (San Francisco: Harper & Row, 1987), 20–34.

7. See especially the analysis in P. Tribble, *God and the Rhetoric of Sexuality* (Philadelphia: Fortress, 1978), chap. 6.

8. Schüssler Fiorenza, *In Memory of Her*, 140–41.

9. This social development is laid out clearly in ibid., 143–51; similarly, Horsley, *Jesus and Violence*, 232–45.

10. As reconstructed in Schüssler Fiorenza, *In Memory of Her*, 149–50.

11. J. C. Anderson, "Mary's Difference: Gender and Patriarchy in the Birth Narrative," *JR* 67 (1987) 188.

12. See Schaberg, *Illegitimacy of Jesus*, 23, 28, 31, 33–34, for the significant lack of intervention by God in those circumstances according to the appropriate biblical texts—in contrast to frequent comments in the theological secondary literature.

13. See further Anderson, "Mary's Difference," 186–90.

14. See Schüssler Fiorenza, *In Memory of Her*, 142. T. Craven (*Artistry and Faith in the Book of Judith* [SBLDS 70; Chico, Calif.: Scholars, 1983[, 121) discerns something similar between Ruth and Naomi in the Book of Ruth, and between Judith and her maid in the Book of Judith.

15. The following discussion is based heavily on Schaberg, *Illegitimacy of Jesus*, 101–10.

16. As noted toward the end of chap. 1 above, this pattern is laid out graphically and discussed in Brown, *BM*, 155–59.

17. R. Alter, "How Conventions Help Us Read," *Prooftexts* 3 (1983) 115–30.

18. Schaberg, *Illegitimacy of Jesus*, 128–30; cf. T. Y. Mullins, "New Testament Commission Forms, Especially in Luke-Acts," *JBL* 95 (1976) 603–8; and B. Hubbard, "Commissioning Stories in Luke-Acts," *Semeia* 8 (1977) 105–20.

19. See further J.-P. Audet, "L'annonce à Marie," *RB* 63 (1956) 346–74.
20. Schaberg, *Illegitimacy of Jesus*, 127, 129.
21. Ibid., 135–36.
22. The problems inherent in that framework are compounded when the infancy narratives are reduced to androcentric christological formulations, which inevitably subsume Mary's person and function into that of her son.
23. Schaberg, *Illegitimacy of Jesus*, 143.
24. Schüssler Fiorenza, *In Memory of Her*, 49–52.
25. Brown, *BM*, 267–68.
26. Schürer-Vermes, *HJP* 2.269–70; more broadly discussed on pp. 257–74.
27. Joachim Jeremias, *Jerusalem at the Time of Jesus* (Philadelphia: Fortress, 1969), 199–201, based on information in the Letter of Aristeas, which compares with Josephus's figure of four groups of five thousand each.
28. TB Taanith, 27a; PT Taanith 4.69a; BT Berakoth, 44a.
29. T. Yebamoth 1.10; PT Yebamoth 1.3a; TB Pesahim, 57a; Kerithoth, 28b.
30. JT Taanith 4.8.69a.53; T. Sotah 13.8; PT Yoma 4 (or 6?).3.43c.58; and see further Jeremias, *Jerusalem*, 194 n. 146, 199 n. 170.
31. T. Betzah 3.8; T. Yoma 1.6; Sifra Emor, 2.
32. Jeremias, *Jerusalem*, 198–99; Josephus, *Life*, 2, and *Ant.* 7.366, confirms the existence of the twenty-four courses for the end of second-Temple times.
33. Josephus, *War* 2.197; *Apion* 2.77; Philo, *Leg.*, 157.
34. Fitzmyer, *Luke* 1.408.
35. On Luke 2:6–20 in particular, see Brown, *BM*, 411, and Fitzmyer, *Luke* 1.392. The one good example Fitzmyer offers as proof text (Luke 1:52) that the shepherds simply illustrate Luke's predilection for the lowly is clearly pre-Lucan, from the Magnificat, on which see below.
36. Brown, *BM*, 421–24.
37. See Fitzmyer, *Luke* 1.396, for concise, incisive critique of the *migdal eder* interpretation.
38. Ibid., 394–96. Similarly Brown, *BM*, 419–20.
39. It is difficult to see how Jesus' reply to the question about whether he would "at this time restore the kingdom to Israel" (Acts 1:6) could possibly be read to indicate that he was somehow rejecting a political dimension of the kingdom (contra, Fitzmyer, *Luke* 1.395.
40. M. Hengel, *"Phatnē," TDNT* 9.54.
41. Jeremias, *Jerusalem*, 303–12.
42. If Jesus were thus portrayed as born in the midst of shepherds as despised outcasts, the birth story would form an appropriate parallel to what many find to be perhaps the most distinctive aspect of his ministry—the association with other such outcasts, namely, "tax-collectors and sinners," beggars, cripples, and prostitutes. J. Jeremias (*"Poimēn," TDNT* 6.490) even suggests explicitly that Jesus' high estimation of shepherds reflects the actuality of his fellowship with the despised.
43. Large numbers were even imported from bedouin areas, as by the Idumean Baba ben Buti (PT Hagigah 2.781); see Applebaum, "Economic Life in Palestine," 670.
44. Fitzmyer (*Luke* 1.396) has more confidence than many would that the possessive pronoun in "their flock" indicates ownership, hence, that the shepherds are not poor. Presumably, with the plural, this would be communal (village or lineage) ownership.
45. Translation from Horsley and Hanson, *Bandits, Prophets, and Messiahs*, 113.

46. Good discussion of sign, but not application to the manger in particular, is in C. H. Giblin, "Reflections on the Sign of the Manger," *CBQ* 29 (1967) 87–101.

47. Following the Septuagint, which Luke and the early church would have known.

Chapter 6/Songs of Liberation

1. See, e.g., Brown, *BM*, 353.

2. See D. Jones, "The Background and Character of the Lukan Psalms," *JTS* 19 (1968) 19–50; and S. C. Farris, *The Hymns of Luke's Infancy Narrative* (Sheffield: JSOT Press, 1985).

3. G. Morawe, "Vergleich des Aufbaus der Danklieder und hymnischen Bekenntnislieder (1QH) von Qumran mit dem Aufbau der Psalmen im Alten Testament und im Spätjudentum," *RQ* 15 (1963) 323–56.

4. From Jones, "Background and Character," 47. Jones ironically draws a conclusion that is evidently the opposite of that to which his analyses point.

5. Suggestions of P. Winter, "Magnificat and Benedictus—Maccabean Psalms?" *BJRL* 37 (1954–55) 328–47; and Brown, *BM*, respectively.

6. R. Tannehill, "The Magnificat as Poem," *JBL* 93 (1974) 274.

7. Brown, *BM*, 351, 254, 363–64; Fitzmyer, *Luke* 1.384–85.

8. Brown, *BM*, 357, 352.

9. Tannehill, "Magnificat as Poem," 273.

10. See Brown, Table 12, pp. 358–60.

11. On the divine warrior, see esp. F. M. Cross, *Canaanite Myth and Hebrew Epic* (Cambridge: Harvard University Press, 1973), chaps. 5–6; and Miller, *Divine Warrior*.

12. The same point about "the arm of the Lord" being associated with the deliverance from Egypt is made from nonpsalmic traditions such as Exod. 6:6 and Deut. 4:34 by Brown (*BM*, 327), followed by Farris (*Hymns*, 121). On its association with the new exodus, see Isa. 51:9; 52:10; Ezek. 20:33–38.

13. See Brown, *BM*, 350–55.

14. H. Birkeland, *'Ani und 'Anaw in den Psalmen* (Oslo: Dybwad, 1933).

15. Cf. Fitzmyer, *Luke* 1.369.

16. E.g., Tannehill, "Magnificat as Poem," 274–75; L. Schottroff and W. Stegemann, *Jesus of Nazareth: Hope of the Poor* (Maryknoll, N.Y.: Orbis, 1986), 19–31.

17. See Ferris, *Hymns*, 122–24 and n. 123, for discussion of the phrases "in the final days" and "at the end."

18. See also the sensible discussion of the aorist verbs in Luke 1:51–53 by Farris (*Hymns*, 114–16); unfortunately his synthetic exegesis of the "reversal" blunts the effect of Mary's declarations.

19. Brown, *BM*, 363; cf. "the offense of the cross" (p. 364).

20. So also, implicitly, Schottroff and Stegemann, *Jesus*, 28.

21. See esp. L. Schottroff, "Das Magnificat und die älteste Tradition über Jesus von Nazareth," *Evangelische Theologie* 38 (1978) 298–313.

22. Brown, *BM*, 363. Brown has recently insisted that he intended more of a "social interest" than some of his readers have detected in *Birth of the Messiah*; see his "Gospel Infancy Narrative Research from 1976 to 1986: Part II (Luke)," *CBQ* 48 (1986) 668.

23. Brown (*BM*, 383) and Fitzmyer (*Luke* 1.379) both assert such an interpretation, even though they recognize that the "Jewish-Christian" song speaks "in generic terms."

24. Brown, *BM*, 383.

25. Farris (*Hymns*, 95) notes that not too much should be made of the parallel in 1 Kgs. 1:48 because of the prominence of this blessing formula in the Psalms.

26. Contra Fitzmyer, *Luke* 1.383.

27. Brown, *BM*, 371.

28. E.g., Fitzmyer, *Luke* 1.384: "On the lips of Zechariah, it scarcely refers to the Roman occupiers of Palestine."

29. Contra Brown, *BM*, 371, and Fitzmyer, *Luke* 1.384, respectively.

30. Fitzmyer, *Luke* 1.384; cf. Jones, "Background and Character," 31.

31. Contra Fitzmyer, *Luke* 1.384–85.

32. Farris, *Hymns*, 93–94.

33. So also Brown, *BM*, 373.

34. So Fitzmyer, *Luke* 1.386.

35. Considering that the name *Simeon* is a diminutive of a word meaning "God/Yahweh has heard" and that *Simeon* was the name of one of Jacob's twelve sons, one is tempted to suggest that the Simeon provided by the narrative context as the singer of this song in Luke 2:29–32 was meant to connote Jacob-Israel himself, particularly in the light of Israel's words in Jubilees 45:3–4, when he finally sees Joseph: "Let me die now that I have seen you. And now let the Lord, the God of Israel, be blessed, the God of Abraham and the God of Isaac, who did not withhold his mercy and kindness from his servant Jacob. It is enough that I have seen your face while I was alive."

36. Farris, *Hymns*, 97.

37. So also Fitzmyer (*Luke* 1.428), who notes that Luke and Paul share this same notion.

38. Brown, *BM*, 440, 460.

39. Contra both Brown (*BM*, 461) and Fitzmyer (*Luke* 1.422–23).

40. See further J. Jervell, *Luke and the People of God* (Minneapolis: Augsburg, 1972), chap. 2.

41. D. L. Tiede, *Prophecy and History in Luke-Acts* (Philadelphia: Fortress, 1980), esp. chap. 1; on the infancy narratives in particular, see pp. 25–33.

Chapter 7/A Modern Analogy

1. Jimmy Cliff's popular song "By the Rivers of Babylon," for example, is a version of the biblical Ps. 137.

2. E. Cardenal, *The Gospel in Solentiname* (4 vols.; trans. Donald D. Walsh; Maryknoll, N.Y.: Orbis, 1976–79).

3. Alejandro, in ibid., 1.32.

4. Tomás Peña, in ibid., 14, 27, 48–49.

5. Ibid., 15.

6. Julio, in ibid., 54–55.

7. Alejandro and Laureano, in ibid., 82, 73.

8. Laureano, in ibid., 62.

9. Ibid., 64–65.

10. Ibid., 65–66.

11. Ibid., 74–75.

12. Ibid., 83.

13. Ibid., 73–74.

14. Ibid., 76; 2.193.

15. The economic and political domination that developed through these stages is increasingly well documented and analyzed in numerous journal articles, scholarly

studies and books, U.S. government records and studies, and reports by international agencies and churches. The discussion that follows will be necessarily brief and sketchy, with an attempt to use representative and relatively well-known illustrations.

16. As cited in J. Pearce, *Under the Eagle* (London: Latin American Bureau, 1981), 9.

17. See further, e.g., W. LaFeber, *Inevitable Revolutions* (New York: Norton, 1983), 59–64.

18. As cited in Pearce, *Under the Eagle*, 20.

19. See LaFeber, *Inevitable Revolutions*, 64–67, 79–81; and D. Dozer, *Are We Good Neighbors? 1930–1960* (Gainesville: University of Florida, 1959), 11–12.

20. For the following, see further LaFeber, *Inevitable Revolutions*, 92–97, 104–11.

21. George Kennan to U.S. ambassadors in Latin America, as cited in LaFeber, *Inevitable Revolutions*, 107.

22. It is fondly known in Latin America as "the School of Coups." The impact of this indoctrination and training was particularly strong on the armies of the small Central American countries. Between 1949 and 1964, a total of 810 officers from Honduras, 958 from Guatemala, and 2,969 from Nicaragua were trained there, as compared with 259, 165, and 178 officers from the much larger countries of Argentina, Brazil, and Mexico, respectively. See W. F. Barber and C. N. Ronning, *Internal Security and Military Power: Counterinsurgency and Civic Action in Latin America* (Columbus: Ohio State University Press, 1966), 145. Not surprisingly, given this U.S. emphasis, military dictators ruled thirteen of the twenty Latin American countries by 1954, a new high for the twentieth century.

23. See further P. Lernoux, *Cry of the People* (New York: Doubleday, 1980), 206–9. Certain U.S. aid does not simply go directly or indirectly to U.S. corporations. On how such aid reinforces the position of local oligarchies, see the testimony of Prof. M. Wolpin to Congress, cited in Pearce, *Under the Eagle*, 46.

24. A comparison of the figures on military aid between 1950 and 1963 with those for 1964 to 1967 is revealing: in these periods, Guatemala, for example, received $5.3 million and $10.9 million, respectively. See further J. M. Baines, "U.S. Military Assistance to Latin America: An Assessment," *Journal of Interamerican Studies and World Affairs* 14 (1972) 481.

25. Prof. Richard Adams, in testimony before the Senate Foreign Relations Committee in 1968, as cited in LaFeber, *Inevitable Revolutions*, 194–95.

26. T. W. Walker, *Nicaragua: The Land of Sandino* (2d ed.; Boulder, Colo.: Westview, 1986), 25–27; LaFeber, *Inevitable Revolutions*, 64–68.

27. The closest Central American analogy to the four high-priestly families that dominated ancient Judea after the death of Herod, of course, are the fourteen families that dominate El Salvador.

28. In 1942, Archbishop Lezcano crowned the elder Somoza's daughter queen of the army, using a crown from the statue of the Virgin of Candelaria. After the elder Somoza was assassinated by a young poet in 1956, he was buried with the honors of "a Prince of the Church." See P. Berryman, *The Religious Roots of Rebellion* (Maryknoll, N.Y.: Orbis, 1984), 55.

29. In 1939, the elder Somoza was received warmly by President Roosevelt, who is reported to have said, "Somoza may be a son-of-a-bitch, but he's our son-of-a-bitch" (cited in Lernoux, *Cry of the People*, 80). The younger Anastasio was particularly close to President Nixon (and some of his wealthy associates such as Bebe Rebozo and Howard Hughes), paid a state visit during his first term, and reportedly sent his mother with a million dollars for Nixon's reelection campaign. See B. Diederich,

Somoza and the Legacy of U.S. Involvement in Central America (New York: Dutton, 1981), 88–89. The Somoza lobby was so strong in Washington that Somoza boasted that he had more friends in the Congress than did President Carter. See LaFeber, *Inevitable Revolutions,* 229–31.

30. See further Walker, *Nicaragua,* 27–29; LaFeber, *Inevitable Revolutions,* 69, 102–3, 160–61. As one North American businessman commented, "You just don't do business here without offering the General a share in it from the beginning" (from *Business Week,* 1978, as cited in Pearce, *Under the Eagle,* 117). "It was an ingenious thing. For 45 years the Somoza family ran this country like their own private enterprise" (banker Arturo Cruz, quoted by W. Hoge in *New York Times,* 26 July 1979, A3).

31. Walker, *Nicaragua,* 31, 110; Lernoux, *Cry of the People,* 82.

32. *Amnesty International Report, 1977* (London: Amnesty International Publications, 1977), 150–53; Lernoux, *Cry of the People,* 83; Organization of American States, Inter-American Commission on Human Rights, *Report on the Situation of Human Rights in Nicaragua* (Washington, D.C.: 1978); LaFeber, *Inevitable Revolutions,* 232; Walker, *Nicaragua,* 32–37.

33. LaFeber, *Inevitable Revolutions,* 231–36; Lernoux, *Cry of the People,* 104–7.

34. On the following, see, e.g., LaFeber, *Inevitable Revolutions,* 111–25.

35. Of its 3 million acres, only 139,000 acres of which were then actually cultivated, the government expropriated 234,000 acres for distribution to landless people.

36. M. McClintock, *The American Connection,* vol. 2: *State Terror and Popular Resistance in Guatemala* (London: Zed, 1985), 28–35.

37. See further LaFeber, *Inevitable Revolution,* 167–71; Pearce, *Under the Eagle,* 68–70; McClintock, *State Terror,* 76–109.

38. B. Manz, *Refugees of a Hidden War: The Aftermath of Counterinsurgency in Guatemala* (Albany: State University of New York Press, 1988), 7, 17.

39. Amnesty International, *Guatemala: The Human Rights Record* (London: Amnesty International Publications, 1987), 6, 53, 66–67.

40. Fuller descriptions or reconstructions are available in several publications; e.g., Amnesty International, *Guatemala,* 59–63. See further, for example, the extensive list by date and village in Appendix 4, pp. 161–68, where the three-month total was 2,186 killings; or the Americas Watch Report, "Creating a Desolation and Calling It Peace," May 1983, p. 17.

41. See further R. G. Williams, *Export Agriculture and the Crisis in Central America* (Chapel Hill: University of North Carolina Press, 1986), 119–21.

42. See further McClintock, *State Terror,* 3–8.

43. Manz, *Refugees of a Hidden War,* 11–12.

44. See further focused and detailed studies such as W. H. Durham, *Scarcity and Survival in Central America: Ecological Origins of the Soccer War* (Stanford: Stanford University Press, 1979); S. H. Davis and J. Hodson, *Witnesses to Political Violence in Guatemala: The Suppression of a Rural Development Movement* (Boston: Oxfam-America, 1982); Williams, *Export Agriculture;* T. Barry, *Roots of Rebellion* (Boston: South End, 1987); briefer discussions and some figures in Berryman, *Religious Roots of Rebellion,* 40–45; Manz, *Refugees of a Hidden War,* 46–52. As the latter points out, the amount of *idle arable* lands on large private holdings is roughly the same as the amount needed for the now landless population.

45. On the cotton boom see esp. Williams, *Export Agriculture,* chaps. 1–2; for its effects on the peasants, see chap. 3.

46. It was also stimulated by Washington-regulated import quotas favoring Central America, U.S. and international agency development projects, and subsidized credit

that benefited the large producers who dominated the expanding beef-export business. For the effects of beef production for export on the peasantry, see ibid., esp. chap. 6.

47. Ibid., 151; for the similar displacement in Nicaragua, see pp. 129–34.

48. On the following, see Manz, *Refugees of a Hidden War,* 7, 145–47.

49. See further ibid., chaps. 6–7.

50. In 1966, Senator Robert Kennedy noted prophetically that "these people will not accept this kind of existence for the next generation. We would not; and they will not. . . . So a revolution is coming . . . whether we will it or not. We can affect its character; we cannot alter its inevitability" (*New York Times,* 10 May 1966, p. 1).

51. E.g., the organizing in the Zelaya area of Nicaragua, where Capuchin priests from the U.S. had been working (Lernoux, *Cry of the People,* 82, 85–87); or in El Salvador, the occupation of idle land belonging to an absentee owner, after repeated attempts to rent it, by members of a basic Christian community (an action crushed by the troops and tanks of the National Guard), recounted in Berryman, *Religious Roots of Rebellion,* 110.

52. Berryman, *Religious Roots of Rebellion,* 188–89; Manz, *Refugees of a Hidden War,* 14; a more recent example appears on pp. 26–27.

53. "Be a Patriot, kill a priest" read handbills circulated shortly thereafter. See Lernoux, *Cry of the People,* 76.

54. Americas Watch, *Guatamala: A Nation of Prisoners* (New York, 1983); Berryman, *Religious Roots of Rebellion,* 201–11; Williams, *Export Agriculture,* 138–39.

55. P. Erdozain, *Archbishop Romero* (Maryknoll, N.Y.: Orbis, 1981).

56. Only about one-fifth of the priests serving in the area were native born, and many of them had studied in Europe.

Chapter 8/Liberating Narrative and Liberating Understanding

1. See, e.g., K. Stendahl, "Biblical Theology, Contemporary," *IDB* 1.418–32.

2. See, e.g., R. E. Brown, "What the Biblical Word Meant and What It Means," in *The Critical Meaning of the Bible* (New York: Paulist, 1981), 23–44.

3. E.g., Brown, *BM,* 178–79.

4. For a sophisticated and dialogic use of a psychoanalytic approach, see W. Wink, *The Bible in Human Transformation* (Philadelphia: Fortress, 1973), 49–63.

5. This hermeneutical position, which builds heavily on the thought of H.-G. Gadamer, particularly *Truth and Method* (New York: Seabury, 1975), is sketched briefly in P. Stuhlmacher, *Historical Criticism and Theological Interpretation of Scripture: Toward a Hermeneutics of Consent* (Philadelphia: Fortress, 1977), 61–91.

6. Gadamer, *Truth and Method,* 268.

7. Ibid., 245, 266.

8. So also L. E. Keck, "Will the Historical-Critical Method Survive? Some Observations," in *Orientation by Disorientation: Studies . . . in Honor of W. A. Beardslee* (ed. R. A. Spencer; Pittsburgh: Pickwick, 1980), 124.

9. E. Schüssler Fiorenza, *Bread Not Stone: The Challenge of Feminist Biblical Interpretation* (Boston: Beacon, 1984), 130–31.

10. J. Barr, "The Bible as a Document of Believing Communities," in *The Bible as a Document of the University* (ed. H. D. Betz; Chico, Calif.: Scholars, 1981), 25–28; J. S. Croatto, *Biblical Hermeneutics* (Maryknoll, N.Y.: Orbis, 1987), 36–50.

11. E. Auerbach, "Figura," in *Scenes from the Drama of European Literature* (Minneapolis: University of Minnesota, 1984; original English trans., 1959), 52.

12.   Ibid., 58.
13.   Pamphlet published in 1788 at Exeter, N.H., by Lamson and Ranlet; more accessible in C. Cherry, ed., *God's New Israel* (Englewood Cliffs, N.J.: Prentice-Hall, 1971), 93–105.
14.   H. White, "Historicism, History, and the Figurative Imagination," *History and Theory* 14 (1975) 54.
15.   Recent reflections on the functions of memory appear in J. B. Metz, *Faith in History and Society* (New York: Seabury, 1980), 184–204; and S. D. Welch, *Communities of Solidarity and Resistance* (Maryknoll, N.Y.: Orbis, 1985), 35–44.
16.   Schüssler Fiorenza, *Bread Not Stone*, 105, 147.
17.   Barr, "Bible as a Document," 39–40.
18.   "Implicit in the movement from memory to tradition to text to scripture to canon is the fulfilled expectation that the material from the past illumines the ever-moving present, that the past is repeatedly paradigmatic" (Keck, "Will the Historical-Critical Method Survive?" 124).
19.   Barr, "Bible as a Document," 40.
20.   Keck, "Will the Historical-Critical Method Survive?" 124.
21.   For the classic exposition of the widely effective "conscientization" process, see Paulo Freire, *Pedagogy of the Oppressed* (New York: Herder & Herder, 1971). The following paragraphs presuppose conversations such as those recorded by E. Cardenal in *Gospel in Solentiname*.
22.   See further C. Mesters, "The Use of the Bible in Christian Communities of the Common People," in *The Challenge of the Basic Christian Communities* (ed. S. Torres and J. Eagleson; Maryknoll, N.Y.: Orbis, 1982), 197–209.
23.   J. A. Sanders, "Hermeneutics," *IDB* Sup., 406.

Appendix/Legends of the Birth of the Hero: A Critical Appraisal

1.   For the publication of the two principal addresses, by A. Dundes and A. Lord, with responses by New Testament scholars and others, see chap. 1, n. 38.
2.   The "hero pattern" is used in developing "a mode of description" for the tales of Israelite figures such as Jacob and Joseph by S. Niditch, *Underdogs and Tricksters: A Prelude to Biblical Forklore* (San Francisco: Harper & Row, 1987), 71–75.
3.   J. G. von Hahn, "Arische Aussetzungs- und Rückkehr-Formel," in *Sagwissenschaftliche Studien* (Jena: Mauke, 1876).
4.   Lord Raglan, "The Hero of Tradition," *Folklore* 45 (1934) 212–31; reprinted in *The Study of Folklore* (ed. A. Dundes; Englewood Cliffs, N.J.: Prentice-Hall, 1965), 142–57; and *The Hero* (New York: Vintage, 1956; original, 1936).
5.   References to Dundes, "The Hero Pattern and the Life of Jesus," will be to the reprint in *Interpreting Folklore*.
6.   Ibid., 231.
7.   See further M. P. Coote, "Response" in Dundes, *Hero Pattern*, 42.
8.   Dundes, "Hero Pattern," 235. Coote ("Reponse," 43) draws the critical implication for Raglan's and Dundes's "hero pattern": "Folk heroes are magnets that attract narratives of different genres and other forms of lore." Thus the "hero tale" may in effect be the product of "collectors and synthesizers (who) try to fit the discrete, often mutually inconsistent tales linked to a single name into cycles and life stories."
9.   Lord, "Gospels as Oral Traditional Literature," 39–40.
10.   Ibid., 39; as clarified by L. E. Keck, "Oral Traditional Literature and the Gospels: The Seminar," in W. O. Walker, *Relationships among the Gospels*, 117.

11. Rank, *Myth of the Birth,* 61. Numbers are inserted for reference purposes.

12. Any further work on these "hero" stories should certainly be done on the basis of the primary texts, or at least recent critical translations of them, rather than on those in Rank's monograph, which are English translations of German translations from the original Greek, Latin, etc. from nearly a century ago.

13. Rank, *Myth of the Birth,* 69–70.

14. Ibid., 87.

15. Cf. also Aelian's version of Gilgamesh, Zoroaster's birth stories, and particularly the story about the Sumerian founder-emperor Sargon, which includes the motifs of virgin or unmarried mother, exposure, and rescue and raising by lowly parents; see further B. Lewis, *The Sargon Legend* (Cambridge, Mass.: American Society of Oriental Research, 1980), esp. 260–67, 273–76.

16. C. H. Talbert, "Prophecies of Future Greatness: The Contribution of Greco-Roman Biographies to an Understanding of Luke 1:5–4:15," in *The Divine Helmsman* (Festschrift Lou H. Silberman; ed. J. L. Crenshaw and S. Sandmel; New York: Ktav, 1980), 129–41. It should be pointed out that Suetonius (c. 70–140) wrote after the Gospels were written.

17. See, e.g., Neumann, *Origins and History of Consciousness,* 173–85.

18. Ibid., 191.

Index